Gwen
You are
Awesome!

Mr Awesome

# THE
# 13 STEPS TO
# RICHES

*Featuring*
*Erik Swanson & Jim Cathcart*

**AUTO**
**SUGGESTION**
**VOLUME 3**

**HABITUDE**
**WARRIOR**

*Foreword by Greg Reid*

Manufactured and printed in the United States of America and distributed globally by BeyondPublishing.net

Library of Congress Control Number: 2021922850

Hardback ISBN: 978-1-63792-208-8

Paperback ISBN: 978-1-63792-206-4

# TESTIMONIALS
# THE 13 STEPS TO RICHES

"What an honor to collaborate with so many personal development leaders from around the world as we Co-Author together honoring the amazing principles by Napoleon Hill in this new book series, *The 13 Steps to Riches*, by Habitude Warrior and Erik "Mr. Awesome" Swanson. Well done "Mr. Awesome" for putting together such an amazing series. If you want to up-level your life, read every book in this series and learn to apply each of these time tested steps and principles."

*Denis Waitley* ~ Author of *Psychology of Winning & The NEW Psychology of Winning - Top Qualities of a 21st Century Winner*

"Just as *Think and Grow Rich* reveals the 13 steps to success discovered by Napoleon Hill after interviewing the richest people around the world (and many who considered themselves failures) in the early 1900's, *The 13 Steps to Riches*, produced by Habitude Warrior and Erik Swanson takes a modern look at those same 13 steps. It brings together many of today's personal development leaders to share their stories of how the 13 Steps to Riches have created and propelled their own successes. I am honored to participate and share the power of Faith in my life. If you truly want to accelerate reaching the success you deserve, read every volume of *The 13 Steps to Riches*."

*Sharon Lechter* ~ 5 Time N.Y. Times Best-Selling Author. Author of *Think and Grow Rich for Women*, Co-Author of *Exit Rich, Rich Dad Poor Dad, Three Feet from Gold, Outwitting the Devil* and *Success and Something Greater* ~ **SharonLechter.com**

"The most successful book on personal achievement ever written is now being elaborated upon by many of the world's top thought leaders. I'm honored to Co-Author this series on the amazing principles from Napoleon Hill, in *The 13 Steps to Riches*, by Habitude Warrior, Erik "Mr. Awesome" Swanson."

*Jim Cathcart* ~ Best-Selling Author of *Relationship Selling* and *The Acorn Principle*, among many others. Certified Speaking Professional (CSP) and Former President of the National Speakers Association (NSA)

"Where else can you find 13 leaders sharing their amazing insights and principles of success, while honoring one of the best books ever published in *Think and Grow Rich* by Napoleon Hill? I know... right here! Pick up your copy of *The 13 Steps to Riches* book series and follow these time tested steps and principles that will change your life if you take action on them."

*Steve Sims* ~ N.Y.Times Best-Selling Author of *Bluefishing - The Art of Making Things Happen*

"Some books are written to be read and placed on the shelf. Others are written to transform the reader, as they travel down a path of true transcendence and enlightenment. "*The 13 steps to Riches*" by Habitude Warrior and Erik Swanson is the latter. Profoundly insightful, it revitalizes the techniques and strategies written by Napoleon Hill by applying a modern perspective, and a fearsome collaboration of some of the greatest minds and thought leaders from around the globe. A must read for all of those who seek to break free of their current levels of success, and truly extract the greatness that lies within. It is an honor and a privilege to have been selected to participate, in what is destined to be the next historic chapter in the meteoric rise of many men and women around the world."

*Glenn Lundy* ~ Husband to one, Father to 8, Automotive Industry Expert, Author of "The Morning 5", Creator of the popular morning show "#riseandgrind", and the Founder of "Breakfast With Champions"

"How exciting to team up with the amazing Habitude Warrior community of leaders such as Erik Swanson, Sharon Lechter, John Assaraf, Denis Waitley and so many more transformational and self-help icons to bring you these timeless and proven concepts in the fields of success and wealth. *The 13 Steps to Riches* book series will help you reach your dreams and accomplish your goals faster than you have ever experienced before!"

*Marie Diamond* ~ Featured in *The Secret*, Modern Day Spiritual Teacher, Inspirational Speaker, Feng Shui Master

"If you are looking to crystalize your mightiest dream, rekindle your passion, breakthrough limiting beliefs and learn from those who have done exactly what you want to do - read this book! In this transformational masterpiece, *The 13 Steps to Riches*, self-development guru Erik Swanson has collected the sage wisdom and time tested truths from subject matter experts and amalgamated it into a one-stop-shop resource library that will change your life forever!"

*Dan Clark* ~ Speaker Hall of Fame & N.Y. Times Best-Selling Author of *The Art of Significance*

"Life has always been about who you surround yourself with. I am in excellent company with this collaboration from my fellow authors and friends, paying tribute to the life changing principles by Napoleon Hill in this amazing new book series, *The 13 Steps to Riches*, organized by Habitude Warrior's founder and my dear friend, Erik Swanson. Hill said, 'Your big opportunity may be right where you are now.' This book series is a must-read for anyone who wants to change their life and prosper, starting now."

*Alec Stern* ~ America's Startup Success Expert, Co-Founder of Constant Contact

"Finally a book series that encompasses the lessons the world needs to learn and apply, but in our modern day era. As I always teach my students to "Say **YES**, and then figure out how", I strongly urge you to do the same. Say YES to adding all of these 13 books in *The 13 Steps to Riches* book series into your success library and watch both your business as well as your personal life grow as a result."

> **Loral Langemeier** ~ 5 Time N.Y. Times Best-Selling Author, Featured in *The Secret*, Author of *The Millionaire Maker* and *YES! Energy - The Equation to Do Less, Make More*

"Napoleon Hill had a tremendous impact on my consciousness when I was very young – there were very few books nor the type of trainings that we see today to lead us to success. Whenever you have the opportunity to read and harness *The 13 Steps to Riches* as they are presented in this series, be happy (and thankful) that there were many of us out there applying the principles, testing the teachings, making the mistakes, and now being offered to you in a way that they are clear, simple and concise – with samples and distinctions that will make it easier for you to design a successful life which includes adding value to others, solving world problems, and making the world work for 100% of humanity... Read on... those dreams are about to come true!"

> **Doria Cordova** ~ CEO of Money & You, Excellerated Business School, Global Business Developer, Ambassador of New Education

"Success leaves clues and the Co-Authors in this awesome book series, *The 13 Steps to Riches*, will continue the Napoleon Hill legacy with tools, tips and modern-day principals that greatly expand on the original masterpiece... *Think and Grow Rich*. If you are serious about living your life to the max, get this book series now!"

> **John Assaraf** ~ Chairman & CEO NeuroGym, MrNeuroGym.com, New York Times best-selling author of *Having It All, Innercise*, and *The Answer*. Also featured in *The Secret*

"Over the years, I have been blessed with many rare and amazing opportunities to invest my time and energy. These opportunities require a keen eye and immediate action. This is one of those amazing opportunities for you as a reader! I highly recommend you pick up every book in this series of **The 13 Steps to Riches** by Habitude Warrior and Erik Swanson! Learn from modern day leaders who have embraced the lessons from the great Napoleon Hill in his classic book from 1937, *Think and Grow Rich*."

*Kevin Harrington* ~ Original "Shark" on *Shark Tank*, Creator of the Infomercial, Pioneer of the *As Seen on TV* brand, Co-Author of *Mentor to Millions*

"When you begin your journey, you will quickly learn of the importance of the first step of **The 13 Steps To Riches**. A burning desire is the start of all worthwhile achievements. Erik 'Mr. Awesome' Swanson's newest book series contains a wealth of assistance to make your journey both successful and enjoyable. Start today... because tomorrow is not guaranteed on your calendar."

*Don Green* ~ 45 Years of Banking, Finance & Entrepreneurship, Best-Selling Author of *Everything I know About Success I Learned From Napoleon Hill & Napoleon Hill My Mentor: Timeless Principles to Take Your Success to the Next Level & Your Millionaire Mindset*

Our minds become magnetized with the dominating thoughts we hold in our minds and these magnets attract to us the forces, the people, the circumstances of life which harmonize with the nature of our dominating thoughts.

(Napoleon Hill)

# NAPOLEON HILL

---

I would like to personally acknowledge and thank the one and only Napoleon Hill for his work, dedication, and most importantly believing in himself. His unwavering belief in himself, whether he realized this or not, had been passed down from generation to generation to millions and millions of individuals across this planet including me!

I'm sure, at first, as many of us experience throughout our lives as well, he most likely had his doubts. Think about it. Being offered to work for Andrew Carnegie for a full 20 years with zero pay and no guarantee of success had to be a daunting decision. But, I thank you for making that decision years and years ago. It paved the path for countless many who have trusted in themselves and found success in their own rights. You gave us all hope and desire to bank on the most important entity in our world today - ourselves!

For this, I thank you Sir, from the bottom of my heart and the top of all of our bank accounts. Let us all follow the 13 Steps to Riches and prosper in so many areas of our lives.

~ Erik "Mr Awesome" Swanson
10 Time #1 Best-Selling Author & Student of Napoleon Hill Philosophies

---

# STAFF SGT. DARIN T. HOOVER, 31

It is our distinct honor to dedicate each one of our *13 Steps to Riches* book volumes to each of the 13 United States Service Members who courageously lost their lives in Kabul in August, 2021. Your honor, dignity, and strength will always be cherished and remembered. ~ Habitude Warrior Team

**Staff Sgt. Darin T. Hoover**, 31, of Salt Lake City, Utah. His military occupational specialty was 0369, Infantry Unit Leader.

His awards and decorations include the Afghanistan Campaign Medal, Certificate of Commendation (Individual), Marine Corps Good Conduct Medal, Letter of Appreciation, Meritorious Mast, Navy and Marine Corps Achievement Medal, National Defense Service Medal, NATO Medal-ISAF Afghanistan, Sea Service Deployment Ribbon and Global War on Terrorism Service Medal. Additional awards pending approval may include Purple Heart, Combat Action Ribbon and Sea Service Deployment Ribbon, according to a 1st Marine Division press release.

# THE 13 STEPS TO RICHES
# FEATURING:

**DENIS WAITLEY** ~ Author of *Psychology of Winning & The NEW Psychology of Winning - Top Qualities of a 21st Century Winner,* NASA's Performance Coach, Featured in *The Secret* ~ www.DenisWaitley.com

**SHARON LECHTER** ~ 5 Time N.Y. Times Best-Selling Author. Author of *Think and Grow Rich for Women,* Co-Author of *Exit Rich, Rich Dad Poor Dad, Three Feet from Gold, Outwitting the Devil* and *Success and Something Greater* ~ www.SharonLechter.com

**JIM CATHCART**~ Best-Selling Author of *Relationship Selling* and *The Acorn Principle,* among many others. Certified Speaking Professional (CSP) and Former President of the National Speakers Association (NSA) ~ www.Cathcart.com

**STEVE SIMS** ~ N.Y.Times Best-Selling Author of *Bluefishing - The Art of Making Things Happen,* CEO and Founder of Bluefish ~ www.SteveDSims.com

**GLENN LUNDY** ~ Husband to one, Father to 8,

Automotive Industry Expert, Author of "The Morning 5", Creator of the popular morning show "#riseandgrind", and the Founder of "Breakfast With Champions" ~ www.GlennLundy.com

**MARIE DIAMOND** ~ Featured in *The Secret*, Modern Day Spiritual Teacher, Inspirational Speaker, Feng Shui Master ~ www.MarieDiamond.com

**DAN CLARK** ~ Award Winning Speaker, Speaker Hall of Fame, N.Y. Times Best-Selling Author of *The Art of Significance* ~ www.DanClark.com

**ALEC STERN** ~ America's Startup Success Expert, Co-Founder of Constant Contact, Speaker, Mentor, Investor ~ www.AlecSpeaks.com

**ERIK SWANSON** ~ 10 Time #1 International Best-Selling Author, Award Winning Speaker, Featured on Tedx Talks and Amazon Prime TV. Founder & CEO of the Habitude Warrior Brand ~ www.SpeakerErikSwanson.com

**LORAL LANGEMEIER** ~ 5 Time N.Y. Times Best-Selling Author, Featured in *The Secret*, Author of *The Millionaire Maker* and *YES! Energy - The Equation to Do Less, Make More* ~ www.LoralLangemeier.com

**DORIA CORDOVA** ~ CEO of Money & You, Excellerated Business School, Global Business Developer, Ambassador of New Education ~ www.FridaysWithDoria.com

**JOHN ASSARAF** ~ Chairman & CEO NeuroGym, MrNeuroGym.com, N. Y. Times best-selling author of *Having It All, Innercise,* and *The Answer.* Also featured in *The Secret* ~ www.JohnAssaraf.com

**KEVIN HARRINGTON** ~ Original "Shark" on the hit TV show *Shark Tank*, Creator of the Infomercial, Pioneer of the *As Seen on TV* brand, Co-Author of *Mentor to Millions* ~ www.KevinHarrington.TV

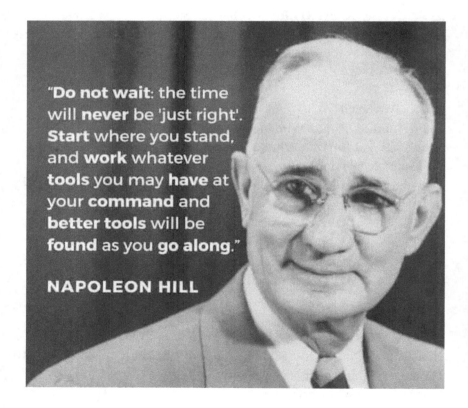

"**Do not wait**: the time will **never** be 'just right'. **Start** where you stand, and **work** whatever **tools** you may **have** at your **command** and **better tools** will be **found** as you **go along**."

**NAPOLEON HILL**

# CONTENTS

# INTRODUCTION

*by Don Green*

## ERIK SWANSON & DON GREEN

Once you give yourself the gift of reading Erik Swanson's newest book series, **The 13 Steps to Riches**, you are sure to realize why he has earned his nickname, *"Mr. Awesome."* Readers usually read books for two reasons – they want to be entertained or they want to improve their knowledge in a certain subject. Mr. Awesome's new book series will help you do both.

I urge you to not only read this great book series in it's entirety, but also apply the principles held within into your our life. Use the experience Erik Swanson has gained to reach your own level of success. I highly encourage you to invest in yourself by reading self-help materials, such as *The 13 Steps to Riches*, and I truly know you will discover that it will be one of the best investments you could ever make.

Don Green
Executive Director and CEO
The Napoleon Hill Foundation

# FOREWORD

*by Greg Reid*

I believe everything is always around us and is always captured in pure energy.

## Tapping into Success Frequencies

Certain people of abundant mindsets know how to dial into the correct frequencies for success. We are all able to dial into the frequencies of the Universe to obtain anything we want by asking the right questions and being inquisitive. Our focus and concentration on the right things become our higher-frequency dials. It's like pulling it down from the ethers until we can learn how to tap into that source and dial into those frequencies. It's similar to radio stations that use radio frequencies. Right now, in the airways, there are so many types of music, such as country music, rap music, classical music, and so many more. If you want to listen to a particular type of genre, you simply need to dial into that specific frequency or as we know it, radio station. It's all in the mechanism and approach to tapping into the correct frequency. We can train ourselves to do this in every area of our life.

Keep in mind, energy has a specific and exact response. It's like when we use "Hey Google." If I said, "Hey Google, show me men's shoes," Google is going to give me a billion variations. However, if I am more specific and say, "Hey Google, show me men's shoes, size 10, color red, within 10 miles of my vicinity," then it will narrow down my choices and give me a better result.

The most successful people in the world tap into this source through the questions of specificity they use. Successful people ask questions such as,

"How can it get any better than this?", "What is the solution to a challenge that I'm facing right now?", or "Who can I open up to my contact list that would build a win-win mutually-beneficial relationship?" By asking these types of questions, magically, the answers immediately come our way. Unfortunately, most people ask these questions in the wrong way or don't even attempt to ask.

The average person asks questions like, "God, why does this always happen to me?" and again, that ambiguous Google-search response comes in the form of billions of correlated, but unspecific information. The information highway laughs at us and says, "This is why you are a dummy; good luck finding the answer to that one," and the Universe continues to give us more of that ambiguity. Consequently, many of us get on the hamster wheel of life where we ask the same old questions that never give us the positive results we are striving to achieve. We're just not framing it in the way we truly desire and want in our daily lives.

### Squashing the Adversaries of Positive Thinking

The application of Auto Suggestion, identified by Napoleon Hill in 1937 through *Think And Grow Rich,* was described as the medium for influencing the subconscious mind and the third step to riches. Auto Suggestion allows us to govern our thought processes and guide them more than our feelings and free-flowing words do. Most people focus on the conversations that come out of their mouths, whereas successful people focus heavily on the conversations that play within our brains. These conversations are the specificity of frequencies described earlier.

I'm very attuned to my thoughts. The biggest challenge we face as a human species is ANTs, an acronym that stands for Automatic Negative Thoughts.

ANTs (Automatic Negative Thoughts) are the reptilian part of your brain that protect you and keep you safe so that you don't walk out of a cave just for a dinosaur or beast to eat you. referencing primal and neanderthal thought processes back in the day. We all have ANTs, and they run every minute of our lives.

Unfortunately, we have 64,000 thoughts a day, and most of them are harmful or the ANTs of our life. For myself, I've formed a defense against ANTs by picturing something much bigger than an ANT, which in this case is an APE. An APE is my acronym which stands for Automatic Positive Experience. My APE (Automatic Positive Experience) is easily connected in my brain as an etch-a-sketch of a song because music positively influences my life. It could be a trip to grandma's house, an accomplishment, graduation, or any major positive life event for other people. As for me, it's simply Billy Joel.

For example, if I'm driving down the road and someone cuts me off, naturally, ANTs creep in, and I want to say something like, "You son of a gun." But then instantly, I trained my brain to squash ANTs with APEs, and I slip into chorus:

*In the middle of the night*

*I go walking in my sleep*

*Through the valley of fear*

*To a river so deep*

*I've been searching for something*

*Taken out of my soul*

*Something I'd never lose*

*Something somebody stole*

The River of Dreams by Billy Joel is my APE. That song and memory cut off all my ANTs and inklings of negativity.

I picture my APE as a giant gorilla standing over an ANT hill and as the ANTs are popping up through the hole, I (now the giant gorilla) stomp on them, squashing their hopes from creeping into my thoughts, so I never let them overcome me.

## Gratitude Filters Everything

Daily, I believe the power of human nature is that we need to seek. We need to seek out people we respect and not people we have influence over, as we need to seek counsel and leadership, not opinions.

So every single day that someone wants to give me their opinion based on ignorance, lack of knowledge, and inexperience, to me, that's an ANT, where I have the self-guidance and Auto Suggestion to squash those opinions. I interrupt those people and say, "Thank you very much, but it doesn't work for me," and I move on.

One of the examples we use in handling the opinions of others (outside influences and forces) is something called the Hand in the Sand. Hand in the Sand is when people give you their input, and it's not to mess you up, but it's just coming from their perspective or to keep you safe in their point of view. So if you grab a handful of sand and say, "I'm working on this project," and they fire back with "This is what you should do" comments, rather than argue with them, say "Thank you very much." Accept it in the palm of your hand like a handful of sand, and if their suggestions work for me, I will keep them. If their suggestions don't work, I let them slip through my fingers like sand and explain that it doesn't work for me. By not having the "yeah buts," I don't have to argue it. I'd say "Thank you very much."

And as people give me their input, I close my hand with the sand that works for me, which becomes my program. That's how I've stayed sober for 34 years. That's how I raised my kid. That's how I do my business. I don't listen to everyone's opinions, but I seek counsel from those I admire, and I apply them wholeheartedly.

Develop Your Personal Success Equation

Though the above examples have worked amazingly for me and my personal victories, I invite you to find your Personal Success Equation (PSE), apply it in your daily life, then pass it on to the world.

One of the most common causes of failure is the habit of quitting when one is overtaken by temporary defeat. —Napoleon Hill

In the book, *Three Feet From Gold*, we teamed up with N.Y. Times Best-Selling Author Sharon Lechter and the Napoleon Hill Foundation to reveal more than the story of one man's persistent pursuit of success. In *Think And Grow Rich*, Hill describes the story of an uncle of R. U. Darby's who had plenty of evidence of tangible riches but lost it because he stopped three feet from the goal he was seeking. After quitting their search after a small discovery of gold, they sold the mine to a junkman for a few hundred dollars. After the junkman sought further investigation from an engineer, they discovered that Darby quit digging three feet too short from the millions of dollars the junkman made in ore.

Imagine starting your goals and dreams and quitting just moments or several feet from your ultimate, most outstanding achievement.

I had just the courage and the fortitude to do something special in my life by applying my own Personal Success Equation. I've had the persistence to publish over 32 best-selling books in over 45 different languages, and I've helped produce more than five motion pictures.

I've identified my Personal Success Equation as:

$$P + T * A (^2) + F = Success$$

P – Passion: What could you do if you could do it for free? Passion is not enough to truly be successful in life.

T – Talent: If you are passionate but aren't good, you won't be successful. A – Action: Apply the action required to back your talents and passions.

A – Association: We are a direct reflection of the people we hang around most.

F – Faith: The journey you are destined for and believe in is possible.

Turn your obstacles into opportunities. Don't give up when you are faced with challenges or obstacles. Don't give up when the going gets tough. We can learn more about someone on their bad days than on their best of days. Never let your mistakes, your setbacks, or your circumstances determine your value as a person.

In this volume of *The 13 Steps To Riches - Volume 3 Auto Suggestion*, you'll learn many different Personal Success Equations from outstanding authors, mentors, speakers, coaches, trainers, and business people who are revered in their areas of expertise. As you learn, focus and concentrate on your inner thoughts rather than your emotional responses. Like the abundant-minded people who repeatedly tap in to the correct frequencies for success, you too, will develop your success- frequencies and obtain your own Personal Success Equation. Don't stop! Don't quit! Keep persisting!

# GREG REID

**About Greg Reid:** For over 25 years, Greg has inspired millions of people to take personal responsibility to step into the potential of their greatness, and, as such, his life of contribution has been recognized by government leaders, luminaries in education and business.

Greg has been published in over 100 books, including 32 best-sellers in 45 different languages. Titles such as - *Stickability: The Power of Perseverance, The Millionaire Mentor, and Three Feet from Gold: Turn Your Obstacles into Opportunities* have inspired countless readers to understand that the most valuable lessons we learn are also the easiest ones to apply.

Greg Reid is best known for being the Founder of Secret Knock; a Forbes and Inc. Magazine top-rated event focused on partnership, networking, and business development.

He is the producer of the Oscar-qualified film, Wish Man, based on the Make-A-Wish Foundation Founder, streaming on Netflix now.

For his work in mentoring youth in his hometown of San Diego, Greg Reid was honored by the White House, where a former President commended Greg for his work for positively impacting the youth through a local mentorship program.

And if that is not enough, recently, Greg was honored with the star on the famous Las Vegas Walk of Stars.

Greg Reid's website: *www.GregReid.com*

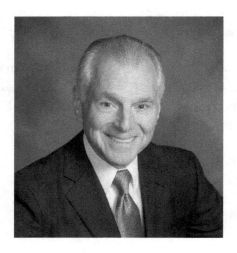

# JIM CATHCART

**About Jim Cathcart:** Jim Cathcart, CSP, CPAE has achieved every professional speaker's dream: a Top 1% TEDx video, President of the National Speakers Association, Sales & Marketing Hall of Fame, Speakers Hall of Fame, The Golden Gavel Award, The Cavett Award, 21 published books, 3,300 paid speeches in all 50 states and 4 around-the-world lecture tours, and honored to be a Celebrity Featured Author in Erik "Mr. Awesome" Swanson's The 13 Steps To Riches - Auto Suggestion #1 Best-Selling book series! He is a University Executive MBA professor and he has also been happily married for 51 years, remained trim and fit despite prostate cancer and a pacemaker in his 60s. He plays guitar and sings in nightclubs and is a life member of the American Motorcyclist Association. Someone said he is what "Fonzie" (from the TV show Happy Days) would be if he had gone to business school. Starting with nothing but dreams and willingness to earn his way, he can clearly show others how to become the person who will attract the future you want.

## Jim Cathcart

# SELF-LEADERSHIP
## NAPOLEON HILL'S CONCEPT OF "AUTO-SUGGESTION"

**Self-Leadership is:**

"How to Get Yourself to Do What Needs to be Done, When it Needs to be Done, Whether You Feel Like it Yet or Not."

**It is how you mold the world around you and within you to assist toward your goal to live an abundant and rewarding life.**

In Chapter 4 of *Think and Grow Rich,* author Napoleon Hill calls this, "The Medium for Influencing the Subconscious Mind. The Third Step toward Riches."

This is about "ALL suggestions and all self-administered stimuli which reach one's mind through the five senses." This applies to what you permit as well as what you choose. The conscious mind is your gatekeeper for what enters your subconscious mind.

Hill recommends:

Read your written desire aloud twice daily and see and *feel* yourself already in possession of what you want.

Faith is the activator; you must *feel* the reward you seek.

Reading the words is useless unless you *feel* the reward.

You must mentally and emotionally *experience* the payoff you seek.

If you don't believe it consciously, then your subconscious won't believe it either.

Faith is the new skill you must learn to master.

We've all heard, "You've got to believe in yourself." Yes, that's nice to say, but how does one do it? The how—that is the master key to riches. Auto Suggestion is how you get there.

I've taught for decades that success must be M.A.D.E.

M - We need a clear Mental Image of what we want.

A - We need to live Affirmations of all types to reinforce our belief.

D - We need Daily Successes to give us real-world success experiences of all types.

E - We need Environmental Influences that grow our belief.

All of these are within your reach.

Wisdom and cleverness cannot shorten the path to success; they simply make parts of it more efficient. You must persist in this until the goal is reached. That's the price. No freebies are possible. Be exact and concentrate until you *feel* what you see. From this daily practice will come the Burning Desire that compels you toward your goal.

Assume the outcome is inevitable if you keep your "magnet" activated. Your magnet is the visual image and the resulting burning desire of what you want. Allow it to turn off and all the other forces of the universe will draw things toward them instead of toward you. Starting over may take you longer. Keep this practice in place daily.

Let the universe bring you what you seek. You must attract it through your mindset and actions. There is enough for everyone in the universe. There always was and always will be.

Your subconscious will reveal the practical plan to get your desire. Don't wait to have a plan, *experience* the payoff in your mind and heart daily now! Expect it!

When the plan arrives, act immediately! See yourself doing the work or service for which you will be paid. Close your eyes and practice this until it is compelling to you. Daily, daily, daily, daily— did I say daily?

### Become the person who will attract the future you desire

Acquire all the traits, habits, and characteristics that will make you the obvious go-to person for the opportunities you want.

J. Paul Getty once wrote a book titled *How to Be Rich*. Note the emphasis, not how to Get rich but rather how to Be rich. Many sad stories exist about poor people who won the lottery yet couldn't keep the riches. They had poor-person habits and thinking. They acquired millions of dollars with no effort and then they squandered it with bad choices. If you don't change your thinking, then any improvement in your circumstances will only be temporary.

### Mental Image

I remember when I was a $525 a month clerk at the housing authority dreaming of future success. One day I fantasized about winning millions in the lottery. But rather than listing all the luxuries and indulgences I'd buy, I wrote out a plan for financially securing my entire lifetime and my family's as well.

On paper, I created a charitable foundation and a set of rules for selecting the family members who would serve on the board of trustees. The service was in a two-year rotation between members of my extended family so that everyone had a chance to participate but nobody could dominate. I made a set of rules that started with, "Any person who is caught lying or acting in a selfish or deceptive way related to this foundation will not only lose their position on the board, but they will be excluded from the benefits of this foundation forever and so will their immediate family members."

With advice from friends and people whom I admired, I crafted a set of rules for the foundation that would assure its survival long into the future and would allow every family member to benefit in meaningful ways from the money. No debt bailouts for spendthrifts, no special gifts for certain people, just financial security, and disaster-relief for all of us.

I never did win the lottery, nor did I create that foundation, but the thinking and preparation I did over those many months laid a foundation for my entire career. Yes, I did go on to earn millions of dollars and to achieve worldwide recognition in my field of motivation and human development. And for all these 40+ years, I've operated with a sound financial foundation.

The vision of what you want is your bedrock. That is what you create your Mental Image from. Then as you clarify the picture in your mind, the steps to make it a reality will come to you. Write them down and take action. Make it real in any way that you can.

Create a vision board or poster with images of what you want your life to be like. Make a folder in your phone of photos and images that give you the feelings you are seeking. Improve it constantly until it is perfect and review it often.

You cannot cheat your way to success. You can deceive others and gain temporary wins, but you'll become a crook. You won't respect yourself, nor will others. Bernie Madoff and other famous swindlers may have lived the high life for a while, but payment must always come.

## Affirmations

Learn a new language, the language of success. Your words shape your mind, and your mind selects your actions. So watch your thoughts with care. Let me give you a few examples of how our words affirm either what we want or what we don't.

- When you say you can't, your mind hears it too. Our chosen words are interpreted by our subconscious mind as directions. It doesn't judge, it just follows and facilitates what it is fed.

If you MUST say "can't", then at least add "yet." Make your limitations temporary, not permanent.

- How do you talk about yourself? What labels have you adopted to describe yourself?

Do you say, "I'm the middle child," "I'm the runt of the litter," "I've never been good at math," "I just don't seem to be very (insert a category: creative, strong, sensitive, etc.," "I don't care about money or prestige, I just want a good life," "I've never been able to keep weight off," "I have big bones or slow metabolism," "You never know when things might go wrong." (Yes, you do.) "You can never be too careful." (Of course, you can!)

All of these are messages to your subconscious as to what to expect from yourself. Most are excuses for not living up to your potential. They are rationalizations that are designed to help you feel OK about being broke, left out, not proud of yourself, etc.

How about something as simple as "I can't remember?" How do you know you "can't?" When did you give up trying? Instead, say, "I don't remember yet." That's the truth, and it doesn't limit you from remembering. "I can't" means it cannot happen. "I don't" means that at present it hasn't happened yet.

- Refuse to criticize others. Don't buy into the soap-opera mentality that life is awful and then you die. Soap-opera TV shows feed on loneliness and fear. They cultivate the belief that nobody can be trusted, all will betray you, nobody is what they seem, and life is about greed, power, and sex. Stop it! Don't go there. Guard your mind and your language. Go toward the Light!

- Cold Calls – In selling, the action of making new calls on people you don't know is a critical element in success. Nobody succeeds by only calling on the people they already know unless they know thousands of them. And, if you wait for them to call you or to expect your call, you will have a lifelong wait. So, businesses encourage what is known as "cold calls."

Why cold? They say it is because the people don't expect to hear from you.

I challenge that. If they don't expect you, or you haven't called on them before, then why not use a term that describes the actual event? Call them what they are "New calls." Not "warm calls," that's just too juvenile. Besides, calls don't have a temperature. They are either new calls or subsequent calls.

So what? Well, if you make it a cold call in your mind then you will react accordingly. You'll feel unwelcome, like an intruder, and you'll be on the defensive from the start. You will be trying to justify the call. If it is simply a new call, then you can focus on your purpose: to find people you can help by selling your product or service.

- Here's another sales term that doesn't work: Closing.

"What?" you ask. "Surely you know that I must ask for the order if I'm to get the sale!" True, but you don't have to close anything to do it.

"Close" means to shut, to end, terminate, discontinue, or finalize. We say, "the case is closed," this is a "closed market", she had a "closed mind", or "Sorry, we are closed. Come back tomorrow." All of these are acts that end or shut out something.

In sales, we want to earn a profit by helping our customer. That means we are forming a new business friendship, not a social one, but one based on mutual financial benefit.

You ask, "Do you mean that I should call it 'Opening' the sale?" No, of course not. But call it what it is: Confirming the purchase. You confirm a sale, you don't end it. A confirmation is the action that makes a purchase official.

Once the sale is confirmed, you begin a new relationship in which you provide benefits to the buyer and they provide payment to you. Nothing closed about it. In fact, you probably want it to lead to a lifetime of purchases and referrals.

Record yourself saying (with feeling!) what you want to become real. Say it like you mean it or don't say it at all. Treat this affirmation as you would treat an apology. Saying the words doesn't count unless the person hearing it believes that you mean it. Listen to yourself saying it, describing what it will be like, feeling the result.

Keep this in mind: whatever you say, you hear it too! Your mind accommodates what your words imply. "I hate selling. I just want to help people." That's the voice of fear speaking. That is self- doubt on display. The implication is that either selling is a bad thing, or you don't believe in your offer strongly enough to overcome reluctance to buy it. Can you truly help people? If what you offer is really worth considering, then why wouldn't you want people to consider it?

## Daily Successes

When I was in the Army, I went through Basic Combat Training. Everything we did was part of a process to make us more effective in armed combat situations. We learned to obey orders from our leaders without hesitation and without challenge. We learned to jump out of bed at the sound of Reveille. We learned to march in formation so well that we acted as one body of men, not separate individuals. Everything counted because, in combat, our lives and other lives were at stake.

In Officers Candidate School, the same discipline was in place. How we made our beds, arranged our uniforms in the closet, shined our shoes, cleaned our weapons, saluted others all counted. Everything counted! We became highly aware of little details and very disciplined about doing what mattered, even the smallest things.

Daily life isn't military service for most of us, but the discipline and confidence that comes from achieving Minimum Daily Standards should be important to all of us. If you don't make your bed each morning, clean up after yourself, wash the dishes instead of leaving them in the sink, keep your personal grooming good and cleanliness excellent, then you will lose respect for yourself. Each small negligence on your part is like a word of discouragement from someone you respect.

Conversely, each small success helps build your confidence bank account and self-respect.

Find something in each key category of your life that you can achieve no matter what else happens that day. Feed your mind, exercise your reason, nurture your friendships, listen to your family members, exercise your body, observe your use of money, improve your work, practice your faith, explore great ideas, and have some fun! Whichever part of life you neglect will sooner or later interrupt the other parts to gain your attention. If you neglect fitness, then you will be forced to make time for illness, etc.

Do ONE thing in each area, no matter how small. If you want to become a runner, put on your running shoes every day and step outside. You don't have to run, but you must form the habit of showing up prepared to run. Once you master the micro-moves, discipline is within your reach.

Keep a record of every dollar you receive and spend. Keep it where you will see it. Become money- conscious and you'll begin to manage money better.

Spend 5 minutes in direct conversation with each immediate family member every day. Not incidental conversation but intentional listening and talking. Spend longer when you can.

Reach out to one friend every day and just ask how they are or tell them that you were thinking about them.

Contribute one better idea each day to your work. Share your improvements with others, but don't expect them to adopt them. Just share them.

Read one passage in the Bible or your faith text each day. Thank God for your blessings and list them each night when you go to bed.

Learn one thing today that you wouldn't have learned without trying. Do a word puzzle or Sudoku math exercise or solve a problem today.

## Environmental Influences

Look around you. What do you see? How does it make you feel? Encouraged or not? Control what you can, adapt to what you cannot change.

You can structure your surroundings to be your helper. To clarify your Mental Image, go and sample what you dream of. Have lunch at a five-star hotel, test drive your dream car, take a snack and sit by the lake where you want to live. Rent a boat for the weekend or the day.

Go to the concert or club where you someday want to perform. Stand on the stage in the convention center or showroom where you will give a speech or receive an award. Buy a poster, or get a fold- out sales brochure, or a scale model of what you want. See yourself owning or using these each day.

Shop for the clothes you hope to afford, sit on the furniture you plan to buy someday. You don't need to go into debt, just get a feel for the items. Put yourself into the picture.

Get around people who share your enthusiasm and drastically reduce the time you spend around pessimists, doubters, and sourpusses. Don't participate in pity parties or criticism and bashing of others. Avoid political debates while you are seeking to succeed.

Choose the movies you watch with your goal as your filter. Don't go to occult or tragic or hateful or victim movies. Read uplifting novels, true stories, auto biographies, heroic, and inspiring works. Listen to positive podcasts, radio shows, webinars, and read blogs that lift you up. Manage your environment, don't let it manage you.

Create a vision board of images, a photo file, a playlist, slogans, tokens, symbols, and metaphors that make your goal more real. Start now to intentionally experience the success you dream about. Make it real, *feel* it.

Here is my personal story:

When I was in my twenties, I never expected to have a life that mattered much. My expectations were that I would get a middle-management office job at the phone company (where my Dad worked as a repairman) and retire at 65, then die whenever the statistics for my age group were up. I didn't have a college degree; nobody I knew had money and no one was encouraging me to achieve big things. My family loved me but didn't actively encourage reading, critical thinking, or aspiring to excellence or success.

One day, after hearing an inspiring message from Earl Nightingale on the radio, I started dreaming bigger. While working as an entry-level clerk in a government agency in Little Rock, Arkansas, I got a course catalog from the University of Arkansas at Little Rock and started listing the courses I would like to attend. There were more than 30 diverse courses that I found interesting, yet I still didn't know what I wanted as my career. I took a couple of night courses but didn't re-enroll.

Soon, I began to read motivational books and listen to recordings. There weren't many at the time, this was in 1972. I read *Think and Grow Rich* by Napoleon Hill, *The Power of Positive Thinking* by Norman Vincent Peale, and *How to Win Friends and Influence People* by Dale Carnegie. I listened to The Strangest Secret by Earl Nightingale and many recordings from Success Motivation Institute and Paul J. Meyer. Then it hit me! I want to do what these people do! I want to work in motivational training and be a speaker like Hill, Nightingale, Peale, and Carnegie.

But I had two limitations: I had never given a public speech and I had nothing worthwhile to say. That's a big limit! So, I started following the advice in each of their books. I set goals: lifetime goals, 5-year goals, 1-year goals, and daily actions to take. I wrote down my dreams and wishes. I clipped photos from magazines and pasted them where I would see them daily.

I changed my circle of friends by including people who also wanted to achieve great things and reduced the amount of time I spent with people who were pessimistic or small-minded. I disciplined myself to use optimistic language and stopped running myself down. I began a discipline of doing at least one good thing in each area of my life daily. There were positive statements and goal descriptions on my bathroom mirror, the visor of my car, and in my notebook. Every day, I listened to motivational recordings… every day.

This continued for five years.

In the first three years of this life change, I went from being a clerk to being the staff assistant to the Board of Directors in the agency where I worked. I was elected president of our employee's association. I joined the Jaycees (Junior Chamber of Commerce) and became very actively involved in volunteer work. At the office, I got a raise, then a promotion and another raise.

One day, a man named Harold Gash came to me after a Jaycees meeting where he and I were both giving presentations. He said, "Jim, you have more potential than any young man I have ever known! You should come to work with me and sell Earl Nightingale's motivational recordings to businesses." I was aghast! Me? Sell? "But I'm not good at selling," I said.

Harold said, "Yes, Jim, you can be an excellent salesman. But first you need to change your thinking." He was right. I had the ability, just not the mindset I needed.

Over the ensuing months, I left the government job and worked full-time with Harold. As I listened to the recordings daily and made calls to tell others about them, I made sales. In fact, I did well and loved the work! Then the US Jaycees national headquarters called me and asked if I would apply for the job of Individual Development Senior Program Manager for the 356,000 members of the Jaycees.

On September 1, 1975, I went to work at the Jaycees HQ in Tulsa, Oklahoma. I was a full-time trainer and speaker in the field of human development, just like my dream goals had stated back in Little Rock in 1972. I flew all over the country and gave speeches to groups as large as one thousand. I wrote training manuals and collaborated with leading experts like Og Mandino and W. Clement Stone (Look them up). I met Cavett Robert, founder of the National Speakers Association. My life profoundly changed.

While at the Jaycees HQ, I still listened to recordings daily, read books voraciously, and had written goals on cards in my bathroom, desktop, closet, and sun visor. I was living a daily regimen of Minimum Daily Standards of behavior that would achieve my goals. I started jogging and working out, lost 52 pounds of fat and became an amateur athlete… at age 30. My life transformed!

In June of 1977, I left the Jaycees and went full-time into professional speaking. Since that time, I have delivered over 3,300 paid speeches to millions of people, done three round-the-world lecture tours, delivered a TEDx talk that has more than 2,400,000 views, authored 20 books, including three international bestsellers, served as president of the National Speakers Association, and received every major award given to professional speakers in the world!

Earl Nightingale called me in 1984 after reading an article I had published, and he subsequently published my audio program, coauthored with Dr. Tony Alessandra, titled "Relationship Strategies for dealing with the differences in people." It sold more than $3.5 million dollars' worth in the first two years on the market! Note: In 1972, I heard him on the radio. In 1974, I was selling his recordings. In 1984, he was selling mine!

Over the years since then, I have become friends with Norman Vincent Peale, Og Mandino, Zig Ziglar, Dr. Denis Waitley, Tom Hopkins, Mark Victor Hansen, Jack Canfield, Brian Tracy, Les Brown, Don Hutson, Cavett Robert, Patricia Fripp, Jeanne Robertson, and many of the great names in human development. I've worked with W. Clement Stone and done *The Fire Walk Experience* with Tony Robbins. I've had my own TV Show on The Success Training Network, hosted a daily radio show, published hundreds of video lessons with Clay Clark, and lectured in 23 major cities across China to hundreds of thousands of people. My books have been published in multiple languages all around the world and I've written college textbooks. I'm a professor for the School of Management at California Lutheran University. And... I could go on, but surely, you get the point. All of this was achieved without outside funding, a government assistance program, a diversity grant or exception to "level the playing field" for me.

I had no college degree, no money to start with, no connections with successful people, no mentor nor encourager to get me started. I was out of shape, overweight by 52 pounds, and had no skills that I could quickly apply to get started. My job was a $525 a month clerkship at a local office of the housing authority. What I have done isn't important except for the fact that: If I can do this, YOU can do this!

Your success will be M.A.D.E. by you.

You already choose which Mental Images to accept. Your words affirm your current state of mind and circumstances. You have daily experiences that reinforce the world you've occupied up to now. Around you are environmental influences at every turn.

**What I'm recommending is that you start making all of them INTENTIONAL.**

Take charge of the influences in your life that are having Auto Suggestion impact on you every day. Make your life what you want it to be!

*Erik "Mr. Awesome" Swanson*

# POWERFUL BEYOND BELIEF

One of the most vital areas of our lives which we can control is our mind. Our mind is such a beautiful and powerful thing. It is powerful beyond belief. The philosophy of Auto Suggestion is truly the medium of influencing our subconscious mind, as Napoleon Hill explains as the third step to riches in *Think and Grow Rich* from 1937.

So, what exactly is Auto Suggestion? Auto Suggestion is the act of words that you say to yourself repetitively, with emotion and conviction, to seep into your subconscious mind. In other words, it's the process in which you are training your subconscious mind to act upon the actual thoughts you feed it. Keep in mind that your subconscious mind does not determine if the thoughts you are feeding it are positive or negative thoughts. It does not determine for you whether these thoughts are true or false, good or bad. Your subconscious mind simply acts upon what you feed it.

This, in and of itself, is either frightening to think about or really great news... depending on how you actually use Auto Suggestion and your subconscious mind. Most people do not use the concept of Auto Suggestion and their success, or lack of it, suffers as a result. It's imperative to YOUR success to implement this concept right away in to your every day habits... or what I call "Habitudes."

Our dominant thoughts truly become our reality. What are your dominant thoughts? What are you allowing yourself to feed into your brain on a consistent basis? You know that saying, "You are what you think about!" It's so true. What you think about most of the day will create your pathway or Auto Suggestion to your subconscious. This is an awesome concept if you use it correctly and wisely. Let me share the 3 steps I follow to assure success in Auto Suggestion.

Step 1: Here is a simple exercise for you to practice daily and keep a record or a journal to log your results. Start to be aware of your thoughts. What I mean by this is for you to literally think about your thoughts. Start to realize and take notice of the thoughts you tend to harbor on and have linger in your mind. Grab a piece of paper and put at the top of one side the words: *Positive Thoughts.* On the top of the other side of this piece of paper write the words: *Negative Thoughts.* Now, start to log your thoughts throughout the day. Start to notice which you tend to lean towards. Are most of your thoughts negative ones, those of limiting belief in yourself? Or, conversely, are most of your thoughts positive and successful thoughts? This will take some training to gear most of your thoughts into the positive realm. But, don't give up. It simply takes practice. Napoleon Hill taught us that this concept of Auto Suggestion works for anyone and everyone. It does not matter where you came from or which side of the tracks you grew up on. He also teaches us to never give up, even if at first you fail. Keep practicing these techniques and you will soon succeed. It is inevitable.

Step 2: The second thing you must do is to start training yourself to only focus on the positive thoughts that come into your conscious mind. Do not allow the negative thoughts to fester or build. By allowing the negative thoughts to build up and consume your conscious mind, you tend to start seeping those thoughts into your subconscious mind in which you are negatively applying the Auto Suggestion concept. I use my Habitude Warrior technique I call the 'Power of 8.' It's super simple to use.

All you have to do is agree to only give yourself 8 seconds to think about that negative thought that creeped into your mind—and then release it!

Vow to yourself that you will only allow positive thoughts to live within you. Giving yourself this permission is absolutely liberating. You deserve to live in a positive and abundant world. It's time you take back your own mindset and create the life you dream about.

Now is the time to start creating a list of affirmations that directly point to the ultimate outcome you are searching for. Let me be clear; this is not simply a list of random affirmations. This list of Auto Suggestion affirmations are geared towards building your subconscious mind to be open for success. They are essential to creating the neuron-pathways to connect your conscious mind to your subconscious mind. These affirmations will need to have emotion behind them. They will need to mean something to you. The more emotion and conviction you have towards these affirmations, the better. Auto Suggestion only works with emotion and conviction!

Here is a list of some of my top 10 Auto Suggestion Affirmations:

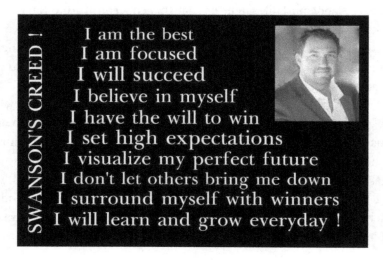

SWANSON'S CREED !

I am the best
I am focused
I will succeed
I believe in myself
I have the will to win
I set high expectations
I visualize my perfect future
I don't let others bring me down
I surround myself with winners
I will learn and grow everyday !

Step 3: Grab your affirmations and start repeating them to yourself throughout the day. Repeat them any chance you get. Actually say the words out loud so that you can hear yourself saying them. This is vitally important. You are now training your brain to accept these thoughts and affirmations into your subconscious mind. Don't stop with only your affirmations. Start to encourage yourself to seek out positive thoughts and use the same technique to enter those into your subconscious mind as well. Trust me, you will get really good at this. Make sure you write your affirmations and any other positive thoughts down on pieces of paper and leave them in places you will find them throughout the day. Also, strategically leave them in places where you can see them before you go to sleep at night and also where you can find them as you get up each morning. Leave them sticking to your steering wheel of your car. Leave them at the office. Put them everywhere and once you find them, say the words out loud with emotion and conviction each and every time you see them.

Let's recap…

## Habitude Warrior's Auto Suggestion 3 Step Strategy:

1) Log in a journal your daily positive and negative thought patterns

2) Create a list of positive affirmations directly pointing to your ultimate outcome

3) Constantly repeat these positive words to yourself with emotion and conviction

Mastering the art of Auto Suggestion will change your life! It's actually a lot of fun. I mean, think about it. How awesome is it to be able to master what you bring into your own mind? Too many people allow others to rent space in their mind and they aren't even charging rent for it. Don't allow others to determine your future and your outcome. Take control of it. In fact, take master control and point your life and success in any direction you desire. Our dominant thoughts truly become our reality!

# ERIK SWANSON

***About Erik "Mr. Awesome" Swanson:*** As an Award-Winning International Keynote Speaker and 10 Time #1 Best-Selling Author, Erik "Mr. Awesome" Swanson is in great demand around the world! He speaks to an average of more than one million people per year. He can be seen on Amazon Prime TV in the very popular show *SpeakUP TV*. Mr. Swanson has the honor to have been invited to speak to many universities such as University of California (UCSD), Cal State University, University of Southern California (USC), Grand Canyon University (GCU), and the Business and Entrepreneurial School of Harvard University. He is also a Faculty Member of CEO Space International and is a recurring keynoter at Vistage Executive Coaching. Erik also joins the Ted Talk Family with his latest TEDx speech called "A Dose of Awesome."

Erik got his start in the self development world by mentoring directly under the infamous Brian Tracy. Quickly climbing to become the top trainer around the world from a group of over 250 hand picked trainers, Erik started to surround himself with the best of the best and soon started to be inviting to speak on stages along side such greats as Jim Rohn, Bob Proctor, Les Brown, Sharon Lechter, Jack Canfield, and Joe Dispenza... just to name a few. Erik has created and developed the super-popular Habitude Warrior Conference, which has a two-year waiting list and includes 33 top named speakers from around the world. It is a 'Ted Talk' style event which has quickly climbed to one of the top 10 events not to miss in the United States! He is the creator, founder, and CEO of the Habitude Warrior Mastermind and Global Speakers Mastermind. His motto is clear... "NDSO!": No Drama – Serve Others!

Author's Website: *www.SpeakerErikSwanson.com*
Book Series Website & Author's Bio: *www.The13StepstoRiches.com*

## *Jon Kovach Jr.*

# ENVISION:
# AS IF YOU ALREADY POSSESS IT

Concentrate!
Fix your mind on the exact thing you desire.
Close your eyes until you see its physical appearance.
See yourself actually in possession of your desire.

It was a mere miracle birthed from the disaster that happened on May 16th, 2019, that my best varsity athletes, whom I coached and trained all season long to qualify for the State Championships, all completely choked in their performances at the Regional Championships. All three of my female high-jump athletes missed their last chance to win a one-way ticket to the State Championships and compete for the gold. However, one of my younger athletes seized this opportunity. A younger freshman girl I hadn't focused on or worked with all season cleared the winning height and earned a ticket to the State Championships.

I knew that this was going to be a long shot for gold. There was no possible way of conditioning her to the varsity level five days before the Championships. She was naturally athletic and mentally tough. In my professional coaching opinion, this was the recipe for a building champion.

The next day at practice, she frantically ran over to the high jump pit, nervous and overwhelmed, and began to recreate her jump. She was shocked when I told her it didn't matter. She had a million questions, and I answered none of them.

I asked her, "What do you want to achieve?" She said, "I want to be a champion."

I replied, "Do you believe you can?" She answered, "I'll do anything."

I informed her that physically she couldn't do anything more to prepare than she already had, but mentally could have whatever she wanted as long as her desire to win was never compromised. She nodded in agreement, and we went to work. For five days, I had her minimally jog a few laps around the track, memorize her steps, do a few jumps, then drink a couple of liters of water. At the end of her physical training sessions, we spent the rest of practice (almost one and a half hours daily) sitting down, closing her eyes, envisioning her desire by imagining and working our way backward from becoming a champion. I called it the Envisioning Exercise.

At first, the other coaches observing my practices were concerned. They asked if I would make her sprint, hit the weight room, or focus on her technique more like they would while training their athletes for the biggest contest of the year. I chuckled each time they inquired and reassured them that this was precisely what she needed. I'm sure they all thought I was crazy. They were right. You've got to be crazy if you want to be different.

If you want to be a champion, don't do what everyone else is doing.

## The Daily Envisioning Exercise

**Step 1**: Visualize yourself in possession of your desires.

The Daily Envision Exercise starts with the end in mind (Habit 2 of the *7 Habits of Highly Effective People,* author Stephen R. Covey). She wanted to win, so I had her spend 10-15 minutes visualizing that moment of winning the competition. With her eyes closed, she imagined the scene—she smiled, cheered, screamed, imagined hugging her mom and grandma. She high-fived her teammates and emulated stepping onto the podium with her medal. Experiencing the win as though it had already happened was vital for her to believe she was a champion.

**Step 2**: Concentrate on the performance.

After 15 minutes of envisioning her desire to win, I had her dream of the perfect performance that ultimately won the competition. She imagined her ideal stride, the exact number of steps in her approach to the high jump mat, the explosive take-off vertical jump, the precisely-timed back arch, the flop and heel kick, and the graceful glide over the lowest-hanging part of the high bar.

**Step 3**: Identify the essentials. Take careful notice of the milestones and checkpoints leading up to the performance of your desire.

After 15 minutes of mentally taking herself through her performance, she focused on the details that led to keeping her focused. She identified those keys as deep relaxing breaths, regular reminders to smile, fast approaches to the bar, firm take-offs, long hang-time, and soft landing. We took note of those essentials and planned them for her performance. I committed to using a whiteboard during her competition and would write reminders to take deep breaths and smile occasionally.

**Step 4**: Repeat the declaration. Repeat and re-affirm your goal by declaring your desire.

The two most powerful words in the English language are, "I am." Those words are the keys to accepting your desires, believing in their existence, and transmuting them into reality through active faith and Auto Suggestion.

*The subconscious mind takes any orders given to it and acts upon those orders, although the orders often have to be presented over and over again through repetition.* —Napoleon Hill

### Desire + Faith + Auto Suggestion = Desire Obtained

It was May 21st, 2019, the Track and Field State Championships. My freshman challenged the top competitors in the sport of high jump. I stood behind the fence with all the other spectators with my large whiteboard sign to indicate my athlete's essentials.

As she warmed up and stretched, she took a look around to soak it all in. I immediately began writing messages on my whiteboard such as "SMILE," "Have Fun," and "Deep Breath!" Each time she read my notes, she would smile, take a breath, shrug her shoulders back, and relax.

The competition began. To our surprise, many girls couldn't clear the opening high-bar height. My athlete cleared the bar on her first jump attempt. When she jumped, it looked as though she was an entire 12 inches above the bar. She smiled, realizing that she had just set another personal record. The event continued; each competitor took their jumps. After the first round of jumps, half the competition faltered.

She jumped again in the second round, clearing the bar looking like she had been high jumping for decades. She cheered again, another personal height record. The competition dwindled to eight athletes, including my freshman.

She took her third-round jump, gliding gracefully over the bar. As she flopped over the bar, her heel nicked the bar, causing it to leap off the stand, but it landed back into place. She had cleared her third height. ANOTHER PERSONAL RECORD!

To my excitement, three athletes remained in the final round. The high jump judge moved the bar up two more inches. I waived my whiteboard at my athlete, and again, she smiled, took a deep breath, shrugged her shoulders back, and approached her final attempt. In this final round, each girl could take a shot at the jump. Each athlete, including mine, had two missed attempts at the final height. It came down to the last jump. She sprinted, jumped her highest, flopped over the bar, and on her descent, that heel nicked the bar again, only this time, knocking the bar off the platform. She landed on the mat, threw her hands over her eyes in disappointment, and looked back at me. I already had the whiteboard waiting for her, which read, "Envision it!"

We waited for the judge to tally up the jump scores. The judge began reading off the names of the winners, starting from 8th place down to 1st. I noticed this woman and an older woman next to me intently watching my athlete. It was my freshman's mother and grandmother, just as she had envisioned. Just then, the judge read my athlete's name, announcing her as a champion! I danced and hugged the two ladies next to me, jumping and screaming in excitement for our girl.

As she stood on top of the podium with her medal around her neck, she looked over at me, her proud coach, and mouthed the words, "I can't believe I'm a champion." I corrected her statement and mouthed back, "I am."

## Create An Action Plan

Desire is your GPS. Faith is the belief that you can obtain your desire, put the keys in the ignition, and start your vehicle. Auto Suggestion takes the vehicle out of park and lets off the brakes while pressing down the acceleration. Auto Suggestion transports you to your desires. It's up to you how hard you press the pedal and how fast you are willing to accelerate to get those desires.

It's so easy to apply Napoleon's success method, written in 1937.

**Step 1**: Read aloud twice daily the written statement of your desire.

**Step 2**: Envision yourself in possession of it.

**Step 3**: Put plans into action immediately.

**Step 4**: Repeat until the desire is obtained.

**Warning:** Failure to do this will be FATAL to your success.

***THESE STEPS ARE NOT LIMITED TO FINANCES. THEY'RE ALSO UTILIZED IN ACHIEVING ANYTHING THAT YOU DESIRE!***

*By following these instructions, you communicate the object of your desire directly to your subconscious mind in a spirit of absolute faith. Through repetition of this procedure, you voluntarily create thought habits to transmute desire into its monetary equivalent.* —Napoleon Hill, *Think And Grow Rich*

Now that I have revealed my desire and drive to become an Olympic athlete in Volume 1, my secret weapon to achieving anything with faith in Volume 2, and my Auto Suggestion envisioning tools in Volume 3, you'll have to read the next volume in this series (***The 13 Steps To Riches: Volume 4 Specialized Knowledge***) to learn what happened to me while competing as a decathlete.

# JON KOVACH JR.

**About Jon Kovach Jr.:** Jon is an award-winning and international motivational speaker and global mastermind leader. Jon has helped multi-billion-dollar corporations, including Coldwell Banker Commercial, Outdoor Retailer Cotopaxi, and the Public Relations Student Society of America, exceed their annual sales goals. In his work as an accountability coach and mastermind facilitator, Jon has helped thousands of professionals overcome their challenges and achieve their goals by implementing his 4 Irrefutable Laws of High Performance.

Jon is Founder and Chairman of Champion Circle, a networking association that combines highperformance based networking activities and recreational fun to create connection capital and increases prosperity for professionals.

Jon is the Mastermind Facilitator and Team Lead of the Habitude Warrior Mastermind and the Global Speakers Mastermind & Masterclass founded by Speaker Erik "Mr. Awesome" Swanson.

Jon speaks on a number of topics including accountability, The 4 Irrefutable Laws of High Performance, and The Power of Mastermind Methodologies. He is a #1 Best-Selling Author and was recently featured on SpeakUp TV, an Amazon Prime TV series. He stars in over 100 speaking stages, podcasts, and live international summits on an annual basis.

Author's website: *www.JonKovachJr.com*
Book Series Website & Author's Bio: *www.The13StepsToRiches.com*

*Amado Hernandez*

# YOU ARE DESIGNED FOR GREATNESS

Auto Suggestion is your internal dialogue. Your personal Auto Suggestion is vital to the way you respond to everything that life throws at you. Auto Suggestion is how you will determine your actions through small, daily steps. Any negative action and reaction will determine if you are fueling your intentions with the right stuff.

Auto Suggestion is having insurance for your life, health, and business because you ensure positive outcomes and responses to tragedies and negativities. In Psalms chapter 23, verse 4; "Yea, though I walk through the valley of the shadow of death, I will fear no evil: for thou art with me; thy rod and thy staff they comfort me." Therefore, Auto Suggestion is the response to my fed intentions.

Religious or not, auto-suggesting courage over fear helps us not to be afraid or be dismayed, for your God (or conviction) is with you, wherever you go. This mantra is challenging to follow, especially if you feel incapable, as I felt when invited to participate in this historical book series. I said to myself that I could not do something that big, but then that little voice came from inside me and said that I could do all things.

My personal Auto Suggestions strengthen me. This is a phenomenal book because that paradigm shift in each of us can open up worlds of opportunity and positive thinking. It happens in your mind, and Auto Suggestion is your immediate response to your Internal Guiding Systems (IGS). Your internal guiding systems are your inner encyclopedia for what you've received and learned throughout your life. IGS is the metamorphosis within yourself, the collection of positives and negatives that all add to your fight or flight instincts.

In *The 13 Steps to Riches*, each of these thirteen volumes holds informational keys of inspiration to change your IGS to a more positive and responsible way of living. You are always at a crossroads of decisions in life, and the more positive Auto Suggestions your IGS is fed, you will listen to that navigational system. Even if you consider yourself a stubborn person, you're going to reap all the benefits of a powerful subconscious.

Success is not final, and neither is failure. I'd rather succeed and have been a success and a failure, than experience no success, having not even tried in the first place.

### Developing the Habitude of Auto Suggestion

Developing Auto Suggestion starts with first acknowledging that you need positive affirmations to fuel your thoughts. Our mind works like a bank. Whatever positive balances you put in your bank will reap more significant dividends later.

Second, I suggest you make a moral decision that you're not going to follow the crowd.

Third, surround yourself with people and mentors who fill your hearts and thoughts with kindness, positivity, and mentorship. I highly recommend some of my friends and mentors, Erik "Mr. Awesome" Swanson, Jon Kovach Jr., Ben Gay III, and anyone else creating positive movements and have results doing them. If you take these types of people more seriously, the change will occur in unbelievable ways.

Where you plant your seeds of Faith, Auto Suggestion will follow. When I was twenty-five, my dad was one of the most intelligent and mature people I knew. When he was around me, I felt smarter. He gave me that confidence. The older I grew, I recognized the wisdom he had passed down from generation to generation. It was amazing to see how listening to their knowledge and understanding fueled them. They've been auto-suggesting principles and values for many years.

When our forefathers wrote the Declaration of Independence, they were not going to be under the tyranny of English rule, auto-suggesting to future generations of Americans that they may all live in a land of freedom. We, too, must write it into our genetic coding so that we, too, will not fall under the tyranny of negativity.

During the pandemic, my fiancé and I were watching Netflix, avoiding the world from the deadly COVID-19 virus. It occurred to me that three months into quarantine, I recalled a quote from one of our Mexican leaders saying, "I would rather die, standing up fighting, than continue living on my knees." I realized that there still was much work for me to do, and that I could do it even amid a pandemic. I told my fiancé that I would start going back to work. "I know I'm not going to die, but if it happens, so be it." I said, "I can't continue doing nothing any longer." For almost four months, I went to the office, where nobody was, and worked where I labored and fought for my prosperity.

My IGS auto-suggested that I decided to apply this freedom-fighting action. Today we're between forty and fifty percent above what we did in 2020, and we're starting to gain a lot more momentum.

The skillset of Auto Suggestion helps to avoid crises and to achieve goals. I started working in engineering in high school until I was twenty-four years old. I worked for Robert McCall's corporation in Los Angeles, the guy that built the London Bridge. I was in charge of the deployment and quality control of the company, and made sure everything was compliant with our procedures.

An opportunity came up in Tulsa, Oklahoma, where they were having problems. They asked me to come and train their staff on compliance. I had difficulty deciding, as I had a wife and kids and would have to move my family across the country. I sought advice from my mother, who would say that I was destined for greatness from the time I was little. She convinced me that this was a minor and temporary decision, compared to my destined greatness. Her advice convinced me not to accept the offer. It was challenging for me to say no to the request because I loved to work, and I knew I could fix the company's issues, but my mom's advice was spot-on for me. I've been destined for greatness my entire life. Then, as I was reading the bible, a verse jumped out at me during this time of crisis. The scripture read, "…you have not, because you ask not…," so I started asking more for greatness.

Another verse reads, "…seek ye first the Kingdom of God and everything will be added unto you…," so I became more focused spiritually. Then lo and behold, after that project in Tulsa wrapped up, they offered me a job back to help build the B-1B Bomber, and they were making the mock-up. Because I had the background of quality control and quality engineering, it was a perfect fit. And now, because I had had more time between project requests, I had more background in mechanics. This request put me in charge of the mock-up development program tasked with delivering it to the US Air Force. Later on, I traveled to the Dyess Air Force base in Ellsworth, South Dakota. Auto-suggesting greatness for my future ultimately brought more excellence and opportunity for me in the end.

Chapter three, Auto Suggestion, in Napoleon Hill's *Think and Grow Rich* says, "No thought, whether it be negative or positive, can enter the subconscious mind without the aid of the principle of Auto Suggestion, except for those thoughts picked up as flashes of inspiration or insight."

My NLP (Neuro-Linguistic Programing) mentor (mindset coach) says that the conscious mind is the practical adult inside of us, the subconscious mind is still the little kid inside us, and the little kid is the workbench. When your Auto Suggestion starts telling the little workers inside what to do with conviction, desire, and faith, you become unstoppable because the little kid inside believes it, too.

### Auto Suggestion derives from desire and faith

At one point, I was in a joint venture, and it was just going from bad to worse. I was getting short on cash and capital very quickly. I went and asked one of my aunts if I could borrow some money. I've always done exceptionally well in my family, so that portion of my family was happy to help me out. However, my aunt told my dad, Roberto Hernandez, who retired at a very young age and was very successful, and he called me. He said, "What the heck are you waiting for to be completely broke and to be standing at the corner naked waiting for something to happen? You are not mediocre. I raised you to live a great life and to be great." To this day, that tough conversation lingers in my mind and gives me the reminding inspiration of who I was designed and destined to become.

In response to his words of wisdom, we built another office building. Our success continued to grow, and I worked myself out of the capital losses and back into more gains.

My dad's words, "You've been designed and destined for greatness," are the most powerful reminders that I've ever had, auto-suggesting my next choice in everything I do. In honor and gratitude to my father, Roberto Hernandez, I dedicate this contributing chapter in *The 13 Steps to Riches*, for his love and mentorship. Thank you for bringing me into this world and teaching me my greatness in the glory of God. Without your words, I would never have become who I am today, Mr. ABC (Always Be Closing).

# AMADO HERNANDEZ

**About Amado Hernandez:** Amado was born in Mexico of humble beginnings and raised in Los Angeles, California. As an avid reader, Amado always focused on self-development. He coaches sales professionals to make six and seven figures in real estate.

Amado believes in a progressive culture, one people-centric where clients' dreams come true and salespeople thrive; at the end of the day, we all want to be respected and pursue our happiness. My goal is to leave a legacy and make a difference in people's lives.

With 33 years of Real Estate experience, Mr. ABC Amado Hernandez successfully operates and grows his Excellence Empire Real Estate Moreno Valley office. Broker/Owner Amado first opened his doors in 1995, and Excellence currently has over 60 offices in Southern California, Las Vegas, Merida Yucatan, Mexico, with over 900 Agents. He is also part owner of a highly successful Mortgage company, Excellence Mortgage, and owner of Empire Escrow Services. Mr. Amado is also involved with his community and currently serves as Director at Inland Valley Association of Realtors and will be the President-Elect for 2021.

Author's Website: *www.ExcellenceEmpireRE.com*
Book Series Website & Author's Bio: *www.The13StepstoRiches.com*

*Angelika Ullsperger*

# THE SCIENCE BEHIND AUTO SUGGESTION

Auto Suggestion, for many people, is a foreign term, yet it is absolutely instrumental in reaching one's full potential. To become your best, you need to understand the inner workings of your mind. By doing this, you can work with your brain to accomplish your desires. Auto Suggestion, at its core, is about reprogramming your mind.

By changing our minds, we can change our brains.

Our brains are filled with many connecting roads, referred to as neural pathways. In short, these connections allow for signals to be sent and received throughout the brain. For everyday travel, such as the drive to work, there may be multiple routes you can take to accomplish reaching your destination efficiently. The brain, however, works in a different manner. For every action you take, the brain has created a specific set of pathways. Every time you execute an action, the pathways relating to that action get stronger. When you don't use a particular neural pathway, it begins to get weaker. If you are having a hard time imagining this, picture a forest. The first time you travel through a forest, you must create the path. Each time you use your new path, the dirt becomes compressed, debris is moved out of the way, and as a result, the path improves immensely as it becomes easier to walk through each time. If you stop walking the path, the forest will begin to grow over it, and the path will slowly fade. If you stop using the path for long enough, it will one day dissolve entirely, leaving no trace. This same principle can be applied to neural pathways.

Have you ever stepped away from something you were good at for a while only to come back and notice you aren't as good as you were? That is an example the neural pathway weakening. After a few hours working at it, you'll notice you've begun to improve again.

The more the pathway is used, the stronger the pathway becomes and, in turn, becomes easier to use.

Not only does this apply to actions, but to thoughts as well. It's easier for depressed individuals to think depressing thoughts because those are the strongest connections in their minds. But let's think for a minute; if we have the power to strengthen or weaken our thought patterns, can't we change them too? The answer is "Yes!"

Like most things, this is easier said than done, but that doesn't make it impossible.

When our minds change, a few things happen. Our beliefs change, the way we think inwards about ourselves changes, and as a result, our actions change as well. All of these have the power to change your life for the better. While it may seem unrelated at first, let me share how I came to this realization.

Hill elaborates on how emotionally-charged thoughts have the most substantial impact. This is true, but unfortunately it works both ways, therefore, it's important for us to be cognizant of the thoughts we have. An example of this occurring is trauma and how it changes the brain.

For years of my life, I was severely depressed from trauma and was left with little motivation, plus a slew of negative thinking. I was convinced that my brain was wired to be depressed, and nothing I could do would change it. I was set on the fact that no matter how hard I tried, my brain would stay the same. While it was true my brain was more wired for depression after everything I've endured, I was wrong about the latter.

Though it may be true that your thought patterns influence how you see the world, you can also influence your brain to alter your thought patterns in a positive way. This took me many years of struggling to understand.

Years passed me by as I stood watching my life in a dissociative state. Still, I was trying to heal and get back to normal living, so I got a job at a small family bagel shop. Every morning before the sun rose, I entered the shop, greeted by the smell of fresh bagels and coffee. I would start my day. I thought I was getting up reasonably early for work, but the woman making the bagels would come in around two am every day. I was in awe of her work ethic. How was she able to get up so early every day yet always give her best? I would love to give her a shout-out in this book, but since I will be mentioning some of her trauma, out of respect, we will refer to her as S. Out of everything that stood out to me, what stood out the most was her positivity. One day we got to talking, and she revealed to me she that had been stuck in an abusive relationship for many, many years. Yet here she was, filled with kindness and positivity, constantly working her hardest, never stopping to complain. After work, she would then drive hours to see her loved ones. I was befuddled. How could she have endured all those years of trauma yet still be so positive and driven??

Filled with curiosity, I had to ask, "How?"

To my bewilderment, she revealed to me it was through working on herself with the help of self- improvement books and listening to podcasts of motivational speakers.

Wait. Podcasts? Motivational Speakers? All of the things I had blown off for years as corny things that mentally healthy people did. I saw those things as things that would never be able to help me, because they didn't understand the struggle.

But that couldn't have been further from the truth. They did understand the struggle; it was me who never tried to understand them. As my head hit the pillow later that night, it finally hit me. There were specific actions taken by all of the motivated, driven individuals I had looked up to. The biggest one being self-improvement resources. All of the people I looked up to filled their minds with motivational podcasts and self-help books. The exact things I had blown off for years.

Being older and wiser, I now understand why they work.

When you fill your mind with positive thinking, you create new neural pathways, and when you're thinking positively, you aren't using the neural connections for negative thinking (thus making them weaker)!

Just as Rome wasn't built in a day, you can't change your mind overnight. You have to continuously work on it. There will be days you feel as if nothing has changed or you have made no progress, but don't stop there. Because every day you work on it, it gets stronger, even when you can't feel it.

Every month, day, week, minute, and second you act with intention, you can rewire your brain.

How does this relate to Auto Suggestion? Well, by strengthening certain pathways, we make it easier for our subconscious mind to automatically suggest a desired outcome.

Thanks to the immense power of the brain, Auto Suggestion really does work.

Many things can be included in this, all with an end goal of a newly productive and more positive YOU. Be open to change during this new time while you slowly introduce a new structure to your way of living.

By giving yourself structure and a growing positive mindset, your default way of thinking will no longer be as negative as it once was. Even in darker times, you will still have this positive side to you, helping you pull through until you can be happy once more. Stick with your routine, and actively replace your negative thoughts with positive ones. Pay close attention to your own self- talk, notice when you are being too negative (including being too negative towards yourself). This Auto Suggestion can change your inner dialogue to think more positively, and once that inner voice changes, your life will begin to change. These repeated tasks, physically and mentally, will act as a complete refresh and potentially a newly blank slate to rewire your inner workings just the way you want them.

Throughout the changes discussed above, it's important to remember that these are big changes, and I want to reiterate that they will not be immediate! In order for them to become permanent additions to your life, you will need to put in the work to locate your negativity, remove that negativity, and replace it with positive structures to base your new life around. While it will take effort, it will be one of the best things you will ever do for yourself. What you desire is far from impossible, so don't ever give up! Because by changing our brains, we can change our lives!

# ANGELIKA ULLSPERGER

**About Angelika Ullsperger:** Angelika is a serial entrepreneur from Baltimore, Maryland. She is a fashion designer, model, artist, photographer, and musician. Angelika has extensive and well rounded professional experience having worked as a business owner, carpenter, chef, graphic designer, manager, event planner, sales and product specialist, marketer, and coach. Angelika is now a #1 Best-Selling Author in the historic book series, The 13 Steps To Riches. She is a lifelong learner with a sincere and genuine interest in all things of the world with a major interest in the formal subject of abnormal psychology, neuroscience, and quantum physics.

Angelika prides herself as someone who has saved lives as a friend, first responder, EMT, and knowledgeable suicide prevention advocate. With a vast knowledge and experience in multiple professions, Angelika is also a proud honorable member of Phi Theta Kappa, The APA, the AAAS, and an FBLA (Future Business Leaders Association) Business Competition Finalist. She is Certified in basic coding and blockchain technology. Amongst the careers and vast experience, Angelika is an adventurer and avid dog lover.

Her ultimate goals and dreams are to make a lasting positive impact in people's lives through her wealth of knowledge and skillsets.

Author's Website: *www.Angelika.world*
Book Series Website & Author's Bio: *www.The13StepstoRiches.com*

## Dr. Anthony M. Criniti IV

# SENSE AND GROW RICH

*Think and Grow Rich* by Napoleon Hill is one of the best classic books to teach someone how to become a financial success (as well as a success in other areas of life). In there, you will find his thirteen steps to riches; each one has its own separate chapter and analysis. The subject of our book is to interpret his third step to riches: Auto *Suggestion*. Admittedly, this concept may be an unusual one for the average person, but if used properly, it can become a powerful tool to achieve greatness.

To really understand the significance of the third step to riches, we must first understand exactly what Napoleon Hill meant by this curious term "Auto Suggestion." In the words of Hill: "Auto Suggestion is a term which applies to all suggestions and all self-administered stimuli which reach one's mind through the five senses. Stated in another way, Auto Suggestion is self-suggestion. It is the agency of communication between that part of the mind where conscious thought takes place, and that which serves as the seat of action for the subconscious mind." (Hill, 2011, p. 106).

I interpret Hill's Auto Suggestion to mean to find ways to purposely inject stimulus from "external *nature*" into the deep parts of the mind. First, let me clarify what I mean by the concept of "external nature." From *The Survival of the Richest*: "The dividing line between its external and internal nature, like that of any other entity, is at the first particle of space outside of the body. The internal nature (or what I will also refer to as "the wealth inside") includes the whole body from its internal organs to its most superficial parts. This is contrasted with external nature, which can be a variety of things, such as astronomical, geological, and meteorological factors." (Criniti, 2016, p. 316). It is easy to think that Hill meant to do this only by sight and sound (via reading and listening) because of the requirement for repetition. However, in Hill's explanation of Auto Suggestion above, he specifically said through the "five senses," which would include sight, sound, smell, taste, and touch.

By incorporating all of the senses into your influence of your subconscious, you are increasing the probability of having a meaningful impact because you are strengthening your feelings for any specific goal. By having stronger emotions mixed with the right thoughts, you can create a more potent formula for your success. Hill continuously acknowledged this powerful combination. He said, "Remember, therefore, when reading aloud the statement of your desire (through which you are endeavoring to develop a "money consciousness"), that the mere reading of the words is of no consequence—unless you mix emotion, or feeling with your words." (Hill, 2011, p. 108).

Hill's mentioning of the relationship between the five senses and Auto Suggestion was not analyzed in *depth* in the short Chapter 4. However, its implications are extraordinary if you can make the proper connections to your goals. The use of each sense will be more or less relevant depending on the specific circumstance of the person who is auto-suggesting. Nevertheless, it is up to that individual to find creative ways to positively influence their own subconscious with the correct stimuli that will help properly shape their mind.

"Be great or go home" has always been my philosophy. *If you want to be the best that you can be, for whatever that means to you, then you need to be immersed in the greatest relevant experiences to attain that specific goal.* This certainly includes being around great leaders in your field. You should want to utilize all of your senses to create a better feeling of what it is to be *great* like them. From listening to their words to smelling the scents of the specific perfume/cologne that they wear, you will increase the strength of your emotions when the thoughts of greatness enter your brain. To enhance the effect, you then allow these thoughts to marinate even in your sleep.

The sense of touch can also be great stimuli for the subconscious. Some examples range from the money that you desire to hold to the handshake of the great leader that you emulate. The more senses that you can bring into your mind, the better the effect could be when you start to incorporate *Hill's* concept of repetition. Let's talk more about this concept next.

One of Hill's major conclusions in this chapter is that auto-suggesting works best when repeated often. Hill explains the significance of repetition further: "Here is a most significant fact—the subconscious mind takes any orders given it in a spirit of absolute faith, and acts upon those orders, although the orders often have to be presented *over and over again*, through repetition, before they are interpreted by the subconscious mind." (Hill, 2011, p. 110).

Hill has a process to make Auto Suggestion work. The following is a quick paraphrase of his three step instructions. First, you need to find a quiet place to be able to focus on envisioning the details of the desired money coming into your life. Repeat these details aloud. Second, you will need to repeat this process twice a day. Third, place a copy of the statement somewhere obvious and read it twice a day until memorized.

Hill's conclusions and instructions require you to invest a lot of time into yourself to become wealthy. This is no different than some of my own conclusions on someone who wants to be a great investor in other areas of life. That is, the top investors always do their homework first. Real investing is not for the lazy; time spent on research, planning, implementation, etc. is what separates the best from the rest. From

Principle 122 of *The Most Important Lessons in Economics and Finance*: "If average investors could make money without any effort, then they would." (Criniti, 2014, p. 154). Hill's requirement for repetition can take much of your time. However, if applied correctly, it could make you very financially successful.

In short, if you want to grow rich, you must first learn how to correctly influence the thoughts in your *own* brain. You also need to fill your head with the right information, especially financially related. As stated in *The Necessity of Finance*: "Ultimately, every student of finance should become the master of his or her financial destiny and make all of his or her own major financial decisions." (Criniti, 2013, p. 179). By learning and implementing the lessons of finance, you can begin to gain control over your financial future.

Hill's Auto Suggestion is a very important tool to help create the right thoughts in your mind to attract riches. He elaborates further on its significance: "The actual performance of transmuting desire into money, involves the use of Auto Suggestion as an agency by which one may reach, and *influence*, the subconscious mind. The other principles are simply tools with which to apply Auto Suggestion. Keep this thought in mind, and you will, at all times, be conscious of the important part the principle of Auto Suggestion is to play in your efforts to accumulate money through the methods described in this book." (Hill, 2011, p. 114).

To conclude, for the average person with lack of confidence in themselves or their ability to attract money, Auto Suggestion can help them the same way prayer can help someone become more spiritual. However, I think that at the more advanced levels Auto Suggestion is not needed as much or at all, particularly when someone has already developed an optimal financial state of mind. *When extreme confidence meets high ability, Hill's secret becomes ingrained in every atom of your body to the point where greatness starts to occur from muscle memory.* Although Hill wrote this book mainly for the regular person, it is important to understand that great people have made daily habits of feeding their minds with greatness, but this might not have looked exactly as Hill's three- step instructions. Thus, Hill's instructions for Auto Suggestion are a guiding point that should be customized to each individual.

Finally, the key to properly auto-suggesting is to continuously feed your mind with the right thoughts *through* as many forms of environmental stimuli as possible. See, hear, smell, taste, and touch financial success and you could truly sense and grow rich!

# DR. ANTHONY M. CRINITI

**About Dr. Anthony M. Criniti IV:** Dr. Anthony (aka "Dr. Finance®") is the world's leading financial scientist and survivalist. A fifth generation native of Philadelphia, Dr. Criniti is a former finance professor at several universities, a former financial planner, an active investor in diverse marketplaces, an explorer, an international keynote speaker, and has traveled around the world studying various aspects of finance. He is an award winning author of three #1 international best-selling finance books: *The Necessity of Finance* (2013), *The Most Important Lessons in Economics and Finance* (2014), and *The Survival of the Richest* (2016). As a prolific writer, he also frequently contributes articles to *Entrepreneur, Medium,* and *Thrive Global.* Dr. Criniti's work has started a grassroots movement that is changing the way that we think about economics and finance.

Author's website: *www.DrFinance.info*
Book Series Website & Author's Bio: *www.The13StepsToRiches.com*

## Barry Bevier

# THE SEED YOU PLANT DETERMINES YOUR HARVEST

My journey into personal development started about 2010. It wasn't until two or three years later, that I was first introduced to *Think and Grow Rich*. My first reading was challenging—What's this secret to wealth Napoleon Hill is writing about? It was during my third reading that it all started to make sense. Each time I read it, I comprehend more, and capture the essence of all the principles, especially mindset. It is now my goal to read *Think and Grow Rich* every year.

What I've realized as I read and understand the teachings of Napoleon Hill, is that throughout my life, I have been using them, unknowingly, and occasionally to my detriment. It was only a couple years ago that I realized I had been unknowingly applying the principles of Auto Suggestion in a way that held me back, kept me from reaching my goals, and hurting me financially.

I now realize that as a younger person, the clues were all around me. I just didn't see them. One of my favorite sayings has become "You don't know what you don't know." Throughout my life, I've had tremendous opportunities presented to me, most of which I willingly took advantage of. Although I had a successful career and made more money than I had ever envisioned, I didn't retain the wealth that could have been associated with the level of income. I was raised in a Christian family on a farm in Michigan. My mother had the mindset that God intended Christians and farmers to be poor (scarcity), and that wealthy people were bad. Other mindsets that I acquired growing up were that making money is not easy, and we have to work hard to achieve success. Those philosophies were embedded in my subconscious and have had a profound impact on my life.

What I've realized is that all of these opportunities allowed me to produce the income, yet not build wealth. Because I had a scarcity mindset instilled in me from my youth, I subconsciously did not allow myself to accumulate wealth. So even though I could make money, I was unable to use it to build wealth. So can Auto Suggestion work both for us and against us? It absolutely does.

Having grown up a farmer, it is easy to relate to Napoleon Hills comment about "…the subconscious mind resembles a Garden Spot in which weeds will grow in abundance if the seeds of more desirable crops are not sown." In my case, because I didn't know better, I involuntarily seeded negative thoughts about wealth, rather than intentionally seeding with thoughts of a creative, positive, and wealthy nature. I seeded thoughts of lack rather than creation of great wealth, of which I was certainly capable.

Starting in the 1960s, my mom was involved with Amway. The Network Marketing profession is a great place to learn personal development. I remember her going to conventions and coming back with sayings like "Every day in every way, I'm getting better and better." And, "If it's going to be, it's up to me." She was working directly with Sterling and Van Kraus, two of the greatest leaders, team builders and earners in the organization at the time. She had a tremendous opportunity. Working directly with their leadership and mentoring, she could have built a very large and profitable organization. Yet she never did much more than a few retail sales every month. While she did have the attitude that she wasn't "a salesperson," it was probably more that she had the subconscious belief that she didn't deserve success and wealth. Not that she couldn't achieve it. I'm sure with the right mindset and desire, she could have.

Napoleon Hill speaks of focusing on the amount of money we desire, and the time in which we will accumulate it. In my journey over the past few years, one of my mentors taught me about the Principle of Precession, and the philosophy that if we chase money, it will evade us. Pursue the activities that, through Precession, create income. So, I'm taking a little different twist on the principle of Auto Suggestion.

Instead of the goal being money, I do my best to focus on a goal that accomplishes greatness for others. And as a result, those activities will generate the wealth we desire. The Principle of Precession is that the desired result occurs 90 degrees to the activities on which we focus. Take for example, a ripple in a pond. It's created by dropping a stone perpendicular, or 90 degrees, to the water surface.

Another example is a honeybee. The worker bees perceived job is to collect pollen and nectar from plants to bring back to the hive and produce honey for food for the beehive. What actually happens is that during the bee's collecting pollen and nectar, it spreads pollen between plants. This allows those plants to bear fruit for our good and the good of the planet.

So as I learn more about the principles of mindset and Auto Suggestion, I'm taking into account the Principle of Precession. I'm in the wellness business. Instead of having a goal of earning, say $100,000 a month, I consider how many people I must impact to generate that income. My goal is improving people's lives, not just earning money.

I can easily figure out how many people I must impact to generate that income and make my focus on them. It's about helping others. It's on creating better health and financial conditions for those that I can reach out to and create an impact for.

I am so grateful to have discovered personal development through network marketing, and events like Secret Knock and Habitude Warrior, where I've had the opportunity to be exposed to great minds. I embarked on this *13 Steps to Riches* project, not because I thought I was a great author, or that what I write would be able to provide incredible insight to others. I accepted the challenge because I knew it would help me get to the next level in my life, and the next level, and the next level. I knew I would meet incredible people along the way. Perhaps that's selfish. Yet perhaps, as I grow through the process, I will be able to have a positive impact on many more people than I would have otherwise.

Although I'm not sure how best to expose more people to the principles of *Think and Grow Rich*, especially when they are raised in an environment where awareness of these ideas is lacking, it is one of my desires to increase younger peoples' exposure to these ideas so they can make their mind a fertile garden spot.

# BARRY BEVIER

**About Barry Bevier:** Barry Bevier is a proud father of two amazing daughters in their mid-twenties, who are pursuing their passions in psychology and architecture in Southern California. He was raised on a family farm near Ann Arbor, Michigan. Growing up, he developed his faith in God, a strong work ethic, a love for nature, and a passion to help others. After completing his master's degree in civil engineering at the University of Michigan, he pursued a career in engineering, which eventually brought him to Southern California.

In 2000, he married the love of his life, Linda. They shared a beautiful life for ten years, until she succumbed to the effects of lupus and 20 years of treatment with prescription medications. Since then, Barry pivoted his career path into educating and helping others. Barry has educated himself in alternative, natural modalities in wellness and became a Licensed Brain Health Trainer through Amen Clinics. He also works with a new technology in stem cell supplementation that releases your own stem cells.

Author's Website: *www.BRBevier.Stemtech.com*
Book Series Website & Author's Bio: *www.The13StepstoRiches.com*

## Brian Schulman

# INCREDIBLE THINGS HAPPEN WHEN WE COME TOGETHER

People revisit places and memories that make them *feel* happy and uplifted. That feeling of bliss comes from a prior association that lives in our subconscious.

Tapping into the power of the subconscious mind and allowing it to deliver profound messages that are encoded through successes results in Auto Suggestion. Auto Suggestion is built from creating a total sensory experience which taps into each individual's emotional response evoking feelings and a subconscious connection.

We think of Auto Suggestion as a tool of advertising; a way to get people to buy something. What if you considered the possibility that Auto Suggestion could sell people on themselves? Now use that power to help people combat negative thoughts, feel less alone, increase their self-confidence, and connection to others.

Why does the smell of Thanksgiving, fresh cookies, or a fire in the fireplace make us smile? Why does smelling a skunk make us break out in hives? Why is it important that success isn't simply success, but tied to emotion as well? How do we create that, with intentionality, for ourselves and others?

Emotion and feeling are what leave lasting impressions.

My two global award-winning, weekly, live shows, Shout Out Saturday and What's Good Wednesday, featured on LinkedinLIVE and several other platforms, are the result of intentionally creating a space that connects emotions and experiences.

I have the singular aim to leave people feeling better than before they joined us on the shows.

Being told four-year-old K was drawing pictures all day and said, "These are for our friends on the homework. Homework is what I call it when I am on the computer!" *SO cute!* "We have so much fun with you all." serves as confirmation that I am creating the types of memorable experiences that make people go from strangers to family; from outsiders to part of a community. The experiences are inextricably intertwined with emotion, creating a subconscious tether that leads guests and audience members like K and her dad back to the shows week after week.

These moments not only link the experience to emotion individually, but for everyone involved; watching and commenting and settling deep into the subconscious mind.

We invite guests to the show who state in the comments, "I can't," and then with the support and encouragement of the community, they step into the discomfort, achieving something they never could have imagined! The power of Auto Suggestion transforms their fear of being LIVE in front of the camera into confidence and assurance. Their subconscious is fueled by the feeling of success and triumph they've experienced.

Due to the nature of the show, the interaction between the audience and the guests leads to collective Auto Suggestion. Anyone can come on LIVE. Having been a part of someone else's emotional experience, people come on and share things they've never shared before, knowing that they can find the same connection. Week after week, there are regulars who not only radiate positive vibes toward others, but are willing to receive in return, because they feel comfortable. The community has not only seen it countless times on every show, but everyone is a part of it. They *feel* it, creating the collective Auto Suggestion.

Sharing our lives, whether it's publishing a book, showing up from the parking lot before graduation, wanting to celebrate with us, asking for prayers and suport when a loved one is sick, exemplify collective Auto Suggestion.

It is the reason a member of my team was unwilling to 'go away' because finding her home, her happy place, felt like finding herself. Neither me or my team knew we were missing her, nor did she know that she was missing us, but the feeling when we are together has left a lasting impression on our subconscious minds.

Feelings and emotions build brand loyalty. Being part of something, feeling like we belong, being recognized and empowered, feeling less alone because of the connections made and the sense of community, drives people to help others *feel* the same.

As a result of the Covid19 pandemic, fear was heightened, and we were forced into physical separation from our loved ones and communities. Uncertainty was the only constant. It forced us from our usual mind-based decision making into emotions, and created the unique opportunity to positively impact people worldwide using LIVE. Through the power of Auto Suggestion to help people believe in themselves, people realized that they were part of a community that cheers and supports them. A ripple effect was created, spreading from one person to another.

Because of my LIVE shows, guests physically or mentally isolated from the outside world were able to reconnect again! Auto Suggestion allowed them to *feel* like themselves again and to have a sense of normalcy in these very 'abnormal' times. This message comes from the subconscious telling them, "SOS and WGW are my semblances of normality; my happy places".

It is comforting to offer guests who are fragile a soft place to land and a beautiful way to be loved. They will return as many times as necessary because a subconscious link is created between what they *feel* and they experience.

In contrast to advertising and marketing (where the message is created to enchant a specific audience) I use Auto Suggestion as a tool of growth by creating memorable experiences. Individual experiences are amplified by the relationships and bonds formed by showing up as yourself, with your unique needs or circumstances. A strong emotional connection is created when people express unconditional love and acceptance, meeting people right where they are in the moment. A sense of belonging to something greater creates 'brand loyalty' with the added bonus that each individual feels empowered to help others.

A lasting impression is created when people show up to support and encourage, by sharing tears and laughter, and by inviting others into a global family where no one feels judged, alone, or inadequate. You are invited to bring your 'negative feelings' and we'll accept them, but ultimately we'll infuse them with positivity in order to create a subconscious connection between them and the emotions they evoke.

Through making sure beloved traditions were preserved (the Halloween episode), childhood experiences weren't lost (the Christmas episode), and celebrating milestones (weddings, birthdays, graduations), I was able to harness the power of positive Auto Suggestion to help people transform their thinking. Adding emotion and feeling with the desire not to miss important events and create memories equals... you guessed it— Auto Suggestion.

With my audience, I'm always finding reasons to celebrate. My goal is to spread happiness and unite my community. It is the chance to feel like part of something big and experience the joy, whether it's for a good cause or a distraction (International Dance Day, Red Nose Day). Every show intentionally feeds the subconscious, much like marketing would, to create a connection between the experience and the emotional response, which in turn, fosters loyalty. I am creating opportunities for people to feel freed, even if only for a moment, of the burdens and responsibilities of adulthood. While the shows are about "Full Force Funness," and letting ourselves be adults who play and find their inner child, we have room for everything. We welcome everyone to bring whatever's going on in their world. We won't let you get stuck in the negative. While I can't remove the realities the Positive Vibe Tribe live with, I can provide a safe space for reprieve. For a few moments, they can smile before they go back to whatever weighs on their hearts.

It is inevitable that when you have the honor and privilege of positively impacting the life of another human being, you transform yourself as a result. I get to be there when those "a-ha" moments happen that spark a flame that lasts well beyond the live show(s).

This isn't something I do for myself. Every week, I create space for others who need it; a place for people to *be*. I've seen it, felt it, and have been told it. I know what it's like to feel like you don't have a community; living on a proverbial island, feeling alone, left out, unwanted, and feeling the need to be cherished. My giving to them is at least equal to their giving to me.

My shows generate Auto Suggestions both for my audience and me. The benefits my community receives are similar to what I'm experiencing and it keeps me and them coming back. Connectivity, community, support, and love are reasons why we all return. We anticipate how we're going to and want to *feel* and we're excited about walking away feeling better than we did before.

Through engagement with my audience, I'm flooded with all the good feelings that are associated with helping, celebrating, or virtually holding someone's hand and as a result, I'm transformed.

People choose to revisit places and memories that make them feel happy and uplifted. Emotion and feeling are what leave lasting impressions.

Why do guests return to the shows? Because of how it makes them *feel*.

# BRIAN SCHULMAN

**About Brian Schulman:** Brian Schulman is known as the Godfather, and Pioneer, of LinkedIn Video and one of the world's premiere live streaming & video marketing experts. He has 20+ years of proven Digital Marketing experience strategizing with IR500 & Fortune500 brands across the globe.

A #1 Best-Selling Author and internationally known Keynote Speaker, Brian founded & is the CEO of Voice Your Vibe, which brings his wealth of knowledge, as an advisor and mentor to Founders & C-Suite Executives by providing workshops and 1-on-1 Mastery Coaching on how to voice their vibe, attract their tribe, and tell a story that people will fall in love with through the power and impact of live & pre-recorded video.

Named "2020 Best LIVE Festive Show of The Year" at the IBM TV Awards, his weekly LIVE shows #ShoutOutSaturday & #WhatsGoodWednesday have aired LIVE for more than 300 consecutive episodes combined and have been featured in Forbes, Thrive Global, Yahoo Finance, an Amazon best-selling book and syndicated on a Smart TV Network. Among his many awards and honors, Brian has been named a 'LinkedIn Top Voice', 'LinkedIn Video Creator Of The Year', one of the 'Top 50 Most Impactful People of LinkedIn' and a 'LinkedIn Global Leader of The Year' for two consecutive years.

Author's Website: *www.VoiceYourVibe.com*
Book Series Website & Author's Bio: *www.The13StepstoRiches.com*

*Bryce McKinley*

# I AM WHAT I SAY I AM!

Auto Suggestion is a great way of speeding up the achievement and realizations of our dreams. Napoleon Hill explains that our subconscious mind can be put to work for us, as whatever we continuously auto-suggest, our mind will eventually be taking for a fact. This happens once it has been truly ingrained in our minds.

He continuous to suggest that you should focus on your ultimate goal by frequently closing your eyes and speak (out loud) your written statement which you wrote down when you read about Principle 1: Burning Desire. When you do this, it is instrumental that you both see and feel as if you are already in possession of your goal, and that you talk about it in detail with gratefulness and passion.

Make sure that you have that written statement of yours always close at hand (on your phone and computer), so that you clearly see it every day. By doing so, you are putting the principle of Auto Suggestion to work!

My statement reads as follows: "I am a real man of God and a capable leader. Today, God comes first. I choose to put His Will above my own. I show others the grace He has shown me and I love others the way He has loved me. I look for every opportunity to add value to those that cross my path. I see people as my priority and not my distraction. I use my talents, my strengths, and my time to not just better my life, but also all those who are around me. I Am the man God has called me to be!"

"I am an entrepreneur! I am a leader! I am a loving husband and father! I am a loyal friend, and I am a positive influence to all who are watching me." "I will give when I feel selfish, I will be courageous when I am fearful, I will remember when I am tempted, and I will be grateful when I feel I am lacking." "I will walk slowly today and savor the small things. I will intentionally look for all the little good things that make up my day."

"Decision by decision, dollar by dollar, choice by choice, I Am Building an enduring legacy." "I will not take myself or my day too seriously. I always enjoy a smile, I relish laugher, I take time to play. In the midst of my work, I will always be on the lookout for an adventure."

"I will invest my time today, I will not waste it." "By the end of this day I will be wiser, I will be smarter, I will be richer and I will be better." "I Am all that I dream of being."

"I think big, I take risks, I swing for the fences. I will not let my critics or the opinions of others dissuade me." "I have purpose and for me God has a plan." "I will not do anything to hinder or delay the incredible things God has laid out for me." "I will emulate the consistency and integrity that has been modeled for me." "No shortcuts and no small lies."

"And So I Pray, Dear Lord, the battles I go through today, I pray for a chance that's fair. A chance to equal my stride. A chance to do or dare. If I should win, let it be by the code with faith and honor held high. If I should lose, let me stand by the way and cheer, as the winners go by. Day by day, I get better and better, until I can't be beat. I won't be beat! Day by day, I get better and better until I can't be beat. I won't be beat!"

Auto Suggestion makes perfect sense to me as I truly believe that we become and behave based on what we spend most of our time thinking about. It has been proven that our brain has no idea whether something is happening in real life or in our minds only, and that is extremely powerful to know because then you can choose what your mind is to think about so that it works in your favor!

Just think about a time when you were watching a horror movie. What did your body feel like and what happened when it got really scary? Higher pulse, breathing changed, posture changed, fear arising? You know what I am talking about, that feeling… and it is all in your head yet extremely powerful as if it were in real life.

Why not make sure that you have more powerful and empowering feelings by using your mind to create them. It will help you generate those highly-stimulating and motivational emotions where your body can't tell the difference from your imagination and real life.

By doing this, you are boosting your energy levels, your mindset, and your emotional state. By continuously working with yourself like this, it gets hammered into your subconscious mind and you will change your whole state of being. Your subconscious mind will start to help you in that direction you have been ingraining, as it knows the importance of it to you. You will, of course, also have to take action and use all the opportunities that come your way, or else nothing will change. The cool thing is that there will be so many opportunities for you to act on, so make sure you make the most of them! It will make you see and hear things related to those thoughts of yours. This all has to do with our Reticular Activating System.

Actions to take:

- Reminder: Remind yourself several times per day about the impact of Auto Suggestion and train your brain to focus on the right things and just let other thoughts flow by.

- Mindset: Train every day so that you are in control of your thoughts.

- Personal Affirmations: Copy mine, or set your own!

- Meditate to quiet your mind down so that you can then decide what it should spend time on.

- Vision board: Live with it and use it several times per day to ingrain it into your mind.

If you're talking to a graduate student, for example, they'll say things like, "I'm getting my master's degree." They talk as if it's ALREADY theirs. They just have to keep showing up to class, and it's theirs, right?

You don't hear them say, "Yeah, I'm going to *TRY* to get my master's degree." Good luck with that. If it's a *sure thing* in their mind, you can HEAR it. Their words are subconsciously MATCHING their expectations.

You need to keep on directing your subconscious, "This is it. This is exactly what I want. No, it's NOT *different* today. This is it AGAIN, and *I expect you to deliver.*"

FINALLY, your subconscious mind, *your faithful servant* goes, "Okay!" It starts to look for all the things that are necessary to achieve your definite purpose. Once it gets *fixated* on the idea, it's all over it.

That's when it seems like the universe metaphysically seems to open up. It starts to deliver the right people into your life, and the right circumstances. You connect with necessary people and resources to help you achieve your purpose.

Consider this: You decide to buy a certain type of car, like a Jeep. You've never really noticed them before. However, as soon as you make the *DEFINITE decision* to buy a Jeep, you'll start noticing them EVERYWHERE on the road.

When you've made a definite decision, the subconscious mind is working on the new idea all the time.

"Your ability to use the principle of Auto Suggestion will depend, very largely, upon your capacity to concentrate upon a given desire until that desire becomes a burning obsession." – Napoleon Hill

# BRYCE MCKINLEY

**About Bryce McKinley:** Bryce is an International Best-Selling Author and one of the Top 5 Sales Trainers in The World! With over 20 years of working with various Fortune 500 companies including but not limited to the likes of Ford, Nissan, Tyco, and ADT. Helping each of them transform their sales process to focus on better conversations and building better relationships.

Over 8,000 transactions in Real Estate later, Bryce is one of the leading experts in wholesaling houses with his 5 Hour Flip method and has been able to close almost every deal over the phone, only ever walking 5 properties.

Author's Website: *www.5HourFlip.com*
Book Series Website & Author's Bio: *www.The13StepstoRiches.com*

Candace & David Rose

# AUTO SUGGEST YOUR POSSIBILITIES

As I've been on the journey of writing this series, I've been able to share things I've learned with many people. And strangely, a response I get when referencing "*Think and Grow Rich*" is people telling me, "I know how to think. And I don't need to be rich, so I'm good thanks anyway." I find that to be a strange response. I mean, who doesn't want to be rich. Imagine all the things you could do with just a fraction of Elon Musk's money. But growing rich isn't just about money. The principals taught by Napoleon Hill can be used to affect all aspects of our lives.

This volume is on the principal of Auto Suggestion. What is that? The way I explained it to my daughter is, it's the process used to tap into your unconscious mind, and use its power to influence your conscious self. Let me share with you a story on how this has helped me and changed my life.

About 15 years ago, I was helping a neighbor build a garage. I had never been afraid of heights so when we were working on the roof, I had no issues being up there doing what had to be done. I was working my way across the trusses when I didn't duck low enough and smacked and cut my forehead. As I stood there and watched, a drop of blood falls the 15 ft down to the floor, I'm not sure why, but suddenly I became scared. The ladder I had been scaling for a few days now didn't seem as sturdy and I really struggled to get down from the roof. Once on the ground, I discovered that my cut was just a scratch, but my life was changed. I'm not sure why or how, but from that moment on, I became terrified of heights. I stayed on the ground the for the rest of the project because I couldn't get back on the roof to help.

This of course affected my life in many ways. My brother needed help on his roof. I had to tell him ,"Nope, I'm too scared." Roller coasters that I had ridden before became too much because they were high up. I had resigned myself to having a fear of heights and that's how my life would continue.

Fast forward about 3 years. I had just started a new job. One that had potential to pay really well. After completing training and heading to the worksite for the first time, I learned that as the "new guy" part of my job included working from a man-lift at heights ranging from 15 to over 100 feet in the air. I now had a choice to make: Either tell them I was afraid of heights (which I'm sure would have been fine and not affected my job) or find a way to overcome my fear and do my work.

So with a burning Desire to do the job I had been asked to to, I climbed into the man-lift for the first time, completely scared out of my mind. My supervisor was going to take me up 60 ft. to perform some maintenance on our equipment. As the basket stared to rise, my fear set it. So I started talking to myself and praying to God, using Faith, that I had been ok with heights before, so, I could do it again. Ultimately, I survived my trip to the sky. But I knew if I wanted to grow with this company, I would have to overcome this fear. This is where Auto Suggestion and the unconscious mind comes in to play. Before work each day, I would repeat to myself, "I can do this" then without thinking, I'd climb in the basket and do it. Each night after work I'd say the same thing. And wouldn't you know after a few months, it became easier and easier! I had convinced myself through Desire, Faith, and using Auto Suggestion that I wasn't scared of heights.

This is the example I use when telling people that the 13 steps can be used for more than just "getting rich" and that these steps can be used to help you overcome fears, learn a new skill or language. So many possibilities beyond just the money.

### ~ *David Rose*

Our minds are amazing vessels. They are like Hermione Grangers bag in "Harry Potter." They expand, shrink, and are ever changing to suit our circumstances They absorb like the best sponge and can hold more than we might ever access in this lifetime. We're often told that the average human only uses approximately 10% of their brain's potential. Do you wonder what you could do with even a portion of that other 90%?

Part of that is what we refer to as our subconscious. We store some of the most important, some of the most sabotaging, and some of the most random things in there. Examples are: trauma, compliments, insults, patterns, as well as useless facts, and trivia.

When I was a teen, I was dishing up some ice cream. A relative said something to me about "if you get fat...." Then one day my mother (completely unrelated) had me put on a swimsuit and she took pictures of me to show me how fat I was, so that I would look at them for weight loss inspiration. What do you think my brain did with that? Well, it stored it. I did not care to look to those photos for inspiration. But my rebel side kicked in somewhere and said, "I'll show you." All in my subconscious. And though I haven't been significantly overweight during the years since then, I'm certainly not skinny. Are there other contributing factors? Of course. However, when contemplating weight loss and pondering on "Why" or "What" may be holding it up, this time when I was younger always comes to mind. And believe me, I NEVER pass up ice cream. It has become an Auto Suggestion to my mind that suggests scarcity and rebellion. All because 30 years ago, someone who had significant influence over me said something that my mind moved into my "saved" folder.

How many of us have several people in our lives that are NEVER the "Glass is half-full" type? How do their lives look?

Do you know why people who read and experience life are generally more healthy, happy, and successful than those who watch television constantly? Yes, some of it is physicality and chemistry. But most of it is literally IN THEIR HEAD.

All of it comes into play with Auto Suggestion. What plays in your subconscious mind while you sleep, brush your teeth? And connect with others....or don't?

Because in your subconscious are the lessons, triggers, and defenses you've learned that can creep up at THE most inopportune times. Or the perfect time. And make or break some REALLY great opportunities.

"The mind is a powerful force. It can make the worst out of the best, or the best out of the worst." —Author Unknown

Edgar Allan Poe said, "Words have no power to impress the mind without the exquisite horror of their reality."

"In the beginning was The Word, and the word was with God, and the word was God." (John 1:1- 14)

There is nothing in this world, your house, the room you're sitting in, etc., that exists without having first been a thought, and then a word.

Every thought you think, every word you speak, becomes first the suggestion and eventually Auto Suggestion that your mind uses to create your reality.

Do you remember in volume 2 of this series, Faith? I quoted Elena Cardone in her book *"Build an Empire: How to have it all"* when she says, "You are either building an empire, or you are destroying one." I promise you that whether you think you can or think you cannot, you are right.

Did you know that the thing you are most afraid of will always show up in your life in multiple ways until you stop re-emphasizing the Auto Suggestion for the thing you fear.

Every time you go to the bathroom, your mind learns the habit and it becomes automatic without you having to think about it. For example: The Auto Suggestion for me is that when I pull into the driveway, I'm headed to the bathroom. Because of this, the second I open our front door, my bladder is ready, and my family knows to clear a path.

In the movie "Focus" in order to manipulate their target, a group of con artists use Auto Suggestion to put the number 55 into his mind. They start the night before and place it everywhere. He does not disappoint, and ultimately loses to them when he bets on number 55.

Every time you think "I love/enjoy that" your mind makes a note. The same happens when you think "I hate/fear that."

Remember, everything that comes to you starts as a thought or a word.

One last thing, a word of caution—Avoid words like: never, none, don't, can't, won't, stop, no— in training you brain for positive Auto Suggestion. They are sabotage words. Our minds naturally overlook them. For example: "I will not run red lights," translates through to the subconscious as, "I will run red lights." When deciding what you want to bring to you, success is more likely if you speak in the positive.

So let me gift you a positive Auto Suggestion to get you started on your way to the life you desire and have faith in:

I wish for you an abundance of LOVE, LIGHT, and MAGIC in your life. Today and always.

~**Candace Rose**

# CANDACE & DAVID ROSE

**About Candace and David Rose:** Candace and David Rose are #1 Best-Selling Authors in the 13 volume book series *The 13 Steps to Riches*. They grew up together and currently live in South Jordan, Utah, with their 6 children, 4 chickens, 4 cats, 1 dog, and a rabbit. They are both Veterans of the U.S. Army. David served as a mechanic and Candace as a Legal NCO. David is currently a Product Release Specialist, delivering liquid oxygen and nitrogen to various manufacturing plants and hospitals throughout Utah, Colorado, Idaho and Nevada. Candace is the owner of Changing Your Box Organization, where she specializes in helping people organize their space, both physically and mentally, with the ultimate goal to help you change your box and find more joy in your life. Both Candace and David are proud members of the elite Champion Circle Networking Association in Salt Lake City, UT., founded by one of our Coauthors of *The 13 Steps to Riches* book series and the Habitude Warrior Mastermind Senior Team Leader, Jon Kovach Jr.

Author's Website: *www.ChangeYourBox.com*
Book Series Website & Author's Bio: *www.The13StepstoRiches.com*

*Collier Landry*

# 'I AM HERE TO TELL MY STORY'

As we exit the theater, my friend Brandon is still in shock. Shaking his head in disbelief at the cinematic experience we had both witnessed, he says, "Man, that don't make no sense, C —such senseless violence."

Nodding steadfastly, I concur, "Yeah, BC, I agree."

"I mean, all that and for what? To prove some BS hatred thinking?!" Brandon continued.

"Well, BC, that's the unfortunate thing about violence. It truly makes no sense, and the devastation ripples throughout so many people's lives, sorta like a butterfly effect."

"Yeah, no doubt, C."

Exiting the frigid cinema building, we are greeted by a suffocatingly hot wave on a scorcher of a day in the San Fernando Valley. We sprint to his mom's car in hopes that a full blast AC would be enough to compete with the 100-degree temperature, quickly proving to be an exercise in futility.

Even though Brandon was a couple of years older than me, we became friends while I was at music school and played on our university football team. Having grown up most of his life in South Central Los Angeles, his mother worked like hell to get him and his sister far away from that life.

It was a life littered with cautionary tales of young black men just like himself, often recruited into the South Central gang culture in lieu of having an appropriate father figure in their lives.

Brandon's mother wasn't having any part of that nonsense. After making sure pop-warner evolved into a full ride to a Division 1A school, his mother was proud her firstborn was now a college graduate.

Being from a sleepy small town in Ohio, and Brandon from the big city of Los Angeles, one might not think we would have a lot in common on the surface. Our upbringings were as starkly different as our skin color. Nevertheless, we had found ourselves sort of kindred spirits at university. Life circumstances aside, Brandon and I had "seen some major stuff."

It was March 2, 1999, and not even a week after my twenty-first birthday. The film we had just seen was American History X, and while our skin was rapidly melding into the faux leather seats, a thought crossed my mind.

"You know what, BC?" I say. "What's that C?"

"I think I want whoever made that film to be the one to help me tell my story," I ponder aloud. "They really understand the consequences of violence. I need someone like that in my life to help me tell my story and the story of my mother's murder".

Brandon laughs, "What, you're gonna be a filmmaker now, opera boy?" jesting me in that brotherly way.

"Hey man, you never know what the future holds," I retort. "As my mother always said, where there's a will, there's a way!"

He chuckles as we speed off.

A few weeks later, I headed back to Ohio for what would most likely be the last of my tenure as a resident of the state. Deciding it was time to leave my traumatic past in the rearview mirror, I packed up my car and hit the open road. I was bitten by the West Coast bug, and I was California Dreamin'.

When I finally arrived in Los Angeles, I had no clue where to go or what to do with my story. I had been slowly carving out a lightweight modeling career, and I pursued every opportunity I found afforded me to in order to get my "big break."

However, as many industry newbies find out when they come to "La La Land," everyone else has a dream and story too. It's a city of the multi-hyphenate wait staff at your favorite restaurant, the actor-singer-writer-director, et al. Everyone has a screenplay they're dying to have you attend a table read for.

Having found solace from the trauma of my youth in the performing arts as an adolescent, I still had no solid foundation or idea of how the entertainment industry worked. In an industry strewn with nepotism, I just knew that I had something special and that persistence was my virtue.

I'd often wonder to myself, "Was I out in LA to be a filmmaker?" I mean, the weather was terrific, and it sure was a lot of fun out here, but what am I really doing? As many artists do, every day is a wash-rinse-repeat cycle of second-guessing, self-criticism, and self-deprecation.

Despite that almost constant, negative, questioning inner monologue every day, I would firmly say to myself, with the most resolve I could muster, "I AM going to tell my story, and that is why I am here." I had stumbled upon the principle of Auto Suggestion.

Today, American History X is still one of my top 5 favorite films ever made. Its themes of senseless violence fueled by hatred and its impact on generations resonated to the very marrow of my being.

Though I'm not a fan of hatred and violence, I empathized with the lead character's journey toward redemption. Perhaps, in the end, I moved to Los Angeles looking for just that—redemption.

I'll never forget when my girlfriend came into my little make-shift office in our Hollywood Hills bungalow. As a model, she was constantly approached by different photographers to shoot, and today was no different.

"Hey babe, so this photographer reached out to me on MySpace," she said as she pranced in in her ever-so-positive way.

"Oh cool, what's their name?"

"His name is John Morrissey. He's a movie producer."

"His name sounds familiar. What has he done?" I ask.

Spouting out a handful of films I was familiar with, she lands on the words "and then some movie called American History..."

I snap into full attention, "American History X" I quizzed as my pulse began to race. "Oh yeah, that's it!" she replied.

"Let's meet him asap!"

John and I became fast friends. I had gushed about his film and how it was a milestone of American cinematic achievement. Flattery can get you far in Hollywood, and I wasted no time asking John if he would help mentor me or give me advice.

Despite having grown very close, I had yet to explain to John the full scope of my real-life story. Sure, there were always surface details that trickled out; my father murdered my mother, he's in prison; I was in foster care, etc.; but I had always shied away from giving the more intimate details of my life for fear of judgment or rejection.

At this point in my 'LA Story', I had become laser-focused on cinematography and took every opportunity to be on a film set, often working for free. Looking back now, this was my abridged version of film school, and I soaked in every opportunity I could to learn the craft of filmmaking.

While standing in my kitchen one day, John said to me, "Collier, I see you've been shooting a lot more now, and that's really cool."

He continued, "I'd like to get back into producing more since I took my hiatus years ago. Do you have any ideas?"

I smiled, recognizing this was the moment I had been waiting years for. "As a matter of fact, John, I do!"

I walk into the other room and grab a scrapbook full of photocopied newspaper articles from the 1990's. These range from my mother's initial disappearance to coverage of my father's murder trial, all neatly organized in chronological order.

I sit down with John and say, "I have a great idea for a television series about the consequences of violence, its repercussions, and the aftermath."

"Tell me more, man, I'm intrigued," he says.

I continue, handing him the binder, "And the best news is I own the rights to the pilot."

He opens the binder. Looking over the bridge of his reading glasses, he says, "This is your story?"

"Yes, sir." Then the words I have repeated to myself every day for over the past decade, "This is the reason I came to Los Angeles. To tell my story."

The following afternoon my phone rings. It's John.

"Crap, brother, I had no idea. I'm so sorry, Collier," he says.

"It's all good, John, it's my life, and there's not much I can change about the past," I reassure him. "But I want to impact the future, so what do you think?"

"Well, I have a friend who is a documentary film director." "Oh really?"

"Yeah, and I think she would be extremely interested in this story," he continued. "Her films have won two academy awards."

"Oh wow, that's amazing," I say, trying to contain my overflowing excitement.

"Yeah," he replies, "She's going to be in town next week for a screening, and I think you should meet her."

"What's her name?" I inquire. "Barbara Kopple." And the rest, as they say, is history.

# COLLIER LANDRY

**About Collier Landry:** As a formally trained musician and photographer, Collier Landry segued into filmmaking as a means to creatively express and deal with his own traumatic story—that of the premeditated murder of his mother by his own father.

Subsequently, Collier is the creator and subject of Investigation Discovery's *'A Murder in Mansfield'*, a documentary directed by two-time Oscar winning director Barbara Kopple. In the film, Collier, who witnessed the murder and at age 12 became the chief witness for the prosecution, returns to Ohio seeking to retrace his past and confront his father, who remains incarcerated and in denial of his guilt.

The film explores not only the collateral damage of violence and its traumatic repercussions, but the beauty of human strength and resilience through seemingly insurmountable odds.

Collier has been featured in *Variety, The New York Times, The Hollywood Reporter, Esquire, USA Today*, is a TEDx Speaker, and a guest on the *Dr. Phil* show. Collier is the host of the 'Moving Past Murder' podcast. He resides in Santa Monica, California.

Author's Website: *www.CollierLandry.com*
Book Series Website & Author's Bio: *www.The13StepstoRiches.com*

*Corey Poirier*

# AUTO-SUGGESTION ISN'T ALWAYS AUTO-MATIC

Of the ideas, and chapters in *"Think and Grow Rich,"* this was the one I perhaps struggled with the most.

This idea of Auto Suggestion, and the idea that I could have any impact, let alone a major impact, over what I created with my mind.

I struggled with it in much the same way I struggled with The Law of Attraction and Manifesting after watching the movie, The Secret.

Ironically, I didn't have as much of a challenge with understanding these concepts, as I did truly practicing them.

Sure, like most people, I watched The Secret and started saying affirmations, practicing auto suggestion, and creating and looking at my vision board daily in my effort to turn my thoughts into things.

I was also certain these suggestions would change my life immediately, and in the biggest of ways.

Also, in much the same way, like almost everyone else who read the chapter on Auto Suggestion in *"Think and Grow Rich,"* I began determining how much money I would accumulate, wrote down a statement of my desire, and set the timeline for its accumulation.

I even repeated my statement over and over. I re-read the statement I wrote about how much and when I would create this abundance on a daily basis. I added it onto my vision board as well. I even decided what I would give in return for the money, as Hill suggests, and how and when I would deliver on that.

What I'm really saying is, I followed all of the steps. Do you know what happened? Nothing.

Well, nothing related to the abundance I was trying to create.

Looking at my vision board after a few months, I realized that I hadn't achieved any of the things I had envisioned for myself, and was trying to suggest into being.

Much like when some of the people who watched The Secret tried to use The Law of Attraction to manifest a new car and didn't have a brand new car with a ribbon sitting out in their driveway the next morning, I ultimately decided this stuff didn't work.

I left the vision board up on the wall, but stopped looking at it.

I kept re-reading *"Think and Grow Rich"* annually but didn't really focus much on this Third Step Towards Riches.

I simply felt that maybe this chapter on Auto Suggestion wasn't as legit as others were saying, or I was missing something that others had figured out.

Finally, two years later, something really interesting happened.

My girlfriend pointed out that she had been looking at my vision board, and noticed something surprising. She asked me to come and look at it with her.

As I stood in front of it, slowly it began sinking in.

Without still looking at the vision board daily and saying the mantras, I had, over the course of less than 3 years, created over 95% of the things on my vision board. And these weren't all small things, either.

**Bestselling Author on a main stream book list?**

Check. One of the books I co-authored had become a *Wall Street Journal* and *USA Today* Best-Selling book. Another of my books had also become a Barnes and Noble, Amazon, Kobo and Apple Books Bestseller.

**Land a TEDx Talk?**

Check. By the time I looked at the board and realized I had envisioned delivering a TEDx Talk, I had already retired from actively pursuing TEDx Talks after speaking on 3 TEDx stages.

**Start a family?**

Check. We already had our first son and were working on our second one while I was looking at my board, despite the difficulties that come with pregnancy at our age.

**Buy our first home together?**

Check. Not only did we buy our first home together, I also bought my girlfriend her first BMW SUV and myself my first Mercedes. This was also on the board.

**Improve my personal and professional centre of influence?**

Check. By this point, I had already interviewed Bob Proctor at his home and had the opportunity to hold his 57-year-old copy of *"Think and Grow*

*Rich*." I also had the opportunity to start working on my latest book while visiting James Redfield (Celestine Prophecy) and staying at his guest house. I had the opportunity to meet with Lisa Nichols and have her compliment my interview style.

All these things would have been unthinkable just years earlier.

On the personal side, I had been spending more time with people who reflected the type of person I wanted to become. You know how they say you are the sum total of the five people you spend the most time with? Well I took that to heart.

**Travel more with family?**

Check. Thanks to my speaking career and client bookings, in the first two years of my son's life, I was able to bring him and my girlfriend to Hawaii, Sedona, New York, Boston, Florida multiple times (Disney of course, Cocoa Beach); all without spending personal money to do so.

Now, I don't say all of this to impress you, but to demonstrate a point.

First, by simply creating the vision board and focusing on it, I was able suggest to myself (and my subconscious) what I wanted to achieve.

The catch was, it didn't happen as quickly as I wanted. Thankfully the Auto Suggestion was still working even after I was done working on it.

**So lesson # 1** for me was this: The Universe doesn't deliver on your suggestion exactly when you expect it to, but it still delivers.

The next thing I noticed was the vision board achievements didn't appear exactly as I had envisioned. For instance, the car image I put on my board was that of a classic Camaro. That car wasn't very practical, especially with a young family, and instead I found myself buying a Mercedes that was both practical and also a vehicle that helped me feel like I had risen above my early life, being raised by a single Mother.

As a side-note, it wasn't about the car but instead what the car represents—that I could create that abundance for myself regardless of where I started.

The house was a different house then I envisioned but the house we live in now is also a better fit for our family.

I had a vision of a boy and a girl on the board to represent family and we instead have two sons.

For the bestseller image on my vision board I placed a Magazine bestseller list. I didn't make that list and instead the Wall Street Journal and USA Today. As they are more well known by my clients, these lists likely offered me more opportunities than the Magazine would have.

Finally, I envisioned myself speaking on a specific TEDx stage and ended up instead speaking at 3 different TEDx stages.

The bottom line is almost nothing I envisioned happened as I had planned, BUT basically everything I envisioned did happen.

This is where I learned **Lesson # 2**: I may think I know what I want, but the Universe knows what I need.

I think there is another important lesson here as well.

You might have to be flexible with the where and when, but the Universe is always listening and working on your behalf.

Oh, and what about the exact amount of money?

Well, even though I didn't receive it in the short amount of time I personally requested, I ultimately not only received that abundance, but I became richer for experiences I had than I likely would have had if it all worked out exactly as I had suggested.

In the end, I read the book ("*Think and Grow Rich*") on Auto Suggestion, I watched the movie on manifestation through Auto Suggestion (The Secret), I created the vision board, and you know what I discovered?

This S**t works!

The key thing is you have to also do the work, and you have to have faith 'while' doing the work. By the time I gave up on Auto Suggestion, I had already planted the seeds, and while I was planting I did have faith it would work.

I just didn't know the pay-off would be later be 'my plan', and I didn't really understand that The Universe always has our back.

# COREY POIRIER

**About Corey Poirier:** Corey is a multiple-time TEDx Speaker. He is also the host of the top-rated Let's Do Influencing radio show, founder of The Speaking Program, founder of bLU Talks, and has been featured in multiple television specials. He is also a Barnes & Noble, Amazon, Apple Books, and Kobo Bestselling Author and the co-author of the *Wall Street Journal* and *USA Today* bestseller, *Quitless.*

A columnist with E*ntrepreneur* and *Forbes* magazine, he has been featured in/on various mediums and is one of the few leaders featured twice on the popular *Entrepreneur on Fire* show.

Also appearing on the popular Evan Carmichael YouTube Channel, he is a New Media Summit Icon of Influence, was recently listed as the # 5 influencer in entrepreneurship by Thinkers 360, and he is an Entrepreneur of the Year Nominee—and, to demonstrate his versatility, a Rock Recording of the Year nominee who has performed stand-up comedy more than 700 times, including an appearance at the famed Second City.

Author's Website: *www.TheInfluencerVault.com*
Book Series Website & Author's Bio: *www.The13StepstoRiches.com*

*Deb Scott*

# THE MEDIUM FOR INFLUENCING THE SUBCONSCIOUS MIND

"Biting into that lemon just made me salivate with bitterness! Yuck!"

Could you taste that lemon or at least feel the bitterness as your read the words? This is a subconscious reaction to your thoughts of what you tell yourself is happening, even if it isn't really happening except in your imagination. The results are real even though it seems like a trick of the mind.

Auto Suggestion is a term which applies to all suggestions and all self-administered stimuli which reach one's mind through the five senses.

If you want to make your million back from what was stolen in a Ponzi scheme (like I do) my Auto Suggestion often sounds like, "Thank you, God, for returning my million dollars back to me in ways I have yet to imagine." Or it might be a simple abundance Auto Suggestion that "success is attracted to me in spiritual and financial ways."

I find ways to make myself remember to say these Auto Suggestions throughout my day. I call this successful sabotage.

I will place notes inside my day timer, on my bathroom mirror, in sock drawers, in my car; wherever I know I have to be, I will place an Auto

Suggestion reminder to keep my conscious and subconscious mind focused on making my dream come true.

Napoleon Hill is clear to state that desire and faith must inject emotion and feeling into your Auto Suggestion. It is not enough to just say the words; they must be alive and trigger an emotional response. The power is in the five senses being activated with the words as the catalyst.

In my example of receiving my million dollars, how will I feel to hold this in my hand, and see it in my bank account? What freedom might this bring me in my lifestyle? How will I celebrate and who will I celebrate with? How will I express my gratitude to God? Questions such as these will create answers which assist the goal to brand this result into my mind, which is always working subconsciously to create the outcome.

We plant a seed, we water the soil, we see the sunshine radiate on the ground, and suddenly, the seed has opened up through the ground into a beautiful, green bud. We may have only planted the seed and God did the watering with sunshine, but we must have planted the seed for God to be able to grant grace on nature. We must do our part for God to do His.

I remember being in the North Shore of Boston, exhausted from shoveling all the snow, weekend after weekend, after my parents passed way alone in this huge home with two dogs. I laid drenched in sweat with my wet coat and pants on the floor thinking, "I need to find a place with palm trees where I never have to shovel again." That one thought turned into many thoughts which I expressed to myself and anyone I met. This then turned into research and trips to where in Florida I thought I wanted to live. The process took a few years to manifest, but manifest it did. I love

living in Venice, Florida. It also doesn't hurt that Tom Brady came down with Gronkowski to join the Tampa Bay Buccaneers!

I want you to write down what you really, really want without judgment of how it will happen. When you write this down, go through each of your senses and see yourself in that place or with that dream; touch everything around you so you know how it feels, and put your heart into the experience of how proud and grateful you are that this has come true for you.

Sometimes you have to let go of the people, places, and things that hold you back from creating the life you desire and most assuredly deserve. In this case, you must be clear, "I desire, God, for You to remove all negative people in my life that destroy achieving my dream of financial successes, peace, and happiness." And make sure to ask, "Please bring people into my life who will help me achieve my financial success, peace, and happiness." We must let go of the past and negativity in our lives to have room for the positive.

Napoleon Hill is clear that:

First: Enter into a quiet place where you can completely focus on how much money (or whatever your goal) and read out loud, "the written statement of the amount of money you intent to achieve." "See yourself already in possession of this money." He suggests writing places, dates, and times for accountably to achieve this goal. He waits for the plan to unfold, and believes with faith this plan will be revealed to him.

Second: "You can see the money you intend to accumulate." Here is where you must activate your imagination to touch, feel, and see what you know you will receive. He emphasizes repeating this experience often throughout the day. This is where I find my "successful sabotage" quite useful in making sure I experience this Auto Suggestion during my day, because I have already planned in advance through proper placement of the Auto Suggestion in locations I know I must be in during my day. The Auto Suggestion is unavoidable. I have set myself up for success.

Third: "Place a written copy of your statement where you can see it night and morning." Feeding your faith is the most productive of the emotions, because you are training your subconscious mind to replace skepticism with confidence. You must be persistent in discipline to read your statement out loud of what you intend to achieve—frequently—into your subconscious mind. Continue this effort with "the faith of a child" until you manifest your desired result.

We often have the pieces of the puzzle for success, but lack the guidance and discipline to put all the pieces together in a way that easily leads us to what we want. Napoleon Hill gives us a plan to put the puzzle pieces together so we don't have to reinvent the wheel. We always have a proven track record to follow.

In my life, I have always wanted to be the best at whatever it was I attempted. This was true in medical sales, to writing a best-selling book, to creating an award-winning podcast, and to become a top-rated sales agent in real estate. I do not intend to do anything I committed to attempt without making sure I can be the best person God created me to be in that venue.

I remember when I was in cardiac surgical sales in Boston, Connecticut, and even in Atlanta. I taped to my dashboard exactly each hospital's account with the dollar amount I needed to achieve to win the President's award that year. I won more awards in one company than any other person had in that amount of time in the history of the company. I had six awards in seven years with one company. In fact, in every medical sales company I worked for, I won awards for outstanding sales success. Outstanding sales success came with hard work, recognition, free trips, and lots of money.

I am new to real estate, although I am a third-generation realtor. It was my family business with my grandfather, father, and mother, which I did not enter until I moved to Venice, Florida. Here with EXP REALTY, my goal is to win their highest sales award nationally, the ICON award, and I am on target to accomplish just that. Although I am honored to be the number-one sales agent in my company in Venice with less than three years of experience, I am five homes away from winning and these five are already under contract. When they close, I have achieved my success. The prestige is fabulous, but I also win sixteen thousand dollars in stock, which is not bad. I am in it to win it, and I use all these tools and many more to ensure my success.

Please understand that following these rules for manifesting your success does not come without obstacles. You will most assuredly encounter jealous people; people who doubt your ability, people who attempt to sabotage your success, and people who lie or maybe even cheat and steal, or defame you. I have experienced all of the above. But if you stay true to who you are and your goals, surround yourself with positive people, and practice these positive Auto Suggestions, you can and will overcome any negativity. You must keep yourself in a high frequency and surround yourself with like-minded people who have similar goals and desires to win.

Auto Suggestion is amazing. Imagine your success and how good it will feel to know you accomplished your goal. Once you have achieved your success, no one can ever take that achievement away from you. Success breeds more success, so rest assured, this is only the beginning of a long history of making your dreams come true.

# DEB SCOTT

**About Deb Scott:** Deb Scott, BA, CPC, and Realtor was a high honors biology major at Regis College in Weston, Massachusetts, and spent over two decades as an award-winning cardio-thoracic sales specialist in the New England area. She is a best-selling author of *The Sky is Green & The Grass is Blue: Turning Your Upside Down World Right Side Up.* She is an award-winning podcaster of The Best People We Know Show. Following in her family's footsteps, she is a third generation Realtor in Venice, Florida. As a certified life coach, Deb speaks and teaches on how to turn bad situations into positive, successful results. As a top sales specialist, she enjoys teaching people "sales without selling," believing that integrity, good communication, and respect are the winning equation to all outstanding success and happiness in life.

Author's Website: *www.DebScott.com*

Book Series Website & Author's Bio: *www.The13StepstoRiches.com*

*Dori Ray*

# IT'S ABOUT TO GET REAL

After only three short months in California, I was excited about heading back to the East Coast. I knew that there was a lot of work to be done and that it had to begin quickly. Every day wasted was a step backwards. Like every other time, I was hoping that this time would be the "Big Comeback" that everyone believed was inside me. I was even beginning to believe it. I saw the principles work with my own eyes. The sudden appearance of the airline tickets back to Philadelphia were a clear sign. However, it wasn't just the flight, it was the clear message that God spoke to me on the way back home! More about that later.

I had determined on my trip to LAX Airport, on what now will go down as one of the "Best Days Of My Life," that California had been a definitely necessary move. It taught me a lot about myself and other people. It proved to me that despite every mistake and setback, I was given new mercy EVERY MORNING!

Speaking of new mercy; while in California, I received a call from my oldest daughter who was a sophomore at Cheyney University. She was always so strong and appeared to be holding it down quite well. She was always the strongest of the three of us, at least for now.

While chatting on the phone, she mentioned her desire to create a fashion blog. Until then, I had never heard the word, but just like the baby leaped in Elizabeth's womb, something inside of me knew that word had a deeper meaning for me. I could not stop thinking about the concept of blogging. I was looking for a way to continue to release the pain of depression. I am a black woman, so therapy was not an option[1].

I loved to write. That came naturally. I remembered reading that you must act on impulses and ideas quickly. I opened my laptop and typed "Brandneweverymorning!" Yep! This was my way out. It fit right into my plan. I had a strong passion for writing and had something to say! I was going to BLOG my way out of depression. It was at this point that I made a deal with God: If I would give FULL DISCLOSURE, HE would, in turn, make Ms. D stay as far away from me as Los Angeles was from Philadelphia!!! I thought I heard him say "DEAL" when in fact, He said "IT'S ABOUT TO GET REAL!"

On March 7, 2012, I began my blog. BRANDNEWEVERYMORNING. BLOGSPOT.COM[2]. I was SUPER EXCITED about the freedom I began to receive by journaling and sharing with the world the naked truth about my MENTAL ILLNESS. I told everything. I shared the effect it had taken on every aspect of my life from being a mother to a business woman. I even shared some interesting information on how it had shattered my intimate relationships. The words just poured out. The more I kept my commitment to share, the easier it became each day to speak, believe, and do the things that would continue to move my life forward! I learned that there were thousands of people around the world who were relating to my journey and who were using my blog as their own platform to freedom from depression. Ultimately, my blog spanned to every continent and reached almost 20K viewers. Today that blog has been translated into an E-Book Daily Journal for those suffering with mental illness and is being sold all over the world.

---

1 Black Mental Health: Statistics, Resources and Services | Wake Forest University (wfu. edu)

2 http://www.dorionpurpose.org to access the blog and the daily journal. Also access other free training and services at this site.

Everything was beginning to work in my favor. I had been using the principles I learned over the past several years from my Mentors and Coaches to begin to rebuild my life. I was blessed to be surrounded by an incredible MASTERMIND TEAM who still believed in me and I was even beginning to believe in myself!

My goal on the flight out to California was to "start over." I wanted to leave the past behind. I quickly learned from my Mentors that "starting over" did not always mean that you had to start something new. It could also mean that you can do the same thing BETTER, or DIFFERENT. I was now going back to Philadelphia ready to Make A Difference. Other people's agendas no longer trumped my own. I was beginning to feel strong. I was definitely ready to jump back into the game of Network Marketing. There was only one problem; I was still flat broke!

Ok, back to the airport trip.

On the way to the airport, my Angel asked if I had any money. Of course I had my handy-dandy food stamp card, but that wouldn't work too well at LAX. He then gave me $10, which was half of what he had in his pocket. My daughter was not in the best of moods that morning. She insisted she was STARVING and that I buy her some food with my last $10. Reluctantly, I purchased the over-priced fries and drink from the airport McDonald's and we headed toward our gate. As we were approaching our gate, I heard the announcer stating that they were looking for people to give up their flight and that they were willing to give a free airline ticket to whoever was willing to make that sacrifice. Because we were in no rush to go home, I decided that my daughter and I would be the ones to sacrifice our flight. That would earn us a free flight back to Los Angeles which at the time I pretended was my intention.

As we approached the counter, we learned that our flight to Philadelphia was overbooked and that they were willing to give us two free round-trip airline tickets to anywhere in the United States if we were willing to give up our flights. We quickly decided that we would be the volunteers. Before we turned to leave the counter, the agent noticed that there was another flight going straight out to Philadelphia that would get us there even sooner. One minor change; the only seats available were in FIRST CLASS! "I guess the two of you are flying to Philly 1st class," she said without even lifting her head. FIRST CLASS! I had $3.14 left and a food stamp card and two first-class tickets back to Philadelphia.

She was simply doing her job when she looked right in my eyes and asked, "Is Philly home for you?" I had traveled extensively by now for business and pleasure. I had answered that question hundreds of times. This time, the answer felt more like a DECLARATION. "YES MA'AM" I said, as I smiled knowing at that moment that I would never return to California as a resident. I was going home, clear, ON ASSIGNMENT! It was at that moment my assignment became crystal clear.... I was DORI ON PURPOSE.

As we prepared to fly back to Philadelphia, I heard God say to me "You are on assignment." Just the thought of that gave me chills. I was known for my leadership skills and also known for my servant's heart but it was all voluntary up to that point. Something about that word in my heart made it seem like from that day on, the choice was no longer my own.

In a strange way, I knew that I was responsible for making this thing happen. DORI ON PURPOSE? If only I had known what that assignment would have entailed, I would have given back the tickets and flown back home coach. But the affirmations that I had been speaking gave me the courage to believe that all of this hard work had not been in vain. I knew the rough times were not over, but I chose to focus on my goals. There was much more for God to say but I chose to focus on the well-dressed black man who was sitting next to me on the plane. He was full of conversation and confirmation. His conversation was uplifting and encouraging. That was exactly what I had been instructed to do, uplift & encourage. As great as that moment felt, something inside of me knew that the rough times were not quite over. I stuffed those emotions in my little box of things to deal with later and chose to focus on my daughter. Her face said it all. She was grinning from ear to ear as a flight attendant offered her a warm towel and a drink before we even took off into the clouds. That McDonald's that had barely settled in her stomach was replaced by a hot meal. I can even remember the smell of the meat and potatoes and hear the crunch of the lettuce we ate. As we settled in and the flight took off, God began to speak a very powerful message to me. He showed me how I left Philadelphia sad, lonely, and confused but was returning clear and "ON PURPOSE".

During the three months in California, I consistently said my affirmations every single day and night! I was beginning to see many of my dreams actualize right before my eyes. I was using my own voice to redirect my life. I went back home a believer! I went back home a willing soldier ready to do whatever it took to be Dori on Purpose. If I had only known what the next chapter was holding, I may not have accepted the "deal" so quickly. Things were about to get real.

# DORI RAY

**About Dori Ray:** Dori "On Purpose" Ray is a native Philadelphian. As a businesswoman, her mission is to help people transform their minds, bodies, and bank accounts!

Dori was educated in the Philadelphia Public School System. She graduated from the Philadelphia High School for Girls in 1982 and Howard University School of Business in 1986 with a BBA in Marketing. Dori is a member of Delta Sigma Pi Business Fraternity and Delta Sigma Theta Sorority, Inc.

Dori leads teams around the world. She is a sought-after Speaker and Trainer within her industry and beyond. She is an experienced Re-Entry Coach as she has helped hundreds of Returning Citizens get back on track after incarceration.

Having suffered from depression for 20 years, she always reaches back to share her story and help break the cycle of silence. Her audience loves her authenticity!

Book Dori for speaking engagements www.linktr.ee/dorionpurpose

Author's Website: *www.linktr.ee/DoriOnPurpose*
Book Series Website & Author's Bio: *www.The13StepstoRiches.com*

*Elaine Sugimura*

# LIVING LIFE OUT LOUD

What is Auto Suggestion and how did it play a role in my life in the past, am I present to it now, and what is the plan for the future? I will share moments where Auto Suggestion was definitely the "key" player in my conscious and subconscious mind. I am here today because of this way of thinking. I am grateful for all that it has created for me—because of me.

What does Auto Suggestion mean to me? It means being kind, loving, motivating, joyful, happy, passionate, positive, powerful, and to believe that I have the divine power to heal myself of anything that comes before me. Checking in with myself with Positive Thoughts vs the Negative narration that many of us tend to focus on. There are three phases of my life where I will share when Auto Suggestion was prevalent and shifted what most would deem impossible.

## The PAST

If you have read the chapters prior to this, many of you already know that I am a breast cancer survivor twice over. Many have asked how I was able to walk through this time in my life with so few tears and with an attitude such that both "fear" and "scarcity" never landed in the deck of cards I was playing with. I did not have time to wallow in my own sorrow as I had a full life ahead of me. There was no time to say, "Why ME?" I chose to take the path of Life Is Worth Living and repeated the following statements and let my subconscious mind lead me.

"Bring it on...I am ready to fight this battle...I am a Survivor!"

"Cancer is afraid of ME I will fight to the End because I Can and I Will!"

"There is nothing I am afraid of; this disease has NO chance of survival!"

"One step forward, each and every day, the cancer is no longer there...it is gone I am healed!"

As these powerful thoughts were racing through my mind, I gained strength to carry on. I kept saying to myself that everything that was happening to ME did not define who I was on the inside. Through the multiple surgeries, scars, and moments of despair, I continued to chant the statements above as I knew if I stood tall and roamed through life with a strong and positive fortitude, everything would be as I wished it to be. My vision, at that time, was to carry on in life as a healthy wife, mom, daughter, sister, and friend. Everyone needed me as much as I needed them. There was no time for masks and charades, life was too short, and the best way UP was to challenge my subconscious mind by envisioning everything from a state of euphoria and success. Specifically, for me, that meant constant mind shifts that had me thinking positive thoughts with a feel-good ending. I wanted to LIVE LIFE OUT LOUD and not focus on death and dying. I shared with anyone and everyone around me, to those who would listen, my positive spin on life; that regardless of the scars, mastectomies, loss of hair, reconstruction, I held my head up high and did not allow cancer to beat me. I chanted daily, "I will beat cancer. I will beat it out of my body and thus my mind, I am recovering, I am recovering, I am healed." Ten years later, I reached a huge milestone—the cancer was in full remission. Isn't this Auto Suggestion at its best?!

The craziness continued and the second cancer diagnosis was not only an aggressive form of breast cancer, but it came at a time when my life was filled with overall greatness, great job, great family and friends, great everything. I found myself stepping right back into the power of Auto Suggestion. I was at the pinnacle of my career and our lives as a family was humming along. I did not want the hummingbirds to stop singing so I buckled myself in and began chanting again.

"You want me, come get me, I am not ready to throw in the towel!" "Bring it on...I am ready to fight this battle...I am a Survivor!"

"Cancer is afraid of ME I will fight to the End because I Can and I Will!"

"There is nothing I am afraid of; this disease has NO chance of survival, I am a survivor, I am a survivor, I am a survivor!"

"I have too much to live for, I shall rise each day and heal myself, the cancer is gone, the cancer is gone, the cancer is gone!"

Through it all, I kept healing myself with my words of encouragement and telling the cancer to take a hike as I, too, had a long hike ahead of me. Life is a game that we all get to play. How we choose to play, whether we are diagnosed with a life-threatening disease or challenged with traumas that affect how we react, often presents the Why ME question. I never had time to think about the negative thoughts as I only made time for the positive. I navigated my life through a complicated course as obstacles continued to pop up everywhere around me. I healed myself of breast cancer both times by mentally preparing myself to only see the brighter side of life. By reminding myself, daily, that everything is coming up roses because of the healthy nourishment I was giving my mind, both consciously and sub-consciously. The cancer is gone, the cancer is gone, the cancer is gone.......

## The PRESENT

As several decades have passed since my last health scare, I can look back and see how Auto Suggestion played a huge part of my healing process. 2022 will be another milestone marker, as it will be thirty years since my first breast cancer diagnosis and twenty years since my second. I am fully healed and no longer in remission. My oncologist stated that I am now 100% cured of my breast cancer. I healed myself by constantly stating the obvious. I will heal, I am healed, I am fully healed, and there is no looking back. I knocked Cancer out of my life, my body, my mind. I am healed.

I am ALIVE, so I know I am capable of creating the results I want to see, experience, and achieve. As many of us have read and learned over the past 18 months, the COVID lockdown brought new unexpected stresses and yes, I had to deal with another health challenge. I was diagnosed with shingles. Not knowing what to expect, I can share that the pain was debilitating. I had already signed myself up for a leadership / transformational workshop and had really started to work on ME as I felt I had lost my MOJO. Everything in my life was shifting into the drift. Somehow, I did not feel powerful, nor confident about who I was. What was happening to the Elaine I knew and believed in? She was lost.

The last 12 months have been eye-opening and by allowing myself to feel the feels, experience the experiences, to do the work it takes to reach the core roots of what drives my subconscious mind; this was the work I was hungry for. It allowed me to focus out and not on the pain I was enduring with shingles. I showed up, I participated, I kept saying to myself, "This, too, shall pass. Yes, this too, shall pass." I have recently learned that to truly create a vision and to manifest the changes it takes to achieve the results, you need to create a "state of mind" that is your inner belief system that there is nothing that will stop you from healing any part of your BEING. I shout to the rooftops so everyone can hear me......

"I am a Powerful, Confident, Authentic Leader! Yes I AM! Yes I AM!"

"Blossoming from a Survivor to Thriver. I am thriving, I am thriving, I am thriving!"

### The FUTURE

All I can say is that Auto Suggestion will always have a place in my conscious and subconscious mind. It is what fuels the fire when I need it most. It is the water to my earth and the ying to my yang. As I close my eyes now, I see the future. It is beautiful, it is peaceful, and it is exactly what I am envisioning it to be. Living LIFE OUT LOUD, beautiful people, beautiful nature, beautiful sounds; everything is healthier, stronger, and healed. I am healed, I am cured, I am living life out loud!

# ELAINE SUGIMURA

**About Elaine R. Sugimura:** Elaine is an accomplished fashion executive turned entrepreneur who has a passion to create leaders amongst leaders. Currently, she owns several businesses and as CEO, she runs a franchise food and beverage organization that requires both strategy and execution. Fun fact: she is an adrenaline junkie—the higher, the faster, the better. Her love for adventure has led her to travel to many parts of the world by plane and automobile. She and her husband, Hiro, share their home in Northern California. They have raised two extraordinary sons and have added two beautiful daughters-in-law to their growing family.

Author's Website: *www.ElaineRSugimura.com*
Book Series Website & Author's Bio: *www.The13StepstoRiches.com*

## Elizabeth Walker

# SPEAK WELL TO YOURSELF

Imagine if other people could hear the way you speak to yourself. Would you still use the same language? Would you be more harsh or less harsh on yourself? Would you speak to others the way you speak to yourself? And how would you react if someone else spoke to you the way you speak to yourself?

The brain is an interesting tool at a human's disposal. You see, it can only do six things! You've all heard of the five senses. The human brain can see, hear, touch, taste, and smell. But unlike any other animal, the human brain can talk to itself. There are great advantages to this when utilized effectively, and significant disadvantages when utilized poorly.

When I was four years old, my maternal grandfather made a strange comment. He said, "Elizabeth Anne Matilda Jane, you have got to blow your own trumpet, because no one else will." I remember thinking to myself, "Pa, I don't have a trumpet." His words stuck with me and still do today, probably because I repeated them over and over to myself in an attempt to understand what he meant.

My paternal grandfather said something similar, "Girly, do you know how good you are? I know how good you are; look at your parents, they are good people and that means that you're good too!" I was about six when this comment played over and over in my head, and it was said to me after an incident where I had gotten in trouble for throwing my soft toys. I didn't think my parents were very good at the time. I was crying and my grandfather comforted me. It was a strange feeling as he usually lived in New Zealand and was not someone I spent a lot of time with, yet this saying stayed with me and even to this day I believe I'm a "good girl."

Over time I learned what "blow your own trumpet because no one else will" meant. My pa was basically saying to me that if I couldn't recognize my own achievements, or talk about them, then no one would recognize them. He also meant that promoting myself would allow me to achieve more; that if I didn't do it myself, no one else would. These learnings from my great grandfathers have stood me in good stead and allowed me to become the woman I am today.

You see, it wasn't actually what they said to me, but the way that I repeated them over and over in my mind. The simple process of Auto Suggestion.

W. Clement Stone says, "Self-suggestion makes you master of yourself." And he is right! Whatever you say to yourself enough times will indeed create your reality. You will become the version of yourself that you speak of in your mind. In fact, the subconscious mind is such an obedient servant that whatever you speak to yourself, it will attempt to make true.

Now really think about this. Do you really believe the words that you're saying about yourself? Are you really hopeless? Are you really a terrible person? Are you really awful at making money?

The answers to all these questions should be no. While you keep saying these things to yourself, they will keep coming true. You are creating your own reality.

One of the things I enjoyed doing with both my parents and grandparents was watching musicals. They filled my heart with joy and in watching them, I found lines to use as effective mantras for auto suggestion.

Remember the musical *Oklahoma*? There's a song in it that goes like this:

> *Oh, what a beautiful morning,*
> *Oh, what a beautiful day,*
> *I've got a wonderful feeling,*
> *Everything's going my way.*

That song has stayed with me since I was seven years old when I saw this musical on the stage in Sydney, Australia. The constant singing of that song for weeks and months after and the repeating of those words has resulted in a mantra that serves me well. Every single time it's a beautiful morning, I know that it's going to be a beautiful day. I know that I'm going to have a wonderful feeling, and I know that everything will go my way!

What a great way to think!

Another favorite is *The King and I* and the song that stuck in my mind from that musical is "Whistle a Happy Tune."

> *Whenever I feel afraid*
> *I hold my head erect*
> *And whistle a happy tune*
> *So no one will suspect I'm Afraid.*

> *While shivering in my shoes*
> *I strike a careless pose*
> *And whistle a happy tune*
> *And no one ever knows I'm afraid.*

> *The result of this deception*
> *Is very strange to tell*
> *For when I fool the people*
> *I fear I fool myself as well!*

*I whistle a happy tune*
*And ev'ry single time*
*The happiness in the tune*
*Convinces me that I'm not afraid.*

*Make believe you're brave*
*And the trick will take you far.*
*You may be as brave*
*As you make believe you are.*

Imagine if every time you felt fear, your brain had been programmed to whistle and it all felt ok! That's exactly what happened for me because of all this singing. What you say or sing to yourself over and over creates your reality.

So I ask you again, what are you saying to you, about you? What are you creating as your reality, by Auto Suggestion?

There was a time in my life where I briefly forgot all the great teachings of my grandparents. I was fifteen years old. The girls in my grade at school and I had all started seeing boys. I'd always hung out with the boys; I was a bit of a tomboy as a young girl and what happened at this age was extremely interesting, albeit distressing to me. Suddenly, the boys I had been friends with started treating me differently. Remember, I was a good girl. I would hang out with them and if one of them was my boyfriend, I'd certainly kiss him. Yet in the ninth grade at school, this all changed. Some of my friends started having sex with boys. Not me though, I hadn't yet made that decision. I was heavily involved with the youth group at my local church and decided that behavior wasn't for me. The group of boys we hung around with decided that wasn't good enough for them and decided to create a label for me. It was "Liz Pig."

They would call me that name out loud across the fence between the boy's school and the girl's school. They called me that name at a swimming carnival that our school held at the boy's school and at first, I thought it was funny, until I realized that they were being mean. I didn't understand why they chose that name. I was a gymnast and a swimmer and didn't at all look like a pig nor did I act like a pig. These boys had been my best friends for a long time. I was so hurt.

Yet as more and more of the girls said yes to the boys' advances and I maintained my no, the worse the name calling got. I started repeating it to myself. Again, just as a child, trying to work out what it meant, only this time it was not an Auto Suggestion that served me.

I allowed myself for three years to believe that I was ugly; that people thought I was messy, and I all but hated myself for being Liz Pig. I met one of the men when I was in my thirties and we chatted about the old days and he said to me, "Remember we used to call you Liz pig?" and I said, "Yes it used to hurt a lot." He said, "Really?" I replied, "Yeah, I hated myself for years because of that." He responded, "Wow Liz, you were probably the only girl in high school that we respected."

Obviously, that was news to me and in short, I reflected on what I had created merely by repeating their words without understanding their meaning.

Just like energy, that cannot be created nor destroyed only transformed, no one creates nor destroys us, only we do.

So, I ask you to make a commitment to yourself today. It may take some practise and it will be worth it. Notice your language to yourself. What you speak in your mind is what you will create in your world. What will you choose to auto-suggest to yourself?

I chose to remember all of those great things from my childhood and focus on them. I whistle a happy tune. I know that if it's a beautiful morning, everything's going my way. I know that I'm a good girl, and I know that I can blow my own trumpet.

The gifts I was given as a child were not available to everyone as a child. What are you suggesting to your children, that they are repeating in their minds? What are you choosing to say to yourself? The thing is, if you're reading this book now, you're probably an adult, and the one thing that you have is choice. Choice about what you say to your children and choice about what you suggest to yourself.

Choose wisely.

# ELIZABETH WALKER

**About Elizabeth Walker:** Elizabeth is Australia's leading Female Integrated NLP Trainer, an international speaker with Real Success, and the host of Success Resources' (Australia's largest and most successful events promoter, including speakers such as Tony Robbins and Sir Richard Branson) inaugural Australian Women's Program "The Seed." Elizabeth has guided many people to achieve complete personal breakthroughs and phenomenal personal and business growth. With over 25 years of experience transforming the lives of hundreds of thousands of people, Elizabeth's goal is to assist leaders to create the reality they choose to live, impacting millions on a global scale.

A thought leader who has worked alongside people like Gary Vaynerchuck, Kerwin Rae, Jeffery Slayter, and Kate Gray, Elizabeth has an outstanding method of delivering heart with business.

As a former lecturer in medicine at the University of Sydney and lecturer in nursing at Western Sydney University, Elizabeth was instrumental in the research and development of the stillbirth and neonatal death pathways, ensuring each family in Australia went home knowing what happened to their child, and felt understood, heard, and seen.

A former Australian Champion in Trampolining and Australian Dancesport, Elizabeth has always been passionate about the mindset and skills required to create the results you are seeking.

Author's website: *www.ElizabethAnneWalker.com*
Book Series Website & Author's Bio: *www.The13StepsToRiches.com*

*Erin Ley*

# POWERFUL BEYOND MEASURE

In *Think and Grow Rich,* Napoleon Hill brilliantly states, *"Through the dominating thoughts which one permits to remain in the conscious mind, (whether these thoughts be negative or positive, is immaterial), the principle of auto-suggestion voluntarily reaches the subconscious mind and influences it with these thoughts."*

So many people are unaware of this powerful control we have regarding Auto Suggestion, also known as self-suggestion. A very simple way to explain Auto Suggestion is to say that the thoughts we entertain the most, through repetition, and which are emotionalized, are passed into our subconscious and become our beliefs, good or bad. If we tell ourselves we are not good at something repeatedly and have the feeling of hopelessness attached to that thought, we will take on the belief that we are not good at it which then becomes a self-fulfilling prophecy. The opposite holds true as well. When we tell ourselves we are good at something repeatedly and emotionalize that thought with a positive feeling, we take on the belief that we are good at it. This explains Henry Ford's quote, "Whether you think you can or think you can't, you're right."

We all come to this planet with purpose and with God-given gifts to share with the world. Babies know exactly what they want and know how to ask for it. As we get older, we begin to listen to authority figures tell us repeatedly what is best for us. Based on that repetition and feeling of faith (because we trust our family, teachers, and others who are the closest influencers in our life) we acquire beliefs in our subconscious without even realizing it. As we receive those beliefs through Auto Suggestion, we begin to act in such a way that reinforces those beliefs. Depending on what we choose to focus on and download as a belief will determine our life's circumstances.

After receiving my cancer diagnosis of lymphoblastic lymphoma in 1991 at twenty-five years old, I read many personal development books that spoke about the significance of the present moment and self-talk, verbal and non-verbal. At that time, I understood that I had to be kind to myself. I needed to give myself grace and show myself compassion. This was something I never thought about prior to the diagnosis. Before, I had only focused on the outer world and what the people, places and things needed from me; who they needed me to be based on their beliefs. I was completely off purpose.

Post diagnosis, I began to realize there is a whole inner-world and the most important thing we can do as we tap into it is to stay in the present moment, repeatedly thinking and speaking only empowering words to ourselves, emotionalized with positive feelings to go with the thoughts and words. My whole *world* changed with this revelation. I became powerful beyond measure. The doctors couldn't understand how they could be wrong over and over again when it came to my health and well-being. I kept defying the odds. Every time they said I was going to die, I lived. For years they insisted I'd never have children due to the intense chemotherapy and radiation regimen. I went on to have three children when I decided to, four years after the protocol ended. Miracles come in threes. The medical professionals and fellow patients referred to me as "the miracle maker." The doctors at Memorial Sloan Kettering Cancer Center started having their patients call me at home. This is how I started Life Coaching in the 1990's. I coached the patients and their families through the diagnoses and the protocol. The doctors reported to me that their patients had less nausea and a brighter outlook on life with a greater sense of wellbeing. I taught them what I learned about Auto Suggestion.

How cool is it to know that we have the power to create our life?! We literally live out what we decide to think and feel. Then, based on that, we take the action that leads to our life *circumstances,* good or bad. Many people go an entire lifetime not knowing this. So many people are home thinking they are unlucky or that they have no chance at a great life. The only reason that continues to be their reality is because that is their dominant thought, coupled with the negative emotion they experience as they think the thought.

You can create a vision statement for your life, beyond your wildest dreams. In *Think and Grow Rich,* Napolean Hill refers to this as a Mission Statement. Put pen to paper. There is a whole psychology behind the idea of pen to paper rather than typing it in a computer. Write exactly what you want in crystal-clear detail. Then bring it alive utilizing your five senses and your sixth sense of intuition. As you visualize your ultimate destiny, hear the music, see the vibrant colors, smell the scent of the perfume and cologne, taste the food on the table, feel the love shared in the hug, and have the feeling as if it's happening right now. This feeling of knowing it's happening positively emotionalizes the thoughts you are thinking, making your vision powerful.

Read your vision statement out loud, bring it alive, and have the feeling as if it is happening right now every morning when you wake up and every evening before going to bed. This repetition is telling your conscious it is important to you, which then gets downloaded into your subconscious as a firm statement of exactly what you want. God, your superconscious, the Universe will then provide the Divine Download, inspired ideas, for you to act upon to bring you to your ultimate destiny. To program your subconscious in this way, via Auto Suggestion, you have to do this every single day without fail. Consistent repetition is key.

I created a crystal-clear vision for my life when I was living with cancer. Then, four years later after getting married, I decided I wanted to have children. I wrote out a crystal-clear vision of myself as a mother with my (now ex) husband as the father with three healthy children. After having two boys, I added that I wanted a girl to my vision statement as well. I bought an adorable infant sized dress and hung it on the door in the family room where I spent the most time. Four months after my second son was born, I found out I was pregnant with my daughter, miracle baby number three. I credit all of this to Auto Suggestion and divine support.

We have the power to decide in an instant if we are going to accept a negative thought or feeling and allow it into our subconscious. We are bombarded with impressions via the five senses all day every day, so it is up to us to decide what we are going to acknowledge and hold onto. When I learned this in 1991, I became diligent about guarding my thoughts and feelings carefully. For me, it was life or death. Actually, for all of us it is life or death. If we allow ourselves to concede to the negative thoughts and feelings and entertain them long enough to have them enter the subconscious and become yet another negative believe such as self-doubt, than we are not living, we are just existing. That's no way to experience this wonderful life we have been given the opportunity to experience.

I would love for you to become aware of what limiting beliefs you are holding on to. What kind of self-doubt and self-sabotage behavior are you experiencing? Write them down on paper.

Awareness is the beginning of all wonderful change. Once you become aware of what those negative beliefs are and where they stemmed from, thank them for showing up to protect you, demonstrate forgiveness, and let them go. Replace the negativity with empowering beliefs through the practice of Auto Suggestion and watch your life light up in the most miraculous way. You deserve to live your very best life filled with love, inner-peace, joy, and abundance. You can begin to make this your reality starting right now by utilizing Auto Suggestion.

We have the power to create our riches in all areas of life, including health, relationships, spirituality, happiness, and wealth, with the help of God. In *Think and Grow Rich*, Napolean Hill said, *"There are no limitations to the mind except those we acknowledge. Both poverty and riches are the offspring of thought."* Based on my experiences in many areas of my life, I know this to be true. There are many Universal Laws. How we communicate with ourselves and our Higher Power (I say God) will determine the life we create. Think, speak, and act only those thoughts, words, and actions that will empower you beyond measure. Always remember to live onward and upward!

# ERIN LEY

**About Erin Ley:** As Founder and CEO of Onward Productions, Inc., Erin Ley has spent the last 30 years as an Author, Professional Speaker, Personal and Professional Empowerment and Success Coach predominantly around mindset, Vision and Decision. Founder of many influential summits, including "Life On Track," Erin is also the host of the upcoming online streaming T.V. Show *"Life On Track with Erin Ley,"* which is all about helping you get into the driver's seat of your own life.

They call Erin "The Miracle Maker!" As a cancer survivor at age twenty-five, single mom of three at age forty-seven, successful Entrepreneur at age fifty, Erin has shown thousands upon thousands across the globe how to become victorious by being focused, fearless, and excited about life and your future! Erin says, "Celebrate life and you'll have a life worth celebrating!"

To see more about Erin and the release of her 4th book *"WorkLuv: A Love Story"* along with her "Life On Track" Course & Coaching Programs, please visit her website.

Author's website: *www.ErinLey.com*
Book Series Website & Author's Bio: *www.The13StepsToRiches.com*

*Fatima Hurd*

# OVERCOMING SCARCITY

I know that Auto Suggestion helps with manifesting what we want, but "Why am I still struggling?" I used to ask myself. I repeat my daily affirmations and meditate and read a lot of self-help books but nothing! I made progress in some areas in life but in others I still needed improvement.

What I failed to realize was that Auto Suggestion is only part of the process.

Even though I was doing the daily morning and evening affirmations, throughout the day I had a million thoughts running through my mind and wasn't aware of all the sneaky negative talk I was auto-suggesting throughout the day. I was hard on myself when something went wrong and instantly felt discouraged. The scarcity mentality didn't help, either. I knew that this negativity wasn't serving me, however, it was difficult to shake that feeling and get back to a higher frequency. I knew the longer I sat in that state, the harder it would be to get out of it. I read the books and I understood what I was reading, but I couldn't quite grasp the concept. So even though I was doing the work in the mornings and evenings, I wasn't taking responsibility to be consciously aware of negative words throughout the day. I was feeding my subconscious, which basically was overriding all the work I was doing daily and ultimately holding me back from making progress.

I think back to how I achieved certain goals in my life and often wondered what the secret was. It wasn't until I read *Think and Grow Rich* that I realize what I was doing wrong.

What I realized is that when even though I was suggesting positive thoughts to my subconscious mind, it wasn't getting 'the memo' because the state of emotion I was in was not aligning with that positive thought.

When I first moved here from Las Vegas, I struggled financially. I still had a studio in Vegas with a lease that was not up for a few more months, and I was driving every other weekend to Vegas to do photoshoots. But the cost of doing business and the sessions I booked was a wash. I remember being in a scarcity mindset.

I did my meditations and daily affirmations, but nothing! I tried to focus on how to make money but I had no creative juice. I was done; I needed to pay my rent for the studio and I had no money. Yes, I could ask my husband, but asking him would only put us in debt, and I didn't want to do that. I needed to figure out how to make money fast!

One day, a friend called me and asked if I wanted to do her 40-day meditation workshop, which cost $27. I didn't have a lot of money, but what the heck, I had nothing to lose. I said yes!

What his guided meditation workshop did was to remind me what I had forgotten in my despair— the secret ingredient to manifesting was gratitude. Every day I had a shift in my mindset. I started to direct my attention to what I already had and feel true gratitude for it. I focused only on the positive things in life and to be immensely grateful for everything. I remember being overwhelmed with joy as my list grew longer and longer for all the things I was grateful for. As I focused on doing my daily affirmations, my state of mind was at peace and filled with joy and love for everyone and everything!

I followed the steps from *Think and Grow Rich* on Auto Suggestion and infused it with my FAITH, LOVE, and GRATITUDE, walking in that Faith that God had my back!

Another day, a client of mine called me. He had just bought his wife a new house and he was so excited getting ready to surprise her. He placed a huge canvas order with pictures I had taken for them a few months earlier. His wife booked a maternity and newborn session with me. This was their third child and finally, she had given birth to a little boy. My client was to the moon and back in love with his cute little family.

It was definitely a surprise! I never expected to receive such a huge order. Especially canvases at the time. I hadn't sold any canvases with my photography after moving to California; without a studio I stopped doing in-person sales. Sometimes I tried to figure out where the money would come from but that was not my job. My job was to trust that God had a plan for what I asked for and trust that he had it covered. I was able to pay off my lease and get out of my studio, and finally, be done with that chapter of my life.

Using the positive affirmations and keeping an open mind allowed me to receive the downloads that helped create the opportunity that lead to the transfer of money for the services I rendered.

I learned this by surrounding myself with people who were where I wanted to be, who always reminded me to be careful with the words that I spoke. Sometimes we don't realize how many negative words we use in our vocabulary daily, and as insignificant as that may be, after a while, it catches up and becomes our belief. Who we are is a result of what we tell ourselves every day.

One of the biggest challenges I had in my life has always been around money. Most of the time it was always scarce. Even growing up, it was one of the things my parents always fought about. To change that took work!

I had to remind myself that it wasn't going to be overnight as mentioned in *"Think and Grow Rich."* As the famous Emil Coue formula goes, "Day by Day, in every way, I am getting better and better!"

This became my mantra whenever I had to be forgiving with myself for allowing the negative thoughts to creep into my subconscious, in order to keep from feeling discouraged.

Being in a positive mindset all the time was difficult, but this mantra helped with allowing me to be graceful and just know that I was in control of what I wanted in my life.

I took the formula that I found in *"Think and Grow Rich, Autosuggestion"* and followed the instructions in the book with the purpose of giving orders to my subconscious mind every day without fail, and I found much SUCCESS!

Negative habits are also a big contributing factor to our thoughts! I had a bad habit of always coming home and complaining about work to my husband. Then I realized how eventually I would end up hating whatever job I had at the time; I didn't realize it at the time, but every time I spoke ill about my job (even if I was just venting), it was still sending a message to my subconscious of how miserable I was until the job became unbearable. When I realized what effect talking about my bad days was having on my thoughts, I quickly brought it to an end.

My goal is to teach my children these tools so that they have control of their lives. I wish someone would have taught me how to use Auto Suggestion positively way earlier in my life!

However, I am very grateful for the opportunities that brought this book, *"Think and Grow Rich!"* into my life.

There are so many great books out there, but I feel that the universe has a hand in bringing into your life the books that really will transform your life, and *"Think and Grow Rich"* has been one of those books for me!

# FATIMA HURD

**About Fatima Hurd:** Fatima is a personal brand photographer and was featured in the special edition of Beauty & Lifestyle's mommy magazine. Fatima specializes in personal branding photography dedicated to helping influencers and entrepreneurs expand their reach online with strategic, creative, inspiring, and visual content. Owner of a digital consulting agency, Social Branding Photography', Fatima helps professionals with all their digital needs.

Fatima holds ten years of photography experience. An expert in her field, she helps teach photography to middle school students and she hosts workshops to teach anyone who wants to learn how to use and improve their skills with DSLR and on manual mode. Hurd is also a mother of three, wife, certified Reiki master, and certified crystal healer. She loves being out in nature, enjoys taking road trips with her family, and loves meditation and yoga on the beach.

Author's website: *www.FatimaHurd.com*
Book Series Website & Author's Bio: *www.The13StepsToRiches.com*

*Frankie Fegurgur*

# RETIREMENT STARTS WITH A TRIP TO THE LIBRARY

Americans are suffering a retirement crisis. One in four have $0 saved, and ten thousand baby boomers turn sixty-five every day, leading experts to believe that Social Security will be insolvent in 8-13 years. Compounded with longer life expectancies, record inflation and healthcare costs, and increasing tax burdens means our situation is exponentially dire. The over seventy million living baby boomers are surpassed in population only by the millennials, who are delaying key milestones such as marriage, kids, and home purchases.

Millennials largely attribute these delays to the soaring cost of college and raising a family, while also caring for their aging parents and/or grandparents. They are 'sandwiched' between their responsibilities and are suffering financially, physically, and emotionally. Most other developed countries aren't far behind, although there have been some interesting propositions, including working longer, revamping pensions, and even expanding government benefits. Only time will tell which countries will find a sustainable solution. Despite these challenges, I believe that we are living in the greatest time in human history.

It's easy to feel overwhelmed by the present-day crises, but the tools to thrive in this new world are more accessible than ever. People like you are actively seeking answers and sharing their knowledge. So how is the retirement crisis relevant to Auto Suggestion, and exactly where does your local library come in? Auto Suggestion is consciously introducing new beliefs into your subconscious mind. Regardless of whether these beliefs are true or not, the subconscious accepts and actualizes them. You can leverage Auto Suggestion to improve any aspect of your life, from your health to your hobbies. For the purposes of our discussion, I'll be focusing on how to use decisive Auto Suggestion to create better financial outcomes in your personal and business life.

I became intrigued by how this principle might complement my work in retirement planning. You see, I knew that the most logical, math-based financial strategy wasn't worth the paper it was printed on, unless the client implemented it. Unfortunately, building a better financial plan isn't as simple as going into the proverbial library of the mind and checking out a few books. For many retirees, to shift financial paradigms reinforced with decades of negative 'evidence' might require an entire remodel of the facility. That's because just as money permeates all aspects of our daily lives, so does our attitude about who deserves to possess it.

I remember early in my career inviting someone to talk about saving for their future. They reflexively responded, "I don't make enough to save enough!" and that really stuck with me. Their scarcity infiltrated their speech and even their body language. I can often estimate how much money someone has by how they carry themselves, especially in a restaurant or store. In a restaurant, they typically read the menu from right to left, ordering based on the cost. They are especially tense after the meal when the check is presented. They probably also tip less. It's much more obvious when I see children in the store with their parents. Tell me you've never witnessed a child plead for a toy or other novelty, only to be met with "We can't afford that!"

This situation may have been all too familiar growing up in your household. Especially if you saw other kids getting the very thing you were told wasn't available to you. This is where the library analogy comes in, however I'm not referring to your local public library. I'm talking about the vast and potentially infinite library housed within your subconscious mind. For each area of your life that you'd like to improve, your subconscious records your previous experiences as well as your emotional interpretation of those experiences. It then catalogues that data as guidebooks to influence your beliefs, attitudes, and behaviors. It understands and communicates ideas utilizing pictures, symbols, and metaphors. By visualizing this fascinating system as a physical library, you are priming your mind for greater change. Why else do you go to the library? To learn AND apply what you learn, of course!

Unless you want to subsist on dwindling government benefits and the charity of others, you'll need to amass a proper nest egg. You may not have the slightest idea where to begin, but with an intentional, persistent practice, you'll learn to provide clear instructions to your subconscious. The first step is to write down the exact amount of money you desire. This isn't about trying to impress people with your net worth. If you want to earn more money because you think it will fix you, you'll never be at peace. If instead you are embracing a new level of receiving, then you're ready. Any doubt or worry that you feel is understandable because until this point, you've used fear to protect yourself. This is a good indication that you need to charge your Auto Suggestions with positive emotions and faith. You've got to let the library know that this is important to you. Address your subconscious in the morning when you wake up, and at night just before you fall asleep. Your mind is more likely to accept new beliefs during those times, assuming you've made the proper suggestion.

If you try to implement a money Auto Suggestion that is too far outside the realm of your current reference material, you'll get denied. It's like trying to check out a book with someone else's library card; the system won't believe it's yours. Instead, try breaking your Auto Suggestions into steps, allowing you to engage with your desire with incremental progress. Also try changing the verbiage to something that seems more plausible. For example, proclaiming, "I am a millionaire" when you aren't even a 'thousandaire' will cause security to escort you off the premises. If instead you say, "I have a millionaire mindset" your subconscious will go to work on researching habits that align with your statement. Listen to that inner wisdom for the right phrasing of your suggestions and stay disciplined. This self-awareness combined with faith and repetition will generate momentum, locking in your new behaviors as non-negotiable.

A concern about Auto Suggestion that I heard recently was that repeating the same thought over and over seems like overthinking. Rest assured, Auto Suggestion is not overthinking, it's deliberate thinking. It is a reflection of your intention and self-confidence. Overthinking is a perpetual round-robin of anxiety, draining you of your creative energy. It causes you to take every detail as a bad omen and paralyzes you. Instead, we want to unleash our gifts. Not only will Auto Suggestion create positive beliefs around financial freedom, it will remove old beliefs that kept you distracted and broke. Your past financial mistakes and struggles serve as a point of reflection— they are not your destiny. Once you understand how your library functions, it's your conscious mind that determines where you go in life. You know deep down the person you are capable of being, and consistent beliefs will lead to consistent results.

It's natural to wonder how long you must practice Auto Suggestion before achieving financial freedom. Even though you set a deadline for when you'll have the precise amount of money that you desire, leave space for it to happen sooner. Sure, you probably won't wake up on day three with a million bucks, but you will be pleasantly surprised by your recent financial decisions. Once you focus on generating wealth, your subconscious will prioritize your command and compel you to take action. If you are looking to supplement your morning and evening routine, I've got some simple ideas. These are free to use, take only seconds to set up, and can further align your intentions with your activity. Record yourself speaking your affirmations. You could even overlay your voice onto some relaxing music. Then loop the recording and play it softly at night while you sleep, preferably with headphones. For a visual trigger, label your cell phone alarms with your affirmations. Here is an example for a 6:30 am alarm, "I'm so grateful to wake up to another $1,000+ a day direct deposited!" You could set alarms just for waking up, or throughout the day as an opportunity to get grounded in the present. Next, change the names on all your app folders. Instead of the generic 'finance' folder, label it "I am rich." Each time you go to open an app, you'll get a quick win!

Americans are careening toward a retirement crisis, and many people you know are struggling to adjust to the new economy. It doesn't have to be this way; your personal example will inspire others to become successful and self-sufficient. I work with so many retirees who earn more money now than they ever did in their primary careers. If it's possible for them, it's possible for you. Begin your research in the library of your mind. Speak your truth with faith. Behave as if you're already the person you desire to be, and you'll be amazed at how just a few minutes a day will totally upgrade your money story.

# FRANKIE FEGURGUR

**About Frankie Fegurgur:** Frankie's "burning desire" is helping people retire with dignity. Frankie distills the lessons he has learned over the last 15 years and empowers our youth to make better financial decisions than the generation before them. This is a deeply personal mission for him—he was born to high-school-aged parents, and money was always a struggle. Frankie learned that hard work, alone, wasn't the key to financial freedom and sought a more fulfilling path. Now, he serves as the COO of a nonprofit financial association based in the San Francisco Bay Area, teaching money mindfulness. He, his wife, and their two children can be found exploring, volunteering, and building throughout their community.

Author's website: *www.FrankMoneyTalk.com*
Book Series Website & Author's Bio: *www.The13StepsToRiches.com*

*Freeman Witherspoon*

# INFLUENCING THE SUBCONSCIOUS MIND

God uniquely created man which includes his subconscious mind. It, however, must be told what to do as the subconscious mind acts on what you feed it. The information that comes into the body is what the subconscious mind feeds on to produce results. There are five gateways to which information gets into the subconscious mind. These five gateways are the five sensory organs. These gateways function to enable the mind to receive and respond to information. The medium through which this is done is what is called Auto Suggestion, which we are going to be looking at in this chapter.

You might be asking yourself, what is this Auto Suggestion? It is a suggestion to self. It is just a process that takes place in the part of the mind where thought takes place and hence influences the subconscious mind. This principle of Auto Suggestion helps the subconscious mind function, either negatively or positively based on what we suggest to it.

What we can understand from this is that we have control over the very things that we suggest to the subconscious mind. If we can learn to apply this same principle to our lives, then we can influence the subconscious mind and produce great results. It is very possible to become successful and increase wealth if the right principles are followed. Remember that success is not just for some people. Success is for anyone who dares to apply the 13 steps. One of these principles is the principle of Auto Suggestion.

Many people in the world today are not successful because they are telling themselves the wrong things. Earlier, I mentioned some of my hardships in growing up and how I was raised by my grandparents. Watching them each day was such a growing experience. However, I discovered something, and that is I saw that they were struggling to make it in life. Financially, things were a bare minimum. I watched how they struggled to get meals together and pay the bills to keep a roof over our heads.

What I resolved to do was to find and utilize all available resources to get out of that situation. At a young age, I decided to take on extra jobs in the neighborhood to make ends meet. The purpose was just to somehow help my grandparents through what was happening at that time. This experience changed everything around me. My perspective of life changed and a great burden for change was birthed within. This pushed me to think differently and do things differently. My approach to life shifted. This shift repositioned me in every way.

I discovered that if I was going to change what was happening at that time, I needed to take a different path. Understanding this, I had to make myself believe that I was born for something bigger and greater. The moment this revelation and understanding came, I started to maximize the principle of Auto Suggestion. This is when I decided to take charge of my thoughts. I had to convince myself that I was able to achieve greatness and become whatever I set my mind to. This was the beginning of the transformational journey.

And just as Napoleon Hill asserts in his book, *Think and Grow Rich*, "If you truly desire money so keenly that your desire is an obsession, you will have no difficulty in convincing yourself that you will acquire it. The object is to want money, and to become so determined to have it; you convince yourself you will have it." Knowing that a man can achieve anything he envisions, I experienced a paradigm shift. This became the framework of my thought pattern. My thinking changed and I began to focus on changing my position in life. The principles I drew out brought me to a place of high-mindedness. I began to think outside the box. The moment I did this, I began talking to myself. I had to convince myself that I can and will become better and greater than my current family situation allowed. What a shift it was!

It motivated me to seek better opportunities out of life. The first step of this quest led to a career in the U.S. Army. While serving, I focused on education and also enrolled in business workshops and seminars. I convinced myself that I was going to break the cycle of mediocrity in my family line and become a legacy maker. After getting my subconscious mind to embrace the altered realism that I was going to achieve this great feat, then a clear focus and a keen sense of insight set in.

You see, the moment your subconscious mind is convinced that you are going to become successful, the desire will not cease to flow. Many people often fail to achieve greatness because they have managed to convince themselves that they cannot do it. The reason they fail is not that the principles are not working, but because they have convinced themselves that they cannot achieve it. In other words, they are using the principles in a negative sense.

This is the core principle I use to change my life. As I assured myself that I was going to become bigger, better, and greater, ideas for achieving these dreams began to materialize. The desire ignited my passion and I became sensitive to new ideas. All of the businesses that I am currently managing emerged as a result of this principle.

As you are reading this, you might be desiring to achieve great things, accumulate great wealth, become famous, or to start your own business. Whatever your aspirations, they are within reach. In Mark 9:23, Jesus asserted that if one can believe, all things are possible to the one who believes. In the same light, when you believe or dream to achieve something, it is possible. You have to suggest these dreams to yourself each day until they become a part of you. Understand that this has to be repeated continuously until it becomes a personal revelation. This has to be done daily until it is personalized. The productivity of that dream becomes effective when it becomes a personal acknowledgment.

You have control over your position in life. Friend, whatever you intend to achieve in life is very possible if only you can visualize and employ the principle of Auto Suggestion. You are going to be amazed at how much you can achieve through this principle. I have seen the power of this principle in action. I wrote down every dream I wanted to achieve and the amount of money I wanted to have in my account, and then I started visualizing it. That is what created a new atmosphere for me altogether. This proves to me that the principle works.

Whatever you want to become or achieve is very possible. Jesus showed us that possibilities are limitless as long as we have faith. So learn to maximize your faith when it comes to applying the principle of Auto Suggestion. The first thing to do is to write down everything you are desiring, and then visualize achieving them. The final thing is to repeat them to yourself daily. Repeat them until they induce an obsession within you. Become super focused on it. Keep repeating it until you believe it. The moment your subconscious mind accepts them as reality is when the shift starts.

Change is very possible. You can change your current situation through the use of Auto Suggestion. I have seen my life move from next-to-nothing to where I am today. If you dare to apply the principle of Auto Suggestion, you will be amazed by how much change will come into your life. After applying this principle, you will become more productive, more efficient and more effective in working towards your goal. Apply the principle of Auto Suggestion today and become whatever you are dreaming of becoming.

# FREEMAN WITHERSPOON

**About Freeman Witherspoon:** Freeman is a professional network marketer that manages several online businesses. He considers himself a late bloomer to network marketing. Prior to partnering with network marketing organizations, he served for over 20 years in the military. He has incorporated his many life experiences into managing successful business models.

Military service afforded him the opportunity to travel throughout the world. He has lived in Heidelberg, Germany, Seoul, South Korea, and many places throughout the United States. Freeman currently lives in Texas with his wife and three dogs; a Dachshund named Dutchess, a Yorkie named Boosie and a Pomchi (Pomeranian-Chihuahua mix) named Caesar.

Author's website: *www.FWitherspoonJr.com*
Book Series Website & Author's Bio: *www.The13StepsToRiches.com*

*Gina Bacalski*

# THE BED PERSON

From a very young age, I have collected motivating sayings and photos and hung them on my wall where I could look at them as I went to sleep at night. I have changed it up as my goals, dreams, and aspirations evolved over the years.

When I was in college, I used to go swing dancing almost every weekend with a few people that I had made friends with in my building. One evening, my favorite dance partner, Daniel, walked into my room to hurry my progress with my makeup so we could leave. He stood before my bed and looked at my motivational wall.

"You are what you think about all day." He read out loud from a quote I had there. Cocking his head to the side, he narrowed his eyes a bit in thought. Suddenly, his eyes opened wide, his head shot up, and he loudly declared, "Damn it, I'm a woman!"

Just before the pandemic hit the world, I became absolutely obsessed with the Korean Pop Super Group, BTS. In addition to learning all their discography and even some of their choreography, I also enjoyed getting to know the members of BTS from the vast abundance of material available of my "seven Korean boyfriends" from the internet and YouTube. I learned that not only do they all have beautiful voices and faces, but also keen minds and deep hearts. In an interview I found one pandemic driven day, Kim NamJoon, or RM, the group leader, main rapper, producer, and lyricist for BTS described his creative process. He explained that for him, and most people, you can't sit down in front of a computer and force yourself to be moved to write or work out a problem or what have you. He then went on to explain about the three "B"s of inspiration: Bed, Bus, or Bath.

Bus People get inspired by walks through nature, car or bus rides, riding bikes, or those types of things. I've heard about other writers or artists that will have to pull their cars over and quickly write down the next chapters of their works or quickly sketch something. RM is a Bus Person. Before his fame prevented it, he would ride the bus everywhere he went. Now, mask and hat shod, he rides his bike all over Seoul, Korea. He also does what the fan base has lovingly named "NamJooning," which is going on walks in parks or somewhere in nature, walking through museums, or hiking. The Korean and English tapestry he weaves with the lyrics of BTS songs is astonishing and admired by industry experts the world over.

Bath People get inspiration when they are in baths, saunas, showers, or a good day at the spa. My husband is a Bath Person. You put him in the sauna for an hour and he's solved the world's problems when he emerges. He also always has very important things to tell me when he gets out of the shower.

And then there are Bed People. I am a Bed Person. I get inspired when I lay down, close my eyes, and let myself be.

Min Yoongi, or Suga, his stage name, another member of BTS, is also a Bed Person. In every iteration of his *Genius Lab* where he writes most of the music that BTS sings, he has to have a couch "big enough to lay down on" just for this purpose. He'll read, play video games, or simply nap and then jump up and start working. But needs a place to "Bed" that's close to his workstation.

When I'm writing a novel and I get stuck on a scene, I will literally stop writing, get up from my desk, go across the hall to my bedroom, lay down on my bed, close my eyes, and write the scene in my mind. Then I'll get back up, sit in front of my computer once more, and finish writing the scene.

In addition to getting inspiration with how and what I write, I also get inspiration in in other areas of my life. I'm thoroughly convinced that Napolean Hill was a Bed Person. He talks about doing the Auto Suggestion exercises right before going to bed.

Even before my discovery of *Think and Grow Rich*, I had already started an Auto Suggestion meditation practice. Mr. Hill has since helped me perfect it.

On the wall of my bedroom, I keep my vision wall. I have my motivational quotes, but I also have photos of things that I aspire to have and to be. Right before I go to bed, or at times when I need some direction, I will sit or lay on my bed, and look at and meditate on my Vision Wall.

Like Napolean suggests, I clearly picture in my mind what I want. It's easier for me having an actual picture of the thing or aspiration that I want. Then I will put an emotion with it, and let the two swirl in my mind and heart.

I have a good friend and mentor named Levi McPhearson, and he taught me a little trick with the emotion of gratitude. Gratitude is one of the only positive emotions that can be felt in the past, present, and future. You can rewrite a negative emotion of the past by filling it up with the emotion of gratitude. Likewise, you can pre-feel the emotion of gratitude when thinking of something you want to attain or a situation you want to go a certain way. I use gratitude in all my in Auto Suggestion Vision Wall meditations.

I actually do one more step beyond the gratitude and aspiration heart swirl. After I've let the chemistry of the mixture ripple around me, I sit in "it" for long moments. This is where the three B's come in to play. For me, I sit in "it" on my bed, but that might not work for everyone. Maybe someone needs to sit in "it" as they take a walk, go for a drive, lay in a bath, or take a shower.

Whichever B suits you best is the one to do, but then one of the most important parts happens; the listening. After I do my laying and sitting, I *listen*. I listen to myself, to the thoughts that come to me as I'm doing my sitting. Those thoughts almost inevitably are the next steps that will get me to the thing that I aspire to gain, the item or aspiration I've been picturing with gratitude and swirling around my heart. I will listen, then I will write them down, and that becomes my To Do list for the following day. Maybe it's to make a phone call to specific person; maybe it's to post a certain thing about my business on a social media platform. It might not make sense and it doesn't always have to, but I listen, write, and then do anyway.

And guess what? I did get sound-check, VIP floor seats to BTS's LA, Permission to Dance stadium concert, and yes, I am a two-time, number one, best-selling author!

I wonder what will come next?

# GINA BACALSKI

**About Gina Bacalski:** Gina is a Real Estate Agent, licensed since June 2018. Her background is in Early Childhood Education where she received her Child Development Associate from the state of Utah and has an AS from BYU-Idaho. For the past seventeen years, Gina has thoroughly enjoyed her experience in the service industry helping families in the gifted community.

In 2019, Gina helped Jon Kovach Jr. launch Champion Circle and is now CEO of the organization. She brings her genuine love for people, high attention to detail, and strives to exceed client's expectations to the Real Estate industry and to Champion Circle.

Gina married the man of her dreams, Jay Bacalski, in San Diego, in 2013. The Bacalskis love entertaining friends and family, going on hikes, and attending movies and plays. When Gina isn't helping her clients navigate the real estate world, she will most often be found dancing and listening to BTS, watching KDramas and writing fantasy, sci-fi and romance novels.

Author's Website: *www.MyChampionCircle.com/Gina-Bacalski*
Book Series Website & Author's Bio: *www.The13StepstoRiches.com*

## Griselda Beck

# YOUR POWER TO CREATE AND BE ANYTHING YOU WANT

Auto Suggestion: The power of declaration and the subconscious repetition of that declaration used to influence one's own thoughts, feelings and behavior to create a new reality. Put simply, it is a powerful tool used to turn dreams into reality. In other words, creating something out of nothing.

I recall one of the early sessions I had with my love and relationship coach when I recounted a story that had happened over the weekend. My partner at the time took a photo of me on my phone. We had a strict no-faces-in-naughty-pics policy, but he said, "Babes, I want you to see what I see." I remember looking at it after, and what I saw was amazing. It was a beautiful, sensual woman, looking so happy. When he asked if he could have the pic, I said, "ABSOLUTELY NOT! No faces!" He looked at me so perplexed as I was not nude, nothing was technically showing and he said, "What's the difference between that and a bathing suit?"

My coach asked, "...and...what's the difference?" I said, "It's lingerie...it's private! I would simply die if it got into the wrong hands." She asked me, "What do you see?" I said that I loved the picture, but I could never show this in "public" or to ANYONE for that matter. It was just for me. To see myself as he saw me. She assured me it was the way EVERYONE saw me. I was so worried about "What would 'they' think?" She proceeded to tell me that all she saw when she looked at that picture was a Confident,

Radiant, Powerful woman, who knows who she is and what she wants. All I could see was beautiful and porn-like material.

She ended this part of the session with, "I would love for you to one day feel confident enough to see yourself with innocent eyes, without judgment or shame." That day she guided me to write some empowering messages to myself. I came home and wrote them on post-it notes, which I placed on my bathroom mirror. I used to read them everyday aloud, at first. Over time, I would see them and just "know" what was on there, as if they were merely a simple symbol as a reminder of the message that was already inside me.

Eighteen months later, I was speaking with someone about how empowering boudoir shoots were. She shared some pictures and I shared mine. Her feedback was powerful, goddess, sensual and beautiful! She wasn't wrong. The woman before me in that very same picture I once saw as "porn" was so beautiful, free, radiant, and inspiring. And then in that instant, not even thirty seconds later, I realized I had just done the thing I was stretched to do so many months before! I couldn't even see what I saw back then. The picture was so innocent. The Victoria's Secret catalog had much more provocative and revealing shots. This was nothing but captured beauty. WOW! There's nothing wrong with me. I'm a beautiful being, and I am radiant and confident and stunning. What a difference a shift in perspective makes when you peel back the years of conditioning, shame filled messaging and programming, release the fear of judgment from others and TRUST YOURSELF.

I was able to easily share that picture now without regard because I had been repeating to myself over and over again that "I am perfect as I am," "My sensuality and my beauty are source of my power, light and love that radiates from within," "My presence inspires, brings light and joy to the world," "I am good," "I am enough." At some point I woke up and it was true. It just was; no filter, no need to hide, no holding back. I had authentically emerged.

The power of suggestion can serve to change the way you see yourself or that person, place, salary, promotion, dream or thing you dream of and see as impossible or unattainable, into believing that you're the only one who can and it is meant for you. It is yours—*By believing it, you create it, you become it.*

One day you wake up and you're the CEO, and you realize this as you're looking out of the floor-to-ceiling windows from your corner office. One day you wake up and you have that family you've always wanted, which you realize as you experience the joy you once felt while daydreaming of this moment. One day you wake up and you're face to face with the love of your life. One day you wake up and you're in the Blue Lagoon in Iceland you just saw on TV a few years back and thought to yourself, "Wouldn't it be nice if…"

*Today, all I see is someone who gets to take center stage. someone who gets to stand up for others and be everything she was meant to be.*

A few things that have worked for me are:

**Write it out.** I write the things that I want down on a piece of paper. There is something about the thought flowing through to your fingertips and guiding that pen in a permanent way that solidifies something in my brain. It receives the message that this is going to happen, kind of like hitting the "Save" button before closing a file on your computer. It saves it to our subconscious mind.

**Say it OUT LOUD.** Saying it out loud is all in the power of declaration, saying that this shall happen, it shall be, and giving it a date creates a subconscious agreement that you will create it. The key is to be unattached to when and how it actually happens. Once again, this is akin to hitting the save button one more time in your subconscious mind.

**Speak it. Share it.** When I start speaking it out loud, opportunities begin to present themselves.

**Display it.** Start putting it in a place where you are repeating it and reading it to yourself over and over and over again. I've made notes on my bathroom mirrors that I see every day. I love using colorful chalk markers. My subconscious mind is constantly taking in these messages. I have sticky poster boards along the walls in my room with some of my key goals and mantras that I am solidifying in my mind. While I don't read them every day anymore, every now and then I glance up and I see them, subliminally transmitting to my subconscious. My own words are being fed back to my subconscious, and they are hitting the save button daily, solidifying that this shall be, this is truth, and in time it truly shall be. I like to call this "marinating."

**Align with it.** With these messages being so active and "loud" you'll start to align yourself with like-minded people who may open those doors. You'll start to get very clear about what does and does not align with your intention anymore. Suddenly, spending hours watching TV, may not sound so appealing. There have been times when I am focused on a goal, and when turning on the TV, nothing appeals to me. During these times, I much prefer to be in a space of planning or taking committed action towards my vision.

When we use the power of Auto Suggestion, feeding your own words back to your subconscious mind in every way possible, we create change. When you put these messages out into the world, they come right back to you, loud and clear. You don't get distracted; the message is in you. Even when you're not thinking about it, you're thinking about it, doing it and being it.

This is how it worked for me. At some point I looked up, and it was already done. I was already the keynote speaker, an executive, started my own business and made a $10,000 day. These things that at one point ALL felt so big and so far away, and yet they all came true in time.

That's the power of Auto Suggestion!

# GRISELDA BECK

**About Griselda Beck:** Griselda Beck, M.B.A. is a powerhouse motivational speaker and coach who combines her executive expertise with transformational leadership, mindset, life coaching, and heart-centered divine feminine energy principles. Griselda empowers women across the globe to step into their power, authenticity, hearts, and sensuality, to create incredible success in their business and freedom in their lives. She creates confident CEOs.

Griselda's clients have experienced success in quitting their 9-5 jobs, tripling their rates, getting their first clients, launching their first products, and growing their businesses in a way that allows them to live the lifestyles and freedoms they want. She has been featured as a top expert on *FOX, ABC, NBC, CBS, MarketWatch, Telemundo*, and named on the Top 10 Business Coaches list by *Disrupt Magazine.*

Griselda is an executive with over 15 years of corporate experience, founder of Latina Boss Coach and Beck Consulting Group, and serves as president for the nonprofit organization MANA de North County San Diego. She also volunteers her time teaching empowerment mindset at her local homeless shelter, Operation Hope-North County.

Author's Website: *www.LatinaBossCoach.com*
Book Series Website & Author's Bio: *www.The13StepstoRiches.com*

## *Jason Curtis*

# THE ENTREPRENEUR'S SECRET TO FOCUS

Napoleon Hill stated, "Your ability to use the principle of Auto Suggestion will depend, very largely, upon your capacity to concentrate upon a given desire until that desire becomes a burning obsession."

I align with this definition and believe that Auto Suggestion is a level of focus. The better you focus, the easier it will be to apply principles of success. I have found this to be particularly true in life. Whether I need to concentrate on completing business tasks or focusing on my family, the more I can double down and get it done, the better the outcome.

In present times, as I've gone through the journey of entrepreneurship, the more noise that seems to come to me. The better I am at focusing on my passion, the easier it to tune out that noise.

### The Best Daily Habitude (Habit + Attitude)
### That Drives Your Success

The best daily habitudes that I can do are expressing my daily affirmations through internal thoughts, speaking them out loud, and physically writing. If I express it even in just one of those ways, I have a good day. Imagine being consistent with all three of these powerful affirmations. If I express my daily affirmations in those three ways multiple times a day,

I find myself unwavering in what I want to accomplish that day. It's a remarkable feeling of fulfillment.

The Nike adage of "Just Do It" directly reflects the power of Auto Suggestion. Start once a day, then when that becomes a habit, do it twice daily and then get to the point that whenever you need a pick-me-up, you state your affirmations. Gradual adoptions of the "Just Do It" motivation will result in more outstanding outcomes than if you were to try and adopt all the suggested steps above at once. Little-by-little and inch-by-inch, you'll reach your destination in a cinch.

Try expressing your daily affirmations in thought, out loud, and in writing.

Identify three affirmations you'd like to focus on daily (i.e., I am happy, strong, healthy, etc.). Say them aloud three times. Write them down three times.

I have been the most surprised with how much easier I can focus on why I am an entrepreneur and what I want to do as I serve my clients. It's so simple that anyone could feel this way, too.

### Overcoming Obstacles and Distractions

My most significant recommendation on creating positive Auto Suggestions in your life is to be the kind of person who completes tasks all the way through. I find myself less overwhelmed when I allow myself the proper time and energy to complete a job I am working on before moving to another task. If you must move on before a task is done, complete your steps as far as you possibly can.

My secret weapon when it comes to maintaining positive Auto Suggestion regarding obtaining riches is reminding myself several times per day about the impact of Auto Suggestions and training my brain to focus on the right things. Anyone can do this and add it to their arsenal for success as well.

It's crucial to train every day so that you are in control of your thoughts. Focus on making positive actions instead of reacting to every circumstance in your life. You can use prayer or meditation to quiet your mind and focus on the decisions that need to be made. I also highly recommend that you review your vision board frequently and ingrain your desires to have the resiliency to guide you to your goals.

The first thing I do is wake up early, so I don't allow myself to be frantic and anxious as I start my day. I also try to be as deliberate as I can in every task I do. Lastly, I focus on the positive outcomes that will come to fruition as I handle my daily tasks.

# JASON CURTIS

**About Jason Curits:** Jason has been a serial entrepreneur for fifteen years and has enjoyed serving and helping his fellow entrepreneurs build their businesses and win in this game of life—on purpose! Jason created On Purpose Coaching because he knew, through his life experiences, that he could create an impact in others. He focuses on helping his clients create better relationships with their customers. This fosters trust and rapport while generating customer loyalty.

Jason is a Navy veteran of six years. He has sailed the seas and oceans in serving his God and country. Curtis and his wife, Brianna, have been married for eight years, and they have two children.

Author's Website: *www.JasonLaneCurtis.com*
Book Series Website & Author's Bio: *www.The13StepstoRiches.com*

## Jeffrey Levine

# MY SECOND CHANCE

When I was in high school, my teachers had me read parts of a book for homework and sometimes pop quizzes would catch me. Because I would sometimes read the pages quickly and not review them, my grades were not as good as I would've liked. This happened year after year.

I remember in seventh grade, my teacher gave us three chapters to read in a book and told us we would have a test the next day on them. After reading the three chapters once, I felt that I had a good understanding of them. Even though I had plenty of time to read the three chapters again, I didn't do it. Again, the test score was not what I wanted. I always wondered how the other students had studied that material and had higher grades. Did they read the three chapters again, or were they smarter? I just didn't know.

I also remember preparing for my speech competition in ninth grade. Because I really liked my speech, I thought I had a really good chance of winning. Because of my sports and family chores, I really didn't have a lot of time to practice, and my results again were the same. Even though I didn't win, my teacher knew I could do better and for some reason gave me a second chance. He told me to practice my speech over and over until I could say it in my sleep. Luckily, because it was a weekend, I had plenty of time to practice. I aced it and won the class contest.

Now it was time to go against the sophomores, juniors, and seniors in the next week.

Because I was going to be on a large stage in front of the school, I was passionate about winning. I literally worked on my speech every waking moment. I could see myself winning and that gave me the inspiration to keep practicing. Even though I was very nervous because I was shy and reserved, I aced it again and won the competition. By practicing over and over and over again, it made a big difference in my results. I had the confidence and I could see myself winning in my mind, before it happened.

In my senior year, I had a very challenging English teacher. Since I didn't play for his freshman football team, I felt there was a chip on his shoulder about me. He was known to fail seniors by giving them a 69 instead of a 70. I was very concerned going into my final exam. I needed a 70 to pass. However, I only had a 68 going into the exam.

I had hundreds of pages of books to review for the exam, and this was a real challenge. Luckily, I had a whole weekend to study . I decided to take 50 pages at a time and study them over and over and over until I had a great understanding of them. I covered all the pages on Saturday. Even though I felt pretty good on Saturday about my understanding, on Sunday, I followed the same process and even knew the material better. By doing this, I passed with flying colors and I graduated.

During my sophomore year in college, I took another speech course, due of my success in high school. However, the competition was much stronger than before. There were some very good presenters. Because I didn't follow my previous protocol of practicing over and over, the speech was a disaster. I begged the teacher to give me another chance. Reluctantly, he gave me a second chance. Knowing that I was given another chance, I practiced and practiced my speech. I gave it over and over with my friends and now felt that I was ready. I also saw myself performing perfectly in front of my class. When the day finally arrived, I was really ready. Just as I had visualized, it happened the same way in person and I won the competition and received an A. It was a huge self-confidence builder.

Since I had success in college and did well in my pre-law courses, I applied and was accepted into law school.

I remember the first day of law school. We had a general assembly and the Dean said, "Look to your right I, and look to your left. At least one of you will not be here next year." I was in shock.

What was I getting myself into? Did I make a mistake ? Why am I going to a law school anyway? My parents always taught me to graduate from college and get a good job. These were all the thoughts that were coming up.

In my contract class, we had a practice exam and I received a grade of 58. Since this caught my attention, I needed to do something different. I decided that if I could get a study partner, my grades may be different. During the Christmas vacation before my final exams, I stayed at the school to study. Since Roy from my class was the only student on campus, we decided to study together and that was very helpful. Roy, who was extremely bright, always had the answers to my questions. Even though everything was going ok with my exams, I now faced my last exam. The property teacher stated that the exam was going to be easy, but I couldn't take that statement at face value. What if he was playing with us and made it impossible? Because I feared the worst, I stayed up all night and studied the material over and over until I knew it cold. Although I knew the material inside and out, it was by far the hardest exam of all. It was almost impossible. Despite having failed one-third of the class, I passed. I am glad I studied the material over and over and over again.

After graduating from law school, I now had to study for the New York State Bar. It was one of the toughest in the country, even for students who graduated from New York law schools. Out-of-state law students, like me, did very poorly because of the low passing rate. This was a big challenge. I signed up for a bar review course, and still was overwhelmed with the amount and complexity of the study material. There was very little of the material that I already knew. Even though I studied hard, I received a failing grade six weeks later. When I was allowed to review my exam, I realized I didn't know the material. However, during those six weeks, I made a new friend named David, who also failed. Because David was so bright, I was shocked that he had failed. But he did!

Once the next bar review class started, we were inseparable. Every night, we would talk and go over the material. I would answer his questions and he would answer mine. While studying, we both realized that there were three practice questions we didn't understand. We decided to attack them one at a time. After a few days, we understood the first one. Since they were only two days left until the exam, could we figure out questions two and three? Unbelievably, the night before the exam we successfully understood questions two and three. We were very lucky, because questions one, two, and three were the first three parts on the exam. What a great start to a challenging exam. The good news is, six weeks later, I passed. The key to success is to do it right the first time. That means study the material over and over.

The one way to make sure you don't need a second chance for success is to follow a few key steps.

1) Fix in your mind what you want to accomplish. Be very specific and clear in vivid detail. If it is a car, know the model, the color, and test drive it. Have a picture of you in it and use as many sensory factors as possible.

2) Affirm what you want precisely and keep repeating it until it becomes part of you.

3) Visualize it as it is already happened. If you want that car, see yourself driving it out of the dealership. Feel how proud you would be driving up your driveway. See the smile on your face.

4) Script it exactly as you want it to play out. Read it over and over with emotion. Record it and play it over and over again all day.

By using these techniques with repetition, you will be programming your brain for the success you want. You have a wonderful mind. Feed it, and it will feed you.

One other helpful hint in getting whatever you want is the use of your higher faculties. These are perception, will, reason, imagination, memory, and intuition. My favorite two are intuition and imagination. It is with your intuition that you pick up vibrations and translate those vibrations in your mind. Your intuition permits you to know (and know that you know) what is happening around you. My intuition is always correct and I use it to make my decisions. Imagination is my favorite intellectual factor. Everything is created twice. First with imagination in your mind, and second, when it manifests in your material world.

You do have a great tools to achieve your success. Don't wait. Start using them now and success is right around the corner!

# JEFFREY LEVINE

**About Jeffrey Levine:** Jeffrey is a highly skilled tax planner and business strategist, as well as a published author and sought-after speaker. He's been featured in national magazines, on the cover of *Influential People Magazine*, and is a frequent featured expert on radio, talk shows, and documentaries. Jeffrey attended the prestigious Albany Academy for high school and then went on to University of Hartford at Connecticut, University of Mississippi Law School, Boston University School of Law, and earned an L.L.M. in taxation. His accolades include features in *Kiplinger* and *Family Circle Magazine,* as well as a dedicated commentator for Channel 6 and 13 news shows, a contributor for the *Albany Business Review*, and an announcer for WGY Radio.

Jeffrey has accumulated more than 30 years of experience as a tax attorney and certified financial planner and has given in excess of 500 speeches nationally. Levine is the executive producer and cast member in the documentary *Beyond the Secret: The Awakening.*

Levine's most current work, *Consistent Profitable Growth Map,* is a step-by-step workbook outlining easy-to-follow steps to convert consistent revenue growth to any business platform.

Author's Website: *www.JeffreyLevine.Solutions*
Book Series Website & Author's Bio: *www.The13StepstoRiches.com*

*Lacey & Adam Platt*

# THE FORMULA &
# START AT THE SHALLOW END

### Adam Platt

I decided to go for a little run, that's my exercise of choice. On this run, I decided to do something different. Instead of running with music in my ear or listening to a podcast, I wasn't even taking my headphones. You see, I had something more important on my mind. I had just come back from a self-improvement seminar and one of the presenters shared with us how to create a power statement. Find seven words that you want to amplify in yourself and create a power statement from them. I had my seven words, but I wanted to ingrain them into my mind so I could remember them and recall them with little or no effort. So my goal on this run was to repeat those seven words over and over again until they were burned into my mind.

I started running and repeating, "I am a smart, strong, passionate, kind, powerful, visionary, leader." Those were my seven words, and I kept saying them over and over again. As I repeated them time and time again, something magical began to happen. I still had my phone to track my run and I was going faster and faster on my run. I was getting stronger as I said those power words in my mind. When I was done with my run, I looked at my time and my splits and I had just run the fastest 5k I had ever run, hands down. I have not since broken that record, either. It still stands as my fastest 5k run ever, but more importantly, I had my power words memorized and still use them to this day.

So what happened to me on that run? I used the power of Auto Suggestion. I told my subconscious mind what I wanted; that I was smart, strong, passionate, kind, powerful, visionary, and a leader, and I believed it! It gave me strength and power as I told my subconscious what I wanted it to believe. We can do the same thing with anything we want in this life.

We have so many negative things that we tell ourselves every day. A mentor of mine had given me a little black notebook that I could carry around with me. I was told for one week that whenever I had a negative thought about myself, to write it down in that notebook. It was amazing how many negative things I told myself each day. It gave me the evidence I needed to change my negative thoughts into positive thoughts.

Here is the how this all works: Our beliefs shape our thoughts, our thoughts create our reality, which in turn creates emotions, and our emotions are what we act on. So the formula is Beliefs = Thoughts = Reality + Emotions = Results. You may have heard the phrase that what you focus on grows and what you ignore dies. We often focus on the negative because our subconscious mind is always bombarded by negativity around us. So how do we change those negative thoughts? We focus our efforts to the positive and what we want in life by using Auto Suggestion, just like I did with my power words during my run.

It all starts with our beliefs and changing them to positive things, and the belief that we can achieve what we want in life. What you may want is riches, health, better relationships, or whatever, but if you can change your beliefs to be positive about what you want ,then it will influence your thoughts. This shapes our reality, creates emotions, and then allows us to get the results we are looking for. Another key is the emotion; you must infuse emotions into what you want.

By using affirmations, visualization, and mediations to change our subconscious mind through Auto Suggestion, we teach it to know the positive things we want and to focus on those things. We are then able to listen for the inspired actions to take. By taking those actions with faith that we can achieve them, we can have what we want in this life.

Use Auto Suggestion to go after those big dreams and those big goals in your life. It all starts with how you think and then speaking it to your subconscious mind to make it think how you want it to. Speaking the correct focus and positive results to yourself is the key to success.

### *Lacey Platt*

When I was younger, I remember that subliminal messaging was a hot topic. It was brought to the attention of the world that advertisers had been using something called subliminal messages to cause us to want to buy their products. When we were told this as a society, there was a big uproar, and everybody felt as though they had been manipulated. People felt like it was unfair to use our subconscious mind against our conscious mind to cause us to want to buy something.

When I first heard of the idea of Auto Suggestion, my first thought was it's like subliminal messaging. How could we communicate with our subconscious mind without allowing our conscious mind to be aware of it? It was through further study and understanding that I realized it's not about tricking your subconscious mind into thinking something that your conscious mind does not, but it's about communicating with your subconscious mind on a level that rewrites all the old programming that's been there since we were young.

Think back to when you were a kid. There was probably something told to you by a parent or other adult that was repeated over and over. It was probably something simple and yet your mind grabbed a hold of that and convinced you it must be true. All without evidence or experience to back it up. This is the programming that was created in our brain as we were growing up. We listened to, and adopted, all things told to us by those who were older than us. We didn't question it or even try to comprehend it; it just became a story that we stored away in our subconscious mind. Now as adults, we question that programming from our subconscious mind, and this is where we struggle because our conscious mind is telling us something different. We want to change our ways; we want to do things differently and yet our mind wants to fight us! Our mind says it's easier and better to do it the way we've always done it, which is why a lot of people say, "change is hard." It isn't necessarily the fact of doing something different that is hard, it's reprogramming our mind to accept the ability to do it differently that is "hard."

What we need to do is reboot our minds!! Kick out that old programming and reprogram ourselves to do the things that we want to do!

Here's a little suggestion: Start out easy. Most people want you to jump into the deep end. I'm going to suggest that we start at the shallow end and work our way towards the deeper end. Start somewhere simple like "I like myself." Say this to yourself every morning, throughout the day,

and every night before you go to bed. It gets to be that simple! This is how you start to train your brain to think positive things about yourself and then build into the bigger things. The power of Auto Suggestion really lies in your ability to do it consistently. Struggle with consistency? By starting at the shallow end and working my way towards the deeper end, I was able to create a habit of consistency. I placed a reminder on my phone for every morning to help me to remember to say my positive statement. I also set a reminder in the afternoon and right before bed. As I saw the reminders come in, they reminded me to be committed to myself and to say my positive statement. I still use reminders to this day because it's super powerful! As I have built myself up to bigger things, I've had to rely on the solid foundation I created with consistency. Most of the time today, I say my positive statement probably twenty times a day. Not because I struggle with consistency and don't want to forget, but more importantly, to really solidify and bring it home that these are the things I want in my mind, and they help me to block out the things I don't want. Anytime I find my mind wandering off into the weeds of negative thought, I can quickly reverse my direction simply by saying my positive statement. This is really where the power of your mind can help you to change your mindset.

Get started today! Start with a really simple statement and then repeat it to yourself several times throughout the day. Set reminders! Notice any times when your mind starts to travel off into negativity and quickly reverse it by saying your statement. With practice and consistency, you will start to realize how much more of a positive mindset you have!

# LACEY & ADAM PLATT

**About Lacey Platt:** Lacey is an energetic, fun loving, super mom of five! She is an Achievement Coach, Speaker and new Bestselling Author who enjoys helping everyone she can by getting to know what their needs are and then loving on them in every way that she can. Her ripple effect and impact has touched the lives of so many and continues to reach more lives every single day. Allow Lacey to help you achieve your goals with proven techniques she has created and perfected over years of coaching. Lacey and her husband have built an amazing coaching business called Arise to Connect serving people all around the world.

**About Adam Platt:** Adam is an Achievement Coach, Speaker, Trainer, Podcast Host and now a Bestselling Author. Adam loves to help people overcome the things stopping them from having the life they really want. Adam owns and operates Arise to Connect. Adam believes that connection with yourself, others, and your higher power are the keys to achievement and greater success in life. He is impacting thousands of people's lives with his message and coaching. He lives in Utah with his wife, five daughters, and their dog, Max.

Author's Website: *www.AriseToConnect.com*
Book Series Website & Author's Bio: *www.The13StepstoRiches.com*

*Louisa Jovanovich*

# LOVE IS THE HIGHEST FORM OF VIBRATION

Folktales are old stories that have been retold for generations. I tell my children the stories I hear from motivational speakers, like the unstoppable Lisa Nichols. By hearing the same themes repeatedly in different myths, movies, and legends, we reinforce certain patterns of belief without even realizing it. This is the power of Auto Suggestion. We can either use this power to train positive thoughts into our minds, or negative ones.

Lisa's folktale is a true story. A fifteen-year-old girl goes to her grandmother for advice because she keeps losing her swim races. She's not coming in third or fourth—she's dead last. *Every. Single. Time.*

So her grandmother says, "Winners never quit. Quitters never win." And she explains, "We come from a family of winners and there's not a chance you're going to quit."

The next day, the girl goes to her swim meet. She's running late and when she gets to the check-in counter, the coach says, "Oh no, your team has already gone. You missed your turn."

The girl looks up into the crowd and sees all fourteen members of her family. And she says to them, "What? What are you doing here? You have never come to see me before!"

And they say, "Grandma called."

The coach notices what's going on, looks at his clipboard, and says, "Well, I can put you in with the seventeen and eighteen-year-olds."

Mortified, she says, "No, no, no!" She pictures herself losing once again, this time with an even more embarrassing gap between herself and the competition. She begs her coach, "I'm the worst. Please don't make me!" But the coach insists she swim the race.

So she lines up with the big teens. They're all wearing professional swimming caps but she has her hair in braids. Normally during a race her mantra is, *I don't want to lose, I don't want to lose.* And the universe gives her exactly what she expects: She comes dead last.

But on this day, she makes a tweak to her routine. As the gun goes off, she chants a new mantra in her head: *Quitters never win, winners never quit! Winners never quit, quitters never win!* With every stroke, she repeats the mantra, *Winners never quit. Quitters never win.* She says it until she hits the wall, turns back, and she finishes her second lap. She breaks the surface of the water and no one is there. She looks at the coach and sees his jaw drop to the pavement.

"Oh no," she says apologetically. "Am I supposed to do another lap?"

"You just beat the record," the coach says in disbelief. "How did you do that?"

She feels her head. The braids are still there. This win had nothing to do with the swim caps, or the crowd, or the lane she swam in. She knew this win came from her own mental strength. "I realized I wanted to win," she said.

Do you ever tell yourself you can't do something you want because you fear you will fail? We can be so mean to ourselves. We would never tell a child they are going to lose a race, and yet we tell ourselves hurtful things constantly. The truth of the matter is, we don't even know we're doing it. That's because our brains are on Auto Suggestion.

I get it. We are *busy and always rushing*. We're late for the swim meet. We're behind on the project. We're wracked with insecurity and self-doubt. Meanwhile, our brains are tearing our confidence to shreds. In my past life (before becoming a clarity and confidence coach), I told myself awful things I ended up believing as true. I didn't think I had what it took to be someone special. I made jokes that the only A+ I've ever gotten is my blood type. I believed I was going to mess up with parenting and ruin my children's lives ... and the list goes on. That Auto Suggestion mode is a vision killer. It can keep us from doing what we really want.

For me and for so many others I work with, it's extremely difficult to change out of Auto Suggestion mode. Mostly, we are stuck in the war stories of the past. We feel we don't have the right tools to improve our lives. We make excuses.

And left unchecked, this pattern will keep repeating in the direction it is set. If you have fear: *more fear*. If you have insecurity: *more insecurity*. Auto Suggestion works like a computer. Whatever mantra you enter in, it repeats, and executes.

I was working as a hairdresser and I was not sure how I was going to make it financially, thinking I could never provide for my children on my own. I was afraid I would fail as a parent. I was afraid my kids might end up in a bad situation. *They might try drugs. They might die. I might die*, and then what would they do? I would worry myself to sleep, pleading to God, *"Please, don't let me fail. Don't let my kids go down the wrong path."*

*"Don't fail"* is no vision at all. I was falling into the same trap as the little girl at her swim meets. What's worse, my *"I'm afraid to fail"* mantra was trickling into every aspect of my life. It was replicating like a computer virus. And I was left feeling stuck and afraid. My clients would sit in my chair and listen to my sad story. I'm not going to lie when I say we probably get something out of telling stories about our misery. It's a little like eating a funnel cake at the fair. It tastes amazing as you pull off the greasy bites and savor the sweet flavor, but it's definitely not good for you.

For many years I kept my mind on autopilot, feeling like I was not good enough for success. I recently interviewed a mother whom I believe succeeded as a parent. I asked her what worked. She said her vision for her children was that they would be seen and heard. I realized that was the swim story. That girl went from "I don't want to lose" to "Quitters never win, winners never quit." My story shifted from "I hope I don't fail" to "My kids should be seen and heard." In an instant, the energy in my home shifted.

I'm grateful for that conversation, because that was the day I turned off Auto Suggestion mode and decided to rework my vision. Okay, maybe not *rework,* but I decided to have an *actual* vision! My children get to be seen and heard. I am worthy of love. I believe in myself.

I did some soul-searching, but not the typical kind. I signed up for deep transformational courses to dig deep into where my limiting beliefs came from. That created new possibilities and I got excited to live a life that gave me freedom and purpose. I learned you can't have conflicting beliefs. The serenity prayer became my mantra. I decided to become a "YES person." I made a commitment to replace every fearful thought with a loving thought, using the power of Auto Suggestion. Because love is the highest vibration, I decided I didn't need any proof that I was good enough. I decided to trust the universe has my back. I basically got out of my own way and swam to the finish.

Here's the magic part: We are happy. My story is the same as the young swimmer. My kids told me they wanted my ex and I to get along. I realized that would be part of their happiness as well as my own. So my ex gave me his blessing to move from Florida to California—where I felt my children could be raised in a more supportive environment. It was no easy task, but we are here and are thriving. My children are happy, and that's all I ever really wanted for them. I have two jobs—which I love—I'm still a hairdresser, and I'm enjoying the connections I make as a mindfulness and emotional intelligence coach. I've always wanted to help people be their best selves, and I get to do that daily. I'm healthy. I'm exercising. I'm meditating. And I'm in love with this life. The worry (for the most part) is gone, I use my tools and I manage my mind.

What do you want? Make your vision crystal clear and you'll get results. I'm here to say you have what it takes. Be a YES person. Over-deliver and excel in what you're good at! Forget fear.

# LOUISA JOVANOVICH

**About Louisa Jovanovich:** Louisa is the founder of Connect with Source. She is a mindfulness and emotional intelligence coach. She enjoys helping others identify blind spots and create new beliefs which empower her clients to access a life they have never dreamed possible. She has completed 20 years of personal and transformational growth including Land-mark Forum, Gratitude Training, and is a Clarity Catalyst Certified trainer. She works with entrepreneurs who seek clarity and want to up-level their lives.

Her life experiences and school of hard knocks are what make her a knowledgeable and compassionate leader and enable her to help guide others through the process of looking for answers within in order to find success and breakthrough their limiting beliefs. Her unique coaching techniques help her clients see the truth behind the stories that are keeping them stuck in the reality they created.

Louisa is a single mother of two teenagers living in LA. Her love and compassion towards others are her superpowers, helping others reclaim their confidence, find their voice, and know their worth.

Author's Website: *ConnectWithSource.com*
Book Series Website & Author's Bio: *www.The13StepstoRiches.com*

## Lynda Sunshine West

# THE LIES WE BELIEVE

*Sticks and stones may break my bones, but words will never hurt me.*

I remember that "nursery rhyme" from when I was a kid. I believed it to be true because it was what I learned. It's the biggest lie ever!

One day, while driving to my forty-ninth job working for a judge in the Ninth Circuit Court of Appeals, I was stuck in heavy traffic. I was so frustrated with life, with MY life, and was pondering questions many of us have at some point. With anger in my voice, banging my hands on the steering wheel, and tears running down my face, I yelled, "What is my purpose? What's the purpose of this planet? Why am I even on this planet? I have no value. There's nothing here for me to do." I literally believed I had no purpose or value.

My beliefs about myself started when I was a child. In actuality, they were other people's beliefs about me that I chose to believe and hold onto.

I grew up in a volatile, abusive, alcoholic household where "kids are better seen than heard." After eighteen years of witnessing physical, emotional, and mental abuse from my dad to my mom, I decided to carry the torch and, unfortunately, married someone just like my dad. So the cycle of abuse continued.

"You're so stupid. You're ignorant. People are only nice to you because they feel sorry for you." Those phrases became my daily beatings.

Fortunately, and unfortunately, I stayed with my first husband for two years and two kids. Two years of daily mental and emotional beatings plagued me for decades to come.

At age fifty-one, when I asked myself, "What's my purpose," the answer came in the form of a life coach from Facebook. I had never met her before seeing her Facebook post in a group. Plus, I had no idea what a life coach was or if one could help me, but I trusted that she had my answers. I hired her and we worked together for five months. It was the greatest gift I had ever given myself.

Working with her was an emotional rollercoaster ride. She asked me tough questions every week and gave me homework assignments. I hated her one minute, then loved her the next. Emotional breakthroughs happened on a weekly basis, so much so that people were saying things like, "Wow! You're so different this week than last week."

It was those breakthroughs that made me realize all the pain I was experiencing was from the words I had been told throughout my life. From my parents, to my siblings, to kids in school, to teachers, to employers, I was fed a steady diet of negative words and I allowed those words to penetrate my soul and impact my life.

No more. I decided to take a stand and wasn't going to let my age stop me. At fifty-one, I was on a mission to change my life and become a better person (and the mission will continue until I take my last breath). Being a positive and uplifting person is extremely satisfying, and sharing words of encouragement to uplift rather than break down people fills my heart and soul. I guess you could say I'm addicted to positivity. That's something I'm excited to be addicted to.

As humans, we have the power of choice. We get to choose what we believe, whether it's negative or positive. Sometimes, though, it's hard to believe positive things about ourselves because of all the baggage we've carried around for such a long time. If you're like me, you'll never see the way out of the negativity without help. I needed that help and I reached out when I was ready.

There is a saying, "When the student is ready, the teacher will appear."

The reality is that the teacher is always there; the student just isn't ready yet.

My first teacher came in the form of a life coach. Next was a business coach, then money mindset coach, then marketing coach, etc. Teachers come in many forms. Sometimes they can even come in the form of a barista at Starbucks.

While I had many "teachers" along my journey, none had quite the impact my life coach had. Why? Because it was THEN that I finally raised my hand and said, "I'm ready to change. I need help."

As a Christian, I knew there had to be something more for me to do than pushing papers around a desk and working for a judge. Otherwise, what's the point of this whole wide world?

What's interesting is as I go back in time to when I was five years old, I experienced something a lot of five-year-olds experience. I ran away. But I didn't just run away. I was gone for an entire week.

I had innate wisdom at that very young age that told me there was something wrong where I was living. I knew intuitively that the household I was living in was wrong, so I made a bold stand and ran away. I'll answer the question you're most likely asking yourself and that is, "Where did you go?" Well, I only went to the neighbor's house, but I was gone an entire week with no intention of ever going back home.

Why did I go back home? My mom called the neighbor and said, "Lynda has been gone long enough. You can send her home now."

While I don't remember any of this (I blocked out the first twelve years of my life—and I'm working with someone to help me recover that part of my past), my mom told me the story on many occasions as she laughed about my antics at such a young age.

Let's go back to that time. You're five years old. You run away. No one comes to get you. Day after day goes by (at five, a week is like an eternity, right?) and nothing, no one comes.

That week was pivotal in my brain. For decades, I believed that no one in my family liked me, loved me, or wanted me around. My beliefs about my family were locked in tight from that one major event at five. The fact that no one came to get me solidified my belief.

Years after my mom passed away, I started looking at that scenario and seeing it from her point of view. This is a process I use to help me see both sides of situations, which helps me forgive and be grateful for those who have harmed me.

I now know my mom loved me dearly. She also believed in me. She just didn't know how to show it. My mom knew something about me that I didn't learn about myself until I was fifty-one. Mom knew I was strong and brave. She trusted that I ran away and learned the lesson I needed to learn. By not coming to get me, that was her way of saying, "Lynda, you are strong and brave. I am going to let you exercise your right to stand up for yourself." I know deep down that that's what she was doing.

But, back then, I didn't see it that way. I interpreted it in a way that meant she didn't love me or want me around.

Wow! I carried around those beliefs for such a long time that it became my reality. Mom and I didn't have that mother/daughter "bond" people talk about. I feel the bond more now that she's gone than I did when she was alive. I applied meaning to what her actions meant, and the meaning I applied to her actions became my belief. I'm now grateful for what she did and the lessons she taught me. She allowed me to be me.

Are you taking on other people's beliefs? If so, are their beliefs serving you and helping you to serve YOUR highest purpose while on this planet? If not, there are many ways to change these patterns and to move into a space where you are supported and uplifted to live your best life.

Find a mentor or a coach who can help you move out of a negative head space. You no longer have to carry around all those negative beliefs. You can rid yourself of them right now. You just need to be ready to raise your hand, say "I'm ready," and then take the step. Your teacher is waiting for you, the student, to be ready. You got this.

# LYNDA SUNSHINE WEST

**About Lynda Sunshine West:** Lynda Sunshine West is known as The Fear Buster. She's a Speaker, 10 Time Best-Selling Author, Book Publisher, Executive Film Producer, Red Carpet Interviewer, and the Founder of Women Action Takers. At age 51 she faced one fear every day for an entire year. In doing so, she gained an exorbitant amount of confidence and uses what she learned by facing a fear every day to fulfill her mission of helping 5 million women entrepreneurs gain the confidence to share their voice with the world. Her collaboration books, mastermind, podcast, and many more opportunities give women from all over the world the opportunity to share their voice with the world. She believes in cooperation and collaboration and loves connecting with like-minded people.

Author's Website: *www.womenactiontakers.com*
Book Series Website & Author's Bio: *www.The13StepstoRiches.com*

*Maris Segal & Ken Ashby*

# IT'S AN INSIDE JOB!

Have you ever been stumped when someone asked you, "What do you want in your life?" and could not reply? Declare, with specificity, what you want, commit to a by-when date that it will be accomplished, and repeat the declaration out loud morning and night until it happens! This is wise proven counsel from a great teacher, Napoleon Hill, and it is often easier said than done! In short, Auto Suggestion is an "Inside Job." It's the purposeful use of consistent, daily directed self-talk led with a desire and a vision. This begins from where we are in the present, right now, and connects to the possibilities in our future. It is vision plus intention coupled with a deep belief and a strong feeling in our bones that it is to be.

When Auto Suggestion is combined with committed action steps, large and small, our vision becomes our reality. These are seemingly simple steps, so clear, with the understanding and faith that we have everything we need inside of us to make such a declaration and see it come to life. Yet there are numerous roadblocks which can hinder our innate power to realize such a declaration. There are no victims here. These roadblocks, which we place in our own way, are based on our fears and self-doubt generated from moments or events that happened in our past. These self-constructed roadblocks can stop us from realizing our dreams and being our best selves for our family, friends, colleagues, and teams.

Who is listening to our declarations? We are! Our subconscious mind is always open and listening. Words matter! The voice and words of our conscious mind, negative or positive, directly impact our actions and dictate how we show up in our external world. Our conscious mind speaks, judges, projects, sabotages, and in some cases, hides our intentions. Our subconscious mind drinks the wine of our words, savors our declarations, and always accepts what our conscious mind depicts as being absolutely true. Our brains are unable to process negative and positive at the same time. That was a big aha for both of us and we realized it's a waste of time to focus brain power on the negative especially when it keeps us in the past. The secret is that we can choose what we feed our subconscious and can empower our positive thoughts from a daily place of gratitude and Auto Suggestion.

When you are feeling and express out loud being depressed, the universe says, "Here's more depression." If you are being grateful, the universe will send more opportunities for gratitude in your direction. Standing in that truth, recognize that the underlying magic to this type of declaration is that the divinity, inside us all, always says YES to whatever we are telling ourselves. It is that "inside job" which opens the possibility for us to now enroll others in our vision! With that understanding at our core and daily practice, being heard, creating fulfilling relationships, manifesting abundant personal resources, and living in audacious success, all become attainable.

We've been working together for eighteen years, nearly as long as we've been together as a couple and recently, we took a look back at our lives around this topic of Auto Suggestion from the eyes of our youth. Think back in your own life to learning how to ride a bike, drive a car, sing a song, or build a business. Auto Suggestion played a role in the accomplishment of each new skill. Our declaration was so strong that we didn't allow self-doubt to hold us back and, and with repeated practice, these simple actions, which came from a desire and vision, were accomplished. With our declarations, we "saw" ourselves riding a bike, driving a car, running a company as if it had already happened—now an automatic action in our life. It is our conscious mind and subconscious working in tandem to create possibilities from what we truly desire. We call this "co-creating a future now." In making the declaration from the present moment and subsequent communication between both levels of our minds, we are co-creating with the universe to manifest a future now moment with such intention and emotion that we can hear, touch, smell, and see it complete. From this place, we see possibilities and step into planning and committed action flow.

Working with our client's and our own visions, we've witnessed the power of Auto Suggestion with declarations years before the actual date, and often without any idea of "how." It's not magic, and it is not in the mechanics of "how" that we accomplish what we desire. It's being committed and open to what's possible and embracing all obstacles as opportunities along the way. Flow versus control! Perhaps you're an entrepreneur, educator, parent, or executive; can you see this in your life?

During the development of *America's 400th Anniversary* for the Commonwealth of Virginia, our company was honored to serve as Executive Producer for eighteen months of key signature programs. This commemoration recognized the historic events of 1607 when the English ship, *The Godspeed*, landed on a small island and established the first permanent English settlement at Jamestown, Virginia, a landmark event that sparked the building of America. Close your eyes and imagine now this slice of history from a lens of Auto Suggestion and what it took for explorer Captain John Smith and others to accomplish settling a "new world" as it's often referred to. For the commemoration's finale, working alongside the leadership, we were committed to creating powerful connected moments that featured the role of Native Americans, African Americans, and English in this history with an eye towards the future. Working with people of all ages, we had a vision to accomplish something that had never been done before. Sitting around our conference room table, in co-creating flow, we felt ourselves standing in a yet-to-be-designed setting, visualizing a yet-to-be-created symphony orchestra of four-hundred young musicians and an unidentified chorus of sixteen-hundred-seven voices representing every state in the U.S. We declared what was possible, designed the opportunity and became so present to the future moment (still two years away), that we "felt" ourselves standing in the afternoon sunlight, hearing the music, feeling the participants and crowd energy, and seeing the news headlines. In this very present now, we could hear and feel the power of this creative future moment as if it was actually occurring. So from this desire and vision we began co-creating with our subconscious mind, enrolling, collaborating, and empowering our team, our client, and thousands of participants. Little did we know at that moment of presence, two years in advance, where this experience would lead.

On the day of this national commemorative event, then President George W. Bush and First Lady Laura Bush joined as guests among other leaders. Surrounding them sat the four-hundred musicians and the sixteen-hundred-seven-voice choir. On finishing his address, and after placing items in a time capsule with students (also in our vision), the orchestra began to play The Stars and Stripes Forever. The President turned from the podium and as he started to exit the stage, walked directly beside the conductor. He stopped, looked up at the maestro, and she invited him to the conductor's platform. The President took the baton and began directing the orchestra as if he had done it all his life. The audience went crazy! The human shared history and connectivity created as part of America's 400th Anniversary reached millions via the media. It became an unplanned, spontaneous magic sparked from Auto Suggestion.

We firmly accept that *"we are where we are when we are meant to be."* This has been a guiding principle for all our personal and professional work. We embrace the moments of *presence flow* which allow us to *experience a future moment as if it had already happened.* Whenever we are open to the possibilities that already exist and experiencing them in audible, visual, and perceptible ways, we cross the threshold of Auto Suggestion, allowing us to co-create with the universe of "nows" that can change our world. A declaration carried through to the steps of Auto Suggestion, along with the understanding that it's an "inside job" creates the underpinning for incredible possibilities to be manifested.

It is not a question of IF we will create something, it's only a question of WHAT we will create. When we are clear about what we desire, when we continually program and place it on our personal playlist of hits, the universe responds. Our subconscious mind and conscious mind are not solo voices, they are a dynamic duo inside of us. The conscious and subconscious are talented singers, harmonizing to the same melody which our internal mind promotes, augments, supports and strengthens. Auto Suggestion is an "inside job!"

Reflections:

1. From your past, identify a moment in your life when autosuggestion played a role.

2. What is your desire for your future?

3. From this desire write your vision, declaration, by when and post it throughout your home. Read it out loud and be present to it daily.

# MARIS SEGAL
# & KEN ASHBY

**About Maris Segal and Ken Ashby:** Maris Segal and Ken Ashby have been bringing a creative collaborative voice to issues, causes and brands for over forty years. As strategists, producers, coaches, authors, speakers and trainers, their work with the public and private sectors unites diverse populations across a wide spectrum of business, policy, and social issues in the U.S. and abroad. Their leadership expertise in Business Relationship Marketing, Organizational Change & Cultural Inclusion, Personal Growth, Project Management, Public Affairs, Corporate Social Responsibility and Philanthropy Strategies has been called on to support a range of clients from classrooms and boardrooms to the world stage including; Olympic organizers, Super Bowls, Harvard Kennedy School, Papal visits, the White House, consumer brands, and celebrities across the arts and entertainment, sports and culinary genres.

Ken Ashby and Maris Segal recently launched Segal Leadership Global—a community of collaborative strategists, coaches and trainers creating global connections and possibilities in times of change and One Song—a creative music and song writing leadership workshop series designed as a collaboration team building tool.

Often referred to by their clients as "the connection couple," their philosophy is "our shared humanity unites us and when we lead with our hearts, our heads will follow."

Author's Website: *www.SegalLeadershipGlobal.com*
Book Series Website & Author's Bio: *www.The13StepstoRiches.com*

*Mel Mason*

# LETTING GO OF NEGATIVE AUTO SUGGESTIONS

My mother didn't take care of herself when she was pregnant, and after I was born she lost some of her teeth. Instead of taking responsibility for her own health, she blamed her devastated dentures on me. As soon as I could understand language, she began to tell me I stole her calcium, and that's why she had no teeth. I know it sounds crazy, but I grew up thinking I was a thief. I was a *calcium-taker*—a bonafide selfish person for destroying my mom's good looks.

Obviously, an unborn child doesn't come into the world to steal her mother's calcium, and yet, these are precisely the kind of thoughts we believe if they are repeated to us enough times. Harmful or not, we take the most negative interpretation of an event and make it our mantra.

In the self-improvement business you're going to hear a lot about "limiting beliefs," or those persistent hurtful thoughts that prevent us from personal growth. Internal limiting beliefs take up so much space in our lives that we have no room left for happiness, success, or love. Left unchecked, these thoughts permeate our lives in the form of resentment, repressed emotion, fear, and judgement. You know the thoughts*: I'm not good enough. I am always broke. I'm unlucky in love.*

Whether it's from failed relationships or rotten childhoods, we all have *something* from the past constantly beating down the door and causing havoc in our lives. And these thoughts are sticky; they express themselves as addiction, or hoarding, or gaining weight; because we are acting out those horrible memories that come with the trauma. We all have some things we tell ourselves without thinking, whether they are true or not. Clutter manifests on the outside because the outside is a mirror of the inside. These negative beliefs can pop in our heads like rot any time a nice thought tries to grow a little garden in your brain. Those Auto Suggestions are relentless. They push and pull and rip you apart from the inside out.

It's not just your problem, it's *everyone's* problem. The mind is so powerful. It can work with you when you think positive things, but it can destroy you if you allow its Auto Suggestion message to repeat things that aren't true, such as what I used to tell myself: *I'm not worthy of love.*

As you can imagine, my relationship with my mom was one of victimhood. She felt like I stole her life away, and in return, she often threatened to leave me or just outright left me on the streets somewhere on multiple occasions. Well what did I do with that Auto Suggestion that I was not worthy of love? I let it take me down the road to depression, addiction, and just plain misery. On top of that, I spent more than a decade in a toxic relationship. For years, I held on to the pattern of dimming my light so I wouldn't steal anyone's love, or calcium (or anything else that I might steal).

Unhealthy Auto Suggestions can only manifest pain. Their only function is *dysfunction.* The problem is, the longer you have those thoughts running through your mind, the worse the damage becomes. When I heard the words *you are a thief,* I internalized them and put them on an endless loop, like a broken record. If your unconscious thought is that you are *bad with money, POOF*—before you know it, you have a pile of mounting debt. Think about something too often, and it appears in your life.

Like I said, no human can get out of life unscathed. We all have our piles of clutter to deal with. And we are excellent at avoiding these things with all kinds of distractions. We are masters at covering it up with alcohol! We are virtuosos at diverting ourselves with work! We are professionals at distracting ourselves with other people's piles of clutter!

Of course, no one plans to be unhappy. Some of us don't even notice the big pile of traumatic memories piling up and infiltrating our lives. The thoughts just take over, just as boxes of junk have a way of taking over your garage. You could tidy up and throw away some of those outdated tennis rackets and tangled up electrical cords, but ... maybe later, *I'm busy, right?* Hm. Let's tell the truth. Deep down, we don't want to clean up. We simply aren't ready to sift through the memories tied to the stuff.

I've been helping people get rid of their clutter for a long time. Yet you know what pattern I see the most? Many people worry that if they start dealing with the clutter, and getting present with themselves, they'll have to dig up all the trauma and the loss they went through. They worry they're going to get flooded with emotion and they will be unable to handle it. That's exactly why people avoid it; because it's too uncomfortable. Nobody wants to feel like *that.*

So how do you stop the Auto Suggestions that are ruining your life? Well contrary to popular belief, stopping is the easy part. When I decided to deal with my core trauma, the one that centered around my mother abandoning me, I was so tired of feeling bad about myself. I didn't want to be held back anymore. I wanted to change. And when I started the process of turning my negative Auto Suggestion thoughts into positive affirmations, it only worked because I was ready. The timing needs to be right for someone to change their thought patterns.

You see, digging for the sake of digging is pointless unless you are ready. In order to be ready, you have to recognize those autopilot thoughts which are holding you back. My advice is to wait until you are a butterfly coming out of the cocoon. Don't try to open the cocoon when you're still a caterpillar and push yourself out through that tiny little hole. *You can't force it.* You can't force anyone to change, even if their thoughts are keeping them stuck. The more willing you are for change, the more space you will make for change. You can stop telling yourself stories that consist of limiting beliefs simply by allowing them back in and by letting them come to the surface.

Once you're aware of your thoughts, opinions, and beliefs, you will *have* to do something about them. That's what it usually takes for us humans. We have to be beating our head against the wall until we're bloody before we are finally willing to make a change.

When you are ready, take a good look at your life. Pinpoint the areas that aren't working; the places where you have a lot of negative stories and harmful self-talk going on. If you are struggling to build a healthy relationship and you're always attracting toxic people, you have subconscious programming around not being worthy enough to have a healthy relationship. Your automated message is *I don't deserve to be loved.*

Next, begin to operate consciously rather than unconsciously. Without awareness, we go from the thought to the action without noticing the impulse. But when you slow down and become present, you notice the impulse and you have the power to make a different choice.

On automatic pilot, you might take out your rage on someone, which all stemmed from an auto suggestion that you don't deserve to be loved. You can catch the faulty programming ahead of time. Step back. Examine what's happening here. *Why am I thinking that?* Whatever your excuses are, those are the programs running.

When I work with people, their biggest realization is always, "Oh my God, I can't believe how much I avoid!" Self-reflection gives them a new kind of awareness. Then they break the pattern! You don't need to know all your unconscious beliefs to heal. You don't need to go dig them *all* up and clear them *all* out. Meet yourself where you're at. Whenever those thoughts are ready to be revealed, your release will show up.

Limiting beliefs are the excess weight of negative subconscious programming. They are messy, unsettling piles of cutter inside your mind. When you learn to do the work, digging your trauma out of your subconscious and letting it surface, you become self-aware. Once you do this, it's much easier to deal with your clutter and release it. And you will be so relieved, because clutter is heavy! When you make the shift, you'll be ready when the next trauma comes up—and it will. After all, pain is part of the human experience.

God bless my mom. She's come a long way from the days of blaming me for the disappointments in her life. I have let go of the thoughts that came with being her daughter. I have come a long way, too. It took me a while, but I did it. And now I can finally embrace my mom without cringing.

Nowadays, I keep autopilot turned off. I don't watch TV. I don't listen to the news. I don't want Auto Suggestions imprinting into my subconsciousness. You don't have to be as particular as me, but you can be aware, and you can stay in control of your life. Hey, it's your life. Why not be at peace with yourself?

I always thought daily affirmations were cheesy, but you know what? They work! Replace the auto-pilot thoughts with compliments. Start sending yourself better messages. Shift your limited beliefs by being aware. I'm out of that toxic relationship I told you about. I decided to shine my own light no matter what. I started a new mode that *I am worthy of love*, and I like it much better.

# MEL MASON

**About Mel Mason:** International Best-Selling Author Mel Mason is The Clutter Expert, and as a sexual abuse survivor, she grew up depressed, suicidal, and surrounded by clutter. What she realized after coming back from the brink of despair and getting through her own chaos was that the outside is just a mirror of the inside, and if you only address the outside without changing the inside, the clutter keeps coming back.

That set her on a mission to empower people around the world to get free from clutter inside and out, so they can experience happiness and abundance in every area of their lives.

She is the author of *Freedom from Clutter: The Guaranteed, Foolproof, Step-by-Step Process to Remove the Stuff That's Weighing You Down*

Author's website: *www.FreeGiftFromMel.com*
Book Series Website & Author's Bio: *www.The13StepsToRiches.com*

*Miatta Hampton*

# HIJACKING SELF-SABOTAGE

When was the last time you influenced yourself, when you told yourself that you could accomplish all that you set out to do? It is time to break the chains off your life. It is time to take your life, your business, and your career to the next level. No more telling yourself that you are not equipped, you are not qualified, that you don't have time, and you don't have help. Today is the day that you begin to manifest a better life, manifest a better you. Today is the day that you stop denying yourself of God's best. You can create the life that you want by simple speaking it into existence and pulling your future into your present. You can suggest to yourself that you will build wealth and create a legacy. Involuntary conditioning of your mind combined with faith gives you the ability to create your future with your words. If you could block out all negative thoughts and self- limiting beliefs like, "I am not enough, I don't have enough energy, and I don't have the funds," what kind of life could you have? Are you ready to sow seeds of success in your mind?

I had been a registered nurse and working at the bedside for five years when I realized there was more for me, that I was built for more. I had spent years encouraging other people to live authentically and unapologetically, but I was not doing that for myself. I remember plopping down in the swivel chair at the nurse's station after dealing with a difficulty patient and thinking to myself, "I cannot do this for another twenty years." I had watched women who had worked at the bedside for twenty plus years and they did not appear to be happy. It was as if they felt stuck, like they had entered nursing and now, after years of working in what they thought was purpose, found it a burden. As I looked around, I thought, "Is this my future?" Would I be that nurse who was short with her patients, experiencing compassion fatigue, and watching the clock waiting for my shift to be over? In that moment, I realized I was letting my imagination run away with me and I had created a narrative in my mind about what my future was going to be. I had to monitor my thoughts and the things that I was telling myself. I had to unlock mind blocks that were standing in between my current situation and my future self. There was a shift taking place in my mind, and I was going to catch the wave.

I was terrified when I applied for graduate school. I mean, who did I think I was? The audacity of this little African American girl, born to an African immigrant. I was a first-generation college graduate and now I got the bright idea to pursue my master's degree. I thought, "Am I smart enough? Would I get in?" What was the worst that could happen? I might be denied admission, but it would not be the end of the world. I opened the course catalog and wrote my two-year matriculation plan. I wrote what courses I would take during the fall, spring, and summer semesters for the next two years. After I completed my course plan, I picked up the phone and called the university to schedule a meeting with the admission coordinator.

When the day came for our meeting, I was physically sick. The thought of getting rejected or turned down had my stomach in knots. I went and stood in front of the mirror and said to myself, "You will be granted admission. You will successfully complete the course work and you will graduate." I stood there staring in the mirror, and I said it over and over and over to myself until I believed, and all jitters went away. I got my acceptance letter thirty days later. Something happened the day I stood looking in the mirror telling myself I would get in. I saw myself walking across the stage, shaking the school president's hand and with the other hand receiving my degree. I went through the program with an expectation and rejected the thought that failure was an option. I was able to influence my thinking.

At times I have feelings of self-doubt. I say to myself out loud, "Show me proof that what you are thinking is true," and I draw on the experience I had applying for graduate school. It serves as a reminder that I am capable and that I can do whatever I set my mind to. You owe it to yourself to create the strategy to get to the next level. It is important to remember that wherever the mind goes, the body goes. In other words, whatever you think, be it positive or negative, if you tell yourself these things continuously you will soon believe it. Your innermost thoughts do not know the difference between positive or negative; they only do what you tell them to do. Believing in yourself and your ability requires tenacity, knowing that if you try and fail, you will try again. See and feel yourself in your future or the position; see and feel yourself writing the book; see and feel yourself completing the degree; see and feel yourself as the CEO of your company.

Your thoughts begin in the heart and are reproduced in the mind. That thinking leads to speaking about your thoughts and hearing your thoughts (and even rationalizing them), and this causes you to act on those thoughts creating repetitive, habitual behavior, which ultimately leads to your lifestyle. So my question is, what kind of life do you want to live?

When I decided to start my group coaching program for women called Next Level Woman of Worth Academy (nextlevelwow.com), I had to reframe my thinking and change my thoughts about myself and my business. I had to use involuntary conditioning of my mind combined with faith to create my future with my words. Creating the business while working a nine-to-five was the easy part. The hard part would be building the business. The difficulty would feel evident on those days I found myself working twelve and fourteen hours a day on my nine-to-five with no energy to come home and work on my future. I was a wife, a mother, a full-time employee. Where would I find the time to be an entrepreneur? I remember thinking I am not a quitter, but I might have to succumb to the idea of giving up. Those days left me feeling confused, overwhelmed, and unproductive. I began to question, "Do I have the ability to pull off this entrepreneur thing?" I had to reject the idea that failure was not an option. I had to find a way to eliminate the negative thinking, the stinking thinking that I was experiencing. My thoughts, if not controlled and combated with positive thinking, were sabotaging. So I wrote my daily affirmation and repeated it to myself twice a day and committed to memorizing it.

*"God's abundance is operating in my life. It floods my life with no hesitation and immediately all my needs, goals, and desires are met through endless wisdom, knowledge, and strategy. I will grow in wisdom in business, strategies, and stature, and in favor with God and man, because I believe all things are possible with God. I will be anxious for nothing. I will set my mind on whatever things are good, honest, lovely, just, trustworthy, and if there be any virtue I will think on these things. Good things are happening for and to me in personal life and in business. I have the influence, I have the creativity, I have the network, I have the strategy."*

Take some time to reflect on these five questions:

What do you need to do next to get to the next level? What do you want and how do you intent to get it?

Where do you lack confidence and courage? What are you doing about it?

What does the best version of you look like?

To book me as a speaker email info@drmiattaspeaks.com
Visit nextlevelwow.com to sign up for the wait list for the group coaching program Follow me on Instagram @drmiattahampton
Follow me on Clubhouse @drmiattahampton

# DR. MIATTA HAMPTON

**About Dr. Miatta Hampton:** Dr. Miatta Hampton is a nurse leader, #1 Best-Selling Author, speaker, coach, and minister. Miatta impacts others with her powerful, relatable messages of pursing purpose, and she empowers her audiences to live life on purpose and according to their dreams. She coaches and inspires women to turn chaos into cozy, pivot to prosperity, and how to profit in adversity. Miatta provides tools and resources for personal, professional, and financial growth.

Author's website: *www.DrMiattaSpeaks.com*
Book Series Website & Author's Bio: *www.The13StepsToRiches.com*

## Michael D. Butler

# "IF I AM TO BE, IT IS UP TO ME!"

Those were the words painted in blue 12-inch letters on the top of the wall above the wrestling room door I saw every day my Freshman and Sophmore year in high school.

Toiling through daily practices in a 90-degree wrestling room with sweat dripping onto the wrestling mat, I pondered these words for hours at a time until I internalized them and believed them.

Wrestling did not come easy for me. I was a tall, a full six-feet tall, lanky kid that wrestled at 108 pounds my sophomore year. Unlike most of my peers who began their wrestling careers in elementary school, I didn't begin until my ninth-grade year in high school. Even though I had to play catch up on learning the basics of takedowns, escapes and pinning my opponent, I loved the idea that wrestling was an individual sport. Even though you were on a team, when you were on the mat it was just you versus your opponent. No one on your team could help you defeat your contender.

Internalizing those words, *"If I am to be, it is up to me!"* have helped me more in life than I realized until recently. With every loss and with every win on that mat, it was my success or my failure. No opportunity to play victim here. What could I do differently is what I asked myself, quickly came up with a solution, then I was on to the next goal.

My conviction is that we only rise to the level of our belief. We only rise to the level of our success that we feel comfortable with. We only earn as much as we are comfortable earning. We only network in the circles we feel comfortable and accepted in.

Like the submarine that prevents itself from collapsing at the extreme outer pressure of the entire ocean, we, also, thrive by increasing the internal pressure to protect us from the antagonistic pressure when society and culture try to move us from our core values.

Our internal engine is more important than going to the gym and any focus on outward health.

Our inner barometer only allows us to rise to the level of success and connection that we see ourselves achieving and feel comfortable with achieving. And speaking our truth verbally with our mouth solidifies the realty of truth that is in our heart.

Several Biblical passages make this key point:

> "As a man thinketh in his hear so is he." Proverbs 23:7

> "For with the heart man believes to righteousness and with the mouth confession is made unto salvation." Romans 10:10

> "Life and death are in the power of the tongue…." Proverbs 18:21

The words we speak solidify our fate and prophesy our future. The words we speak solidify our belief and our action. The truth is we can never rise above our level of our belief but our level of belief is tied directly to the words we speak.

## Autosuggestion from My Uncle

My Great Uncle Don was one of my childhood heroes. He believed in me and my brother when we were young. Uncle Don had played college football and we idolized him. I remember one year for Christmas, he bought us a full set of football gear complete with helmets, shoulder pads and jerseys. I can still hear his voice, "Wow look at Michael run, he can sure handle that football...." His voice made an indelible imprint on my mind, my soul, and my future because I knew he believed in me. And because he believed in me, I believed I could do, be, or become anything or anyone I wanted to be.

Not only did he believe in me and communicate that to me every time I saw him, but he also introduced me to the world of personal development. He was a graduate of the Dale Carneige course on *How to Win Friends and Influence People*, and he also introduced me to the work of Napoleon Hill and *Think and Grow Rich*. Uncle Don is still thriving today at 90 years old, still reads 1-2 books a week, and does 100 push-ups per day. He'll always be a hero to me.

The fact is we must consciously take charge of our inner dialogue and be proactive with positive programming, otherwise, our inner programming will, by default, become negative and be influenced by the world's programming. Like the daily charging of our phones and computers, our mind, heart, and soul need daily recharge, jumpstart, and rebooting to not only survive, but thrive in a world that is overwhelmingly negative.

Some keys that have worked for me over the years to maintain high levels of positivity when all around me was negativity are:

1) Have a daily list of positive affirmations.

   My list of daily confessions revolved not just around my academic and sports performance but also around my identity, my self-esteem and my contribution in the world. My daily affirmations will change from time to time throughout the seasons of my life based on the challenges I'm facing and the things I'm believing for for myself and for my family. This started as a list of 20 positive affirmations I taped to my mirror and repeated twice a day until I had them memorized and could recite them in my sleep.

2) Spend time daily feeding your heart, mind and spirit on positivity with books, podcasts, audio books that uplift, encourage, educate and inspire you.

3) Consciously avoid negative talk, negative people and dream killers. Dreams and goals are fragile when they are young and have to be nurtured or they will be destroyed before they ever happen in our life. Do everything to protect your dream and your goals.

4) Daily proactively do one positive thing for yourself and for someone else.

### Auto Suggestion from Yourself for Yourself

It can sometimes be very discouraging to hear a story about someone who had a positive role model or cheerleader in their corner, and you feel as though there is no one around to encourage you through life's ups and downs. But the true power comes from knowing the most important source for autosuggestion comes from within your own heart, mind and soul. Deciding that, "If I am to be, it is up to me" removes all blame, removes all shame and makes your life an entirely new game. Step up, accept the challenge. When no one believes in you, is counting on you, or expecting it from you, you step up and launch the best version of yourself. Open your heart, your mouth, and your message to the world—we're all waiting to see you do just that!

I'm proud to be a global book publisher and speaker, and a recognized authority in the book publishing space, helping authors and speakers evolve and create platforms of influence in an ever-changing marketplace.

As the new CEO of The Mark Victor Hansen Library with over 80 New York Times Bestselling titles, global distribution, and sales with over half a billion books sold, I'm also the Founder at BeyondPublishing.net and have authors who have spoken in 50 countries on 6 different continents. I'm most proud of my 4 grown sons and 2 grandsons.

MichaelDButler.com

# MICHAEL D. BUTLER

**About Michael D. Butler:** Michael Butler has been a guest on *Fox News* and *USA Today* and has gotten his clients onto *CNN, Dr. Phil, TMZ, TLC, Rolling Stone, Entrepreneur Magazine, Inc500, TBN, TruTV, Fox Business* and many others.

His Podcast, *The Publisher Podcast* is heard by thousands globally and features guests from Hollywood and the Literary Industry.

He has published 4 of his own International best-selling books in multiple languages: *The Single Dad's Survival Guide, Best-Seller Status – Becoming a Best-Selling Author in the Digital Age, The Speaker's Edge – Turning Your Part-Time Passion into Your Full-Time Speaking Career* and *It's Complicated – When Finding Love was a Matter of Letting Go.*

He founded and runs 1040Impact.org that rescues kids in human trafficking, educates them and teaches them trade skills to equip them for life in Asia in places like Pakistan.

He is the CEO of Beyond Publishing with authors in 20 countries and over 400 titles by end of 2021.

Author's Website: *www.MichaelDButler.com*
Book Series Website & Author's Bio: *www.The13StepstoRiches.com*

*Michelle Cameron Coulter & Al Coulter*

# A CHAMPION'S CHOICE

How would you do it if you already were a World Champion?

This is one of the most profound and powerful questions I was asked by my coach, months before winning our first World Championship title. What did it take to get there? What did it take to do it? It took believing, visualizing, "Auto Suggestion," being as if.

My duet partner and I had both been in our sport of synchronized swimming for years and had swam on our National team together. We were paired together as partners after the 1984 Olympics where my partner, Carolyn, had won a silver medal.

The year 1985 would have been our first year swimming together as a pair for Canada. We were heading to the United States to compete in our first world championship, and our toughest main competition was identical twins that had been swimming together for 16 years as a pair—and we would swim in their hometown with ten thousand spectators.

Against all odds, we won our first world championship. How did we do it? Yes, hours and hours of training, six-to-eight hours a day. Building strength, endurance, choreographing our routine, pushing our limits of what we could do, meticulously going over perfecting every single second, stretching our creative minds, AND Visualizing (Auto Suggestion).

We would see and feel how would it look like in our minds first, before it would ever be. We would practice visualizing our routine over and over in our minds, see ourselves having the perfect swim; feel what our body was doing with ease and strength, how we would walk out onto the deck, how we would feel confident. Being as if we already were "World Champions." We would practice the parts in our mind before we would actually do it in the water. Auto Suggest before we even did it. We had to BELIEVE first that we could without any doubts.

Let me tell you, yes, those doubts can creep in when you are tired or have a down day. That is why the building of that muscle itself specifically is one of the most important key elements to success and to not underestimate its power.

After winning our first world championship, we had three more years until the Olympic Games. How do you keep getting better you have reached being the best in the world? There is always room to grow, challenges that test you, limits to be stretched. We continued to stack and grow all the key foundational elements.

The year before the Olympics, I was given a license plate that said, "GOLD 88." I drove with that on my car, trained, ate, slept, trained, and believed to my core.

Actually, this is quite cute. I have a niece who, many years after the Olympics said, "What if Auntie Michelle didn't win the Olympic Gold? Would she have had to change her licence plate to "Participant 88?"

The year of the Olympics, we had a pre-Olympic meet in Seoul, Korea. The Olympic pool was not yet complete. We went to the site and stood in the middle of the construction zone, right at the edge of where the pool would be. Right where we would be standing and getting ready to dive in at the Olympics. We visualized and felt exactly what it would feel like. How it would feel to stand on the podium. It was real in our minds, first.

There is a power in SEEING, SAYING, FEELING, and BELIEVING—before it ever can be.

And yes, we did win Gold in 1988.

Now, Many years retired from the sport and four grown children all young adults, I see and utilize the power of Auto Suggestion and visualization everywhere.

The power of our thoughts is incredible.

One particular example that I love is when our oldest daughter was in sixth grade. She had a science-fair project, and she decided she wanted to do it on "The positive and negative effects of our thoughts on our energy."

She did it in two parts.

The first part she did was how what we say actually affects our body. She did this through muscle testing; having her test subject hold up their arm as strong as they could and not let her push it down.

A.  When someone would say, for example, "I am strong and invincible," their body was actually strong and invincible, and it was hard to push down their arm.

B.  When they said, "I'm weak and insignificant," it was easy to push their arm down.

During the second part, she planted bean seeds.

She had a positive group, a negative group, and a control group. They all had the same soil, the same water, and the same sunlight.

- The control group, she left alone.
- The positive group, she said positive things to play positive music to everyday.
- The negative group, she took into the bathroom and yelled at three times a day. She would come out and say, "Mom I hate that part."

It was incredible to see the results.

- The negative group grew about .5 cm a day.
- The control group grew about 1cm a day.
- The positive group grew about 2 cm a day and also had significantly more leaves on them.

That is a Plant! Imagine what we say to ourselves and how that grows.

Another of my favorite reinforced lessons came from my same daughter later that year, again, when she was only ten years old. I was having a tough day and about to leave the house in a mood that reflected that. Suddenly, my daughter stopped me to say, "Mom, remember I love you, and *remember the energy you put out is the environment you create.*"

Wow, I think of that often and realize how it is always true! What kind of environments are we creating?

By being aware of our energy, thoughts, and focus, we can attract more of what we want.

*~Michelle Cameron Coulter*

Auto Suggestion is something I stumbled upon while playing on a volleyball team.

To me, it is getting yourself into the state where you attract what is most prominent in your main focus. This can be done through daily goal setting, meditation, prayer, and repetition—consistent repetition of that exciting thing you want in your life.

I love looking back and seeing how I was learning so many life skills while playing on a team. I ended up playing for the Canadian volleyball team for thirteen years, and I still have many of my goal-setting journals. It is so interesting to see the goals I set each year, and how important Auto Suggestion was to achieving many of those goals.

I remember the first time I made the Provincial Volleyball Team and they asked us what our goals were with volleyball. I was seventeen years old and had not really thought about my future.

I said, "What do you mean?" They said, "Do you want to play college or university, be on the Junior National Team, Senior National Team or even the Olympic Team?"

I really didn't know what they meant. I was playing because I enjoyed the game.

Over the next two years, I fell in love with the sport, and it became a passion of mine to keep improving and represent Canada at the Olympics. This started my journey in Auto Suggestion into motion.

During that time, whenever I saw a glass leaving a round wet ring of water on the table, I would make five rings in the shape of the Olympic Rings, feeding my vision.

Our National coach was hired from Japan and the men's Japanese team was ranked third in the world, while Canada was ranked twenty-first. Only twelve teams make the Olympics, and Canada had never qualified, so we had a lot of work to do.

Our coach was extremely tough and ran hard four-hour-full practices, six days a week, plus two-hour practices in the morning three times a week for fitness and skill development. In the beginning, he was really mean to me and always kept me in drills longer and yelled at me. To a point where I had enough and went to our team captain and said, "That is it. I am quitting."

He said to me, "Why do you think he is working so hard on you? You don't see him spending any time with the guys with no talent. He sees something in you that you have not recognized."

I had suggested to myself that I wasn't good enough when it was that exact opposite. That was a big lesson that day. I was GOOD, and I started believing in myself. I brought my game. From that day forward, I was a starter, and later became the captain.

We travelled to Japan thirteen times during my career. The first time in Japan, they did not respect us. We were put up in a low-quality youth hostel, and only played the National Team one time out of six matches. They beat us badly. We hardly scored a point on them. But, now we knew what we needed to work on. Over the next three years leading into the 1984 Los Angeles Olympics, we kept learning and growing our confidence.

In the spring of 1984, we played in Japan and played them four times. We finally took a match off of them. They put us up in the Hilton, gave us watches and spending money. We had earned their respect and little did they know they had been building our confidence in ourselves.

The most amazing time came down to the last pool-play match in the 1984 Olympics, where we ended up playing Japan to see who would move on to the final four in the world. We ended up beating them three-to-zero to qualify for the semi-finals of the Olympics. What an amazing experience! All because we had been implementing Auto Suggestion in ourselves and as a team. We built on it for four years, moving from twenty-first in the world to number four.

Auto Suggestion is something I learned through sport, and it became a major influence in my life with everything I did and do.

**~*Al Coulter***

# MICHELLE CAMERON COULTER & AL COULTER

**About Michelle Cameron Coulter:** Michelle is an Olympic gold medalist, entrepreneur, mother of four, community leader raising millions of dollars for charities, global inspirational leader, and founder and CEO of Inspiring Possibilities.

**About Al Coulter:** Al is a two-time Olympian in volleyball, captain of Team Canada, world record holder in matches representing one's country in any sport, with over 735 matches, entrepreneur, father of four, and personal best coach, specializing in relationships, team, and resilience.

Michelle and Al are the embodiment of today's leaders. Strong and empowering, they embraced life's challenges with strength and courage. They bring insight, compassion, depth, and inspiration to the table with multiple world championships, three Olympics, an Olympic gold medal, marriage, and four children.

They are sought-after inspirational leaders. Through their speaking, workshops, and retreats, their gift and passion is to inspire possibilities and support people to embrace their greatness in a real, authentic, healthy, and vibrant way—creating thriving community, connection, and one's own gold medal results.

Author's website: *www.MichelleCameronCoulter.com*
Book Series Website & Author's Bio: *www.The13StepsToRiches.com*

## Michelle Mras

# EVERYDAY MIRACLES

*"You have not because you ask not."* - James 4:2-3

I believe in miracles. Do you?

Throughout the end of my forties and into my next decade of life, I experienced a huge range of trauma and health challenges. The lifestyle changes my family and I endured during this time seem remarkable as I reflect back onto what has become our normal.

In 2014, I was involved in an automobile accident that shifted my life and set me on a rollercoaster ride I never anticipated. I was plummeted into a life of silence and the inability to walk without assistance for two years. Those years felt like a few months to me because, unbeknownst to my family and me, I had obtained a traumatic brain injury (TBI) to four parts of my brain. These injuries left me completely cognizant of what was happening and spoken around me, without the ability to react or communicate. I was trapped within my mind.

Have you ever been alone with your thoughts? It seems as if all your inner critics come out to play and stir up insecurities about love, worthiness, and capability. That is what occurred with me. I battled daily with my inner critics. At first, I agreed with them. I fell into the "woe is me" trap.

Maybe I was left in this state because I had no life plan? Perhaps my voice was taken away because I had nothing to contribute? Maybe I became helpless because I squandered my days with worry and lived so stuck in my ruts that there was no time for play?

In my head, I berated myself for not having a plan, not enjoying the simplicity of what life has to offer, and my most guilty habit of being stuck in a rut and expecting the world to adjust to make my dreams come true. I felt unproductive, lazy, stupid, worthless, a burden, and careless to have allowed myself to be in an auto accident.

Somewhere in my journey of being isolated with my thoughts, I realized that I was becoming less aware. I felt my mind slipping away. My health was also slipping. I would become dizzy and my headaches were more severe. My family would say comments that they didn't think I understood, regarding my response time to stimuli. I became very depressed. I preferred death over continuing to live in this state.

Somewhere near the end of the two years of being completely helpless, I was very frustrated. I was placed on the loveseat in our living room, just as I had been placed for the past seven hundred and thirty days. I would sit there until my husband came home to move me. The thoughts of being useless flooded my mind. I made plans to take my life. The irony was tha I was unable to move in order to orchestrate the plan. I was furious! I screamed inside of my mind, "If you hate me so much, kill me already!" While tears streamed down my face, I heard a booming voice say, "You're not dead, yet! Get up!" Some may think that voice was a figment of my imagination; I know it wasn't. The moment I heard the voice, I saw a high speed movie reel of my life. Each point that I thought I was alone and left for dead, there was some unseen being with me. I knew that I would actually be dead if I wasn't being protected. I found myself several feet away from the loveseat I had become accustomed to, on my knees thanking God for all I had endured during my life.

There was another thought that came to me which brought a sense of peace, "I have never been alone." I thanked God for every trial I had experienced, because it prepared me for the next. I promised to no longer question the "why" behind my experiences and to seek gratitude in every day. I asked to be able to speak again so I could share what I learned with others—that life is precious and each of us is worthy of living as our best selves every day.

My recovery from my TBI has been long. I didn't get up and start walking and talking immediately, it took work. I had to train myself out of my old habits of berating myself. I found that there is power in our words. Remember when I told you about my decline in health and reaction time I experienced when stuck in my head? There was no physical cause for it. I convinced my mind, by berating myself over and over again, that I was not worthy of healing. I inadvertently created negative affirmations of being unproductive, lazy, stupid, worthless, a burden, and careless so well, that my body responded.

I knew I needed to restructure my mindset. I found guidance in my mentor, Dr. Paul Scheele. He once said that humans are built to be resilient. Look at a baby learning to walk, "They get up, they fall. They get up, they fall." If babies had the mindset of adults, we would be a "world of crawlers." If words have power, I needed to learn how to take control of how I used those words in my life to heal myself. I needed to rediscover my toddler mindset to believe in myself. It took deep inner work to accomplish this task. My daily mantra in my head revolved around my complete healing or better. I used my imagination to see, feel, taste, and embody how I would be as the newly improved me. I believed that this reality existed; it was simply awaiting me to catch up to it. Every morning before I opened my eyes and every night as I closed my eyes, I would see the me I wanted to be. I knew how it felt to be in my healed body. I became the me I am today within my mind, years before I arrived. Now, I am known for my positive attitude. As a matter of fact, I was recognized by the John Maxwell Team with the Culture Award for that very attribute.

Whether or not you believe in God is your business. I don't consider myself an overly religious person. I simply share what I experienced. My words have power, which means everyone's words have power. I've seen it in action up-close and personal. You have, too! How often have you said to yourself, or even just joking with another person, "I'm always broke. I have horrible luck dating. I won't get that raise. There are no more good men/women in the world. I'll never (fill in the blank)." This negative or self-depreciation talk is a form of Auto Suggestion. We say these words like they just go into the wind without effect, but the emotional ground from which we proclaim those attributes give the words power and in turn, becomes our reality.

*"In the beginning was the Word, and the Word was with God, and the Word was God."* - John 1, NKJ

Earlier, I asked if you believe in miracles. If my story didn't provide enough proof, I challenge you to look for them throughout your days. Miracles occur right before our eyes, but we are too consumed with how much we aren't deserving that we don't recognize the gifts that fall before us, perhaps because they don't reveal themselves in the ways we want them to be presented. Observe the intricacies of a leaf. Watch a bee buzz from flower to flower. Ponder the magnitude of the sky above us and how the clouds move. I ask that you do an experiment with the words you say outwardly and to yourself when no one else is around. Focus on one statement you have been guilty of saying and flip it into a positive statement. Use only uplifting language, like, "I am worthy of (fill in the blank)." Believe it. Live as if it is already in your life. Use as many senses you can muster to feel the sensation of whatever you are worthy of and how you feel once you have it. See the miracles begin to be more evident.

I believe in miracles, big and small. Not because I recovered from my TBI, but rather that I obtained my TBI in the first place. It was a harsh wake-up call in order to live with purpose. I had to lose myself to find the willpower to seek what I wanted out of life. I became intentional with my thoughts and actions. I used to live my life feeling inadequate and powerless. The miracle is that through the rollercoaster ride, I learned to love, accept, and honor myself to be the best version of me every day and to be so—unapologetically!

# ABOUT MICHELLE MRAS

**About Michelle Mras:** Michelle is an International TEDx Speaker, Communication Trainer, Success Coach, co-Host of the Denim & Pearls podcast, the Author of Eat, Drink and Be Mary: A Glimpse Into a Life Well Lived and It's Not Luck: Overcoming You, and Host of the MentalShift show on The New Channel (TNC), Philippines.

Michelle is a survivor of multiple life challenges to include a Traumatic Brain Injury and her current battle with Breast Cancer. She guides her clients to recognize the innate gifts within them, to stop apologizing for what they are not and step into who they truly are. She accomplishes this through one-on-one and group coaching, Training events, Keynote talks, her books, Podcasts and MentalShift television show.

Awarded the Inspirational Women of Excellence Award from the Women Economic Forum, New Delhi, India; the John Maxwell Team Culture Award for Positive Attitude; has been featured on hundreds of Podcasts, radio programs, several magazines, and lends her voice to audiobooks and has a habit of breaking out into song.

Michelle's driving thought is that every day is a gift. Tomorrow is never promised. Every moment is an opportunity to be the best version of you… Unapologetically!

Author's Website: *www.MichelleMras.com*
Book Series Website & Author's Bio: *www.The13StepstoRiches.com*

*Mickey Stewart*

# THE STORY WE TELL OURSELVES

In 1870, a young woman of twenty stood barefoot in the sand on a triangular peak of beach where, fourteen years later, the Boularderie lighthouse would be constructed. She wore a full-length, 19th century dress, complete with petticoats, a Scottish Sontag shawl wrapped around her bodice, and her hair tucked into a white day-cap. A ship approached from her left, heading towards the Atlantic Ocean on its way to Scotland. As the ship sailed by, a handsome Scottish Highlander reached down over the side to where the young lass stood, scooped her up into his arm, and whisked her away to his homeland.

This particular scene is taken from a made-up movie that, from the age of twenty, I adopted as my reality. It resulted in one of my strongest examples of how I applied the power of Auto Suggestion to my life.

In his book, *The Power of the Subconscious Mind,* Dr. Joseph Murphy states, "If you consciously assume something is true, even though it may be false, your subconscious mind will accept it as true and proceed to bring about results, which must necessarily follow because you consciously assumed it to be true."

My personal translation? "If I tell myself a story, my mind will go to work to fetch it for me."

When I was twenty years old, my parents built a new home in Boularderie, which is located on the eastern coast of Cape Breton Island, Nova Scotia, Canada. Positioned on three acres of land, their property faces the beautiful Bras d'Or Lakes, and provides access to a path that leads to a private beach. On this beach, there's a triangular patch of land where the lighthouse stands. I made many trips down to our beach over the years as it's the perfect place to lose track of time, feel the wind against your skin, and get lost in the melodic lull of the waves.

At the time, I was employed as an animator at the Halifax Citadel National Historic Site, which is a four-hour drive from our new family home. In my role as a Scottish soldier's wife, I was responsible for helping recreate the period between 1869 and1871, when the Ross-shire Buffs from Scotland were stationed in Halifax. Often, when I was dressed in my 19th century costume, I would close my eyes and temporarily teleport myself back in time to BEING that girl from one hundred and fifty years earlier; standing barefoot in the sand, on that triangular peak of beach, waiting for my handsome Scottish Highlander to sail by and whisk me off to a faraway land.

My story started to take on a life of its own when my romantic scene of two strangers falling in love played out to the song *"When First I Went to Caledonia"* sung by Scottish singer, Tony Cuffe. The song, whether played through the headphones of my Walkman, or just in my head, not only became the soundtrack to my very own love story, it (more importantly) became a TRIGGER that brought forth powerful images and emotions every single time I listened to it.

During the song, when I heard, *"I spied a maiden from Boularderie over, she seemed to me like the Queen of May,"* it felt personal. Not only did my story take place in Boularderie, but I was born during the month of May! So each time I heard that line, it felt as if somebody had literally taken their hand, reached deep down into my chest and squeezed my heart, leaving me feeling like it would burst from joy.

As the weeks, months (and even years!) went by, I continued to teleport myself back in time to BEING that woman on the beach. My story gained momentum as the vivid images, music, and emotions all blended together to create one powerful, magnetic force; a force that possessed me with a KNOWING that (whether already lived or yet to happen) my made-up mind-movie was TRUE. This was MY Story.

It was now time for my mind to get busy fetching it for me!

I was so convinced that my Scottish Highlander was going to come and take me away to Scotland that I ACTED AS IF it had already happened. For four years, I actively and playfully focused on making this story a part of my everyday being; seeing it each night as I fell asleep, daydreaming about it during my classes, and escaping to it at every possible opportunity. I even rejected offers to go out on dates, feeling as if I would be cheating on my Scottish Highlander, who was finding his way to me.

To paraphrase the words of Dr. Joseph Murphy, "My subconscious mind had no other option than to accept this story as true and proceed to bring about results."

The results?

Mark, my Scottish Highlander, was my very first (and only) boyfriend.

While he may not have literally scooped me into his arms from the side of his passing ship, Mark stole my heart and whisked me off to his homeland of Scotland. (My chapter in *The 13 Steps to Riches, Desire, Volume 1* captures the exciting journey of how we found each other.)

Mark and I are now approaching our twenty-fifth wedding anniversary and have been blessed with our amazing seventeen-year-old son, Cameron. At the time of writing this chapter, I was back home in Boularderie visiting my Mum, where I spent time down at that very beach, beside that very triangular patch of land (facing the beautiful Bras d'Or Lakes), next to that very same lighthouse, meditating and writing.

And, while I was there, the craziest thing happened! It was a realization of mass proportion! As I sat on the beach, looking over at the lighthouse (the exact spot where I imagined myself one hundred and fifty years earlier), I realized that, just three days after we first met, Mark stood on my family beach—LITERALLY stood at that EXACT SPOT of my mind movie!

When I think about the power of Auto Suggestion, it brings me back to when we learned to magnetize a sewing needle back in science class. By rubbing a magnet against a needle in the same direction several times, the needle will become magnetized. For me, Auto Suggestion, which is repeated thoughts, images, feelings, and expectations, is my magnet, and my subconscious mind is my needle. When we use the power of Auto Suggestion (our magnet) to convince our subconscious mind (our needle) that something is TRUE, we magnetize ourselves in the direction of our goal and we start attracting people, things, and circumstances into our life to help fulfil that goal.

Not only did I attract Mark to the spot I imagined him to be, the entire pipe band he was touring with also ended up on that small, triangular patch of sand, all the way from Scotland. Talk about one heck of a powerful magnet!

This realization hit me just five seconds after the first one, like a delayed ripple effect. I got chills and voiced a few 'choice' words as the full awareness of what took place made its connection with me. After four years of reruns of the same show playing in my mind, my powerful Auto Suggestions successfully fetched my handsome Scottish Highlander and brought him to the very spot I imagined!

To this very day, when I listen to *When First I Went to Caledonia,* I can't help but cry from sheer joy, and absolute awe, of how MY STORY became my reality.

"The dominating thoughts which one permits to remain in the conscious mind (whether these thoughts be negative or positive is immaterial) will *reach and influence* the subconscious mind, through the Law of Auto Suggestion." *Think and Grow Rich,* Napoleon Hill.

# MICKEY STEWART

**About Mickey Stewart:** Born in Cape Breton, Canada, Mickey Stewart is a musician, coach, and author who has been a player and instructor of the snare drum and bodhrán for forty years.

Responsible for heading up the drum program at Ardvreck School in Perthshire, Scotland since 2002, Mickey is in high demand to teach throughout the U.K. and North America.

Creator and founder of BodhránExpert.com, her YouTube videos have received more than two million views from students and fans from every country throughout the world.

Over the past eight years, she's been involved in the TV and film industry as a supporting artist. Even more recently, she's begun following her newest passion, which is teaching others how to share their talents with the world.

Stewart lives in Crieff, Scotland with her husband of twenty-four years, Scottish musician and composer Mark Stewart, along with their 16-year-old son, Cameron, who is also a piper.

Author's Website: *www.MickeyStewart.com*
Book Series Website & Author's Bio: *www.The13StepstoRiches.com*

## Natalie Susi

# IT WORKS LIKE MAGIC

*Whatever we tell ourselves is what it is.* Reread that again. Now, read it once more.

Sit with that sentence and see how it lands on you. Maybe say it a few times in your head and out loud. Does it make sense? Does it make you uncomfortable? Do you want to keep reading?

When I say "whatever we tell ourselves is what it is," what I'm really saying is that the story you're telling about yourself, your life, or a particular experience that you're unhappy or happy about is the narrative that shapes your current personal reality. These narratives can be based on positive thoughts or negative thoughts, and they can change in an instant, to either distract us or support us on our life journey.

So if you're reading this and thinking about how you're not enjoying your current reality, it is quite possible to transform this and start experiencing a different reality right now. I can imagine this sounds too simple, but it's true, and it works like magic.

This magical process is called Auto Suggestion, and it is the act of telling yourself what you actually need to hear in order to produce what you actually desire. In some cases, it is also the act of initially lying to yourself with positive thoughts and statements, even when you're feeling the exact opposite. Finally, it also includes connecting those thoughts and feelings to your senses, so you can truly imagine what it looks, sounds, tastes, feels, and smells like to live in your desired reality, so you can begin to manifest it into your real life.

When I was five, I proclaimed that I wanted to be a teacher, and I spent all of my free time as a child "playing school." I grew up in a middle-class family of Italian immigrants on the East Coast. Both of my parents were employees at larger corporations, and while they enjoyed their jobs, they both ascribed to the belief that money was hard to make, that it didn't grow on trees, that it wasn't the root of happiness, and that we weren't going to spend too much time talking about it because it wasn't appropriate. They were very proud of my aspirations to become a teacher, and often assured me that doing something I was passionate about was way more important than making money. I grew up saying things like, "I know I'll never be rich, but I don't care, if I get to do what I love." It was not even in my awareness that you could do what you love AND also make money. I was a middle-class child who would be a middle-class adult, and that was just the reality. When I graduated with my Master's degree, I got a teaching job right away. I started my professional life as a very low-paid teacher, who was having a very challenging time paying rent on the West Coast. Shortly after, I was laid off in the California budget cuts, and I couldn't find a new job.

One night, I was drinking a margarita, and I had an idea to create a low-calorie cocktail mixer that eventually ended up launching on the same day as a similar product, the multimillion dollar success, Skinny Girl Margarita. It was the right time in the market, but I had no idea how to run or build a profitable brand in one of the most competitive industries. I was truly way out of my league. I created, built, and ran that company for eight years, wearing all of the hats right down to delivering the product out of the back of my Hyundai. I also worked three jobs while I was building the business to keep my head above water. Like my parents, I believed money was hard to make, that it didn't grow on trees, and that it wasn't appropriate to say I wanted to be wealthy. I made less than two-thousand dollars a month, and I could never get ahead in life or in business.

I lived from a lack mentality all day, every day, and I told the story about how I was a broke, female entrepreneur all the time to anyone who would listen. I totally identified with this story, and this narrative became my whole life.

One day, I got so frustrated with my own stories that I decided to start studying some of the best personal development content on money mindset. I learned from books like *Think and Grow Rich* and people like Jack Canfield, Tony Robbins, John Assaraf, and T. Harv Eker. I wrote down my beliefs around money, and I started to see how I was uncomfortable expressing out loud that I wanted to make money. I also saw that my true desire to teach stemmed from a desire to help people, and I quickly realized that I couldn't help anyone if I was too busy helping myself.

After completing some of these exercises and meditating on what I really desired, I stumbled upon this simple sentence that changed everything. I told myself, "The more I get, the more I'll give." As soon I said it out loud, I felt a deep sense of peace and relief. My shoulders relaxed, and I was able to take a deep breath for the first time in years. I was in the process of rewriting my money story. I told myself that my parents were always very generous and willing to help people, so it was totally in alignment with our values to give to people who were less fortunate. I reasoned that in order to help more students, more people, and more charities, I had to be in state of abundance versus a state of lack. I started saying another sentence, "I don't just survive. I thrive." Then, I added a few more, "I am abundant. I am generous. I am open to giving AND receiving. I attract wealth. I am wealthy doing what I love to do every day." I put these statements on post it notes all over my house and on my mirrors, and I read them every morning and every night.

These repetitive statements gave me a new narrative and the permission to say out loud that I desired to make more money. Within ninety days, just like magic, I tripled my income while doing what I love to do every day. These small sentences created big, huge changes.

If you'd like to change one of your narratives right now and test out how Auto Suggestion works, check out the exercise below. I have written some examples for each prompt in case it supports you.

1. What is one area of your life (a story, narrative, relationship, or experience) that you'd like to shift right now? *Example: The financial area of my life. I want to stop being/feeling broke.*

2. Describe the negative emotions you experience when you think about this area of your life. *Example: fear, anxiety, frustration, depression, overwhelm around paying all of my bills.*

3. What beliefs have you created from this story? What do you believe to be true? *Example: I am not meant to be wealthy. I am not the kind of woman that gets to be wealthy. It's not appropriate to say you want to make money. Money is really hard to make. I have no idea what it is to make 6 figures, and I never will.*

4. What emotions do you want to feel when you think of this area or story of your life? *Example: Empowered, calm, peaceful, excited, generous, and in the flow.*

5. What does it look and sound and feel like to have the outcome you desire in this area of your life? *Example: It looks like I live in a beautiful space with an ocean view and new appliances that smells like that expensive candle I love from Anthropology. I can hear the ocean when I go to bed at night. I go out to eat and buy delicious food wherever I go, and I am able to comfortably provide free sessions to clients when I want to help someone and also support 2-3 charities*

*that I really believe in consistently every month. I get to teach a UCSD because I want to not because I have to.*

6. What are three short statements that reflect your new belief around this area of your life? *Example: The more money I get, the more I'll give. I attract abundance. Money flows easily to me. I can do what I love to do every day AND be wealthy.*

7. Write your new positive statements down and read them every morning and every night. *Example: I don't just survive, I thrive. The more I get, the more I'll give. I am wealthy and abundant. Money flows easily and efficiently to me.*

I know it seems too simple, but it's true, and it works like magic.

# NATALIE SUSI

**About Natalie Susi:** Natalie has more than 14 years of experience as a teacher, speaker, entrepreneur and mentor. Currently she's a 5-year UCSD professor focusing on communications and the Pursuit of Happiness. As an entrepreneur, she founded and grew Bare Organic Mixers beverage company for 8 years resulting in an acquisition in 2014.

After selling the company, Natalie combined her educational background as a teacher and her experience as an entrepreneur to provide personal development coaching and consulting to individuals, businesses, and creative entrepreneurs. She developed a program called Conscious Conversations and utilizes a step-by-step process called The Alignment Method to support leaders in cultivating conscious teams and businesses through a process of self-reflection, self-discovery, and self-ascension that ultimately increases profits, productivity, and the growth of the individuals personally and professionally.

Author's website: *www.NatalieSusi.com*
Book Series Website & Author's Bio: *www.The13StepsToRiches.com*

*Nita Patel*

# MANTRAS

In 2013, I wrote a letter to my Guru, who was in India at the time, describing a mental and emotional crisis that had been weighing on me for some time. It was a mid-life crisis moment where I couldn't find meaning to life. I didn't know what my purpose was, and I surely knew I wasn't fulfilling it, whatever IT was supposed to be.

Emotionally, I was in a very dark place and no matter how much I tried, it felt impossible to escape this place. I had tried all the things I knew I could do on my own to escape this darkness and momentarily I would find relief, but it would quickly return the next day, even the next hour.

I received my Guru's blessings within days. The blessings shared lots of supportive and uplifting statements. I felt happy in the moment, but there was still a strong sense of anxiousness. I was still lost. And I still had no sense of direction. I continued to hold on to what I could and tried to keep my chin up, but inside I felt everything from emptiness to seeing my life crashing right in front of me. Who am I? And why am I here?

I remember reading an article from a magazine one day about living an authentic life and I thought to myself, what does that mean? I'm 5'1", I wear a size 0, my shoe size is 6.5, and I'm a manager, mom, wife, and daughter. That's how I knew myself. That was my authentic self. My purpose was to go to work, get promoted, buy a bigger house someday, and retire when

I turned sixty-five. Then, I would find my next authentic self and maybe work at an art gallery because that sounded interesting and fun.

I struggled with all my conflicting thoughts for many months. Each day, I lost a little bit of hope. This meant more confusion and more darkness. Finally, I decided I needed answers and I was willing to do the work this time. In the fall of 2015, I wrote another letter. Only this time, I asked for a specific response. I needed to know what I could do to eliminate the darkness and to remove the negativity from my mind, though I'm pretty sure I didn't say it that concisely. They say, when the student is ready, the teacher appears. This was my first experience of that concept. I was ready to do the work and I knew what to ask for, and so I did.

Surprise, surprise! This time, the blessings I received included an action. My guru suggested I pray for pure and positive thoughts and asked me to do one mala (a rosary with 108 beads) while chanting the mantra 'Swaminarayan'. Like OM, Swaminarayan is one of the highest vibration mantras.

I did exactly that! I chanted Swaminarayan 108 times every day.

From that day forward, I can't explain the people, thoughts, inspiration, places, google searches, books, YouTube lectures, online programs, and events that I was met with. But everything has led me to finding myself, to understanding what it actually means to be authentic, and to finding my purpose. My growth has been emotional, spiritual, mental and physical.

This one ask, blessing, and mala transformed my entire life. You may be wondering how this relates to Auto Suggestion or affirmations, as we call them today.

It's the mantra. Swaminarayan. The mantra I grew up knowing, hearing and even chanting, but this time it changed my life.

You never know when or how words affect you. Every day is filled with Auto Suggestions. From the lyrics in the songs we listen to, the news, conversations in our home, to the company we choose to keep. Sometimes it's intentional and other times it happens by accident. Good and bad, positive and negative. It all affects us. Think of it like gravity. Gravity doesn't favor good or bad. It's a universal law that is effective one-hundred percent of the time equally across our earth to all things and people.

Intentional Auto Suggestions can come in many different forms. They can be statements you repeat daily. They can be images you set your intentions upon. Or it can be something you hear completely unintentionally that changes your life. When you hear or say the same thing repeatedly, it eventually leads to believing in oneself.

In the fall of 2017, I created my first digital vision board. I didn't want anyone to know what I was aspiring to manifest, so keeping it on my computer felt safe. A part of me believed that it would magically happen and a part of me didn't believe in it at all. Nonetheless, it didn't hurt to experiment.

As I mentioned earlier, I started listening to people who said it was possible to turn my dreams into reality. I started listening to accomplished futurists and thought leaders. And slowly, bit by bit, I started believing that it was ok to dream big. Taking my purpose to the next, next level felt expansive.

Here is my formula, which I learned somewhere along the way: Set an intention, take inspired action, and receive!

The goals I stated with dates and details, I achieved with ease. Of the items I stated generally, some I still achieved and even better than I could ever imagine. A few of them never came to fruition. Looking back, I can say it's because I missed a step in my formula. But after all, we only receive what's for our highest good. So, if a mansion in Paris, London, NYC, and San Francisco with staff and a private jet to get me from place to place is not for my highest good, it may not happen. But don't worry, I hadn't given myself permission to dream that luxuriously back then, so it wasn't on my vision board. I'll put it on my next vision board with dates and details and keep you posted!

In all seriousness, my sacred mantra, the messages I write to myself on my mirror, the conscious self-talk that occurs all day long in my head, the people in my life, my values, and so much more have allowed me to be here with you today. I'm grateful to everyone who has helped me get to where I am today, and I'm grateful to everyone who will help me get to my tomorrow.

As for you, take inventory of all the Auto Suggestion happening in your life. Set your intention. Take inspired action. And be open to receiving all that is for your highest good.

Swaminarayan.

# NITA PATEL

**About Nita Patel:** Nita is a Best-Selling Author, speaker, and artist who believes in modern etiquette as a path to becoming our best selves.

Through her professional years, Ms. Patel has 25 years of demonstrated technology leadership experience in various industries specifically with a concentrated focus in health care for 14 of those 20+ years. She's shown her art across the world to include the Louvre in Paris. She's a best-selling author and performance coach, pursuing her master's in industrial organizational (I-O) psychology at Harvard. Her investment in psychology theory and practice is what led her to a deep interest in helping others. She has become deeply and passionately devoted to nurturing others and in building their confidence and brand through speaking and consultative practices.

Author's website: *www.Nita-Patel.com*
Book Series Website & Author's Bio: *www.The13StepsToRiches.com*

*Olga Geidane*

# BE CAREFUL WHAT YOU THINK ABOUT!

You have been using Auto Suggestions since you were little!

Your brain loves repetition! It learns best through repeating things. The only problem is, your brain cannot distinguish negative from positive thoughts, as they are not visible! You can't touch or smell them; they come and go without being noticed. And whether you use negative or positive Auto Suggestion, your brain doesn't care. It's YOUR job to recognize what is going on in your mind and make that change.

Here is a paradox about Auto Suggestions: despite using them on a daily basis, some people still don't believe in them. To them, Auto Suggestions are something wishy-washy and not important. However, EVERYONE is successfully using Auto Suggestions, but sadly, in a very self-destructive way.

These are some of the phrases you might use at some point during the day:

- I am always late!
- I am not good at…
- I never manage to do things on time.

- I am often last minute!
- I suck at dating/relationships.
- I am not good with money.
- I often lose things.
- I constantly break things.
- I am not a good driver.
- I am terrible with…
- I always attract some idiots.
- I am never lucky.
- All women are…
- All men are…

Have you recognized yourself saying one or a few of those phrases? Way too often, people repeat the same message to themselves again and again, without realizing that they are making their story stronger every time they say those words.

Auto Suggestions can be positive and can be negative, and the trickiest part about it is to recognize and replace the limiting and self-disruptive messages with empowering and supportive ones. Let's admit that often, some of the phrases we use are just statements of reality and that is ok. Let's just agree that the old reality doesn't have to be your future. Here are some of the examples of how self-disruptive Auto Suggestions can be replaced:

I am always late! > I am getting better at being on time! I am not good at…> I am good at these...

I never manage to do things on time. > I am getting better at meeting deadlines and being on time.

I am often last minute! > I do things in time.

I suck at dating/relationships. > I am learning about myself and relationships. I am not good with money. > I am getting better at managing money

I constantly break things. > I am careful when I move around. I am not a good driver. > I am becoming a much better driver. I am terrible at…> I am improving at…

I always attract some idiots. > I am vibrating at a higher frequency and attracting high-quality people from now on.

I am never lucky. > I am one in a million and I am lucky.

All women are… > whatever your negative story about women is, just replace it with an opposite new belief.

All men are… > identically the same applies here.

When I work with my clients, discovering and replacing their Auto Suggestions is a crucial part of the coaching journey. Often, people think that coaching is about getting help with goals and accountability and the truth is, most inexperienced coaches do exactly that: focusing their client attention only on the end result. Look at it this way: if the progress of the client would depend only on knowing what they want, they would have gotten there without the coach.

The mastery of coaching is to help the client to discover what stopped them BEFORE and ensuring that there is a new paradigm, new Auto Suggestions, story, and beliefs built around their aim, so it is sustainable and achievable.

Can you discover the old Auto Suggestions that stopped you from getting where you wanted to be? Of course you can, just get ready to pay really close attention to what you say and how you feel as a result. Here are a few tips to help you on this journey:

1. Ask your friends and people close to you to point out to you when you repeatedly say some phrases that are negative or self-limiting. Surely we can't expect them to be specialists in this, but it will help you.

2. Whenever you discover a negative Auto Suggestion, make sure you write it down. Ideally, cross it away and rewrite a new, supportive Auto Suggestion. Reread what you wrote and ask yourself, "If that was someone else's message to themselves, is it strong and powerful enough? Is it positive and inspirational?"

   People struggle with finding new Auto Suggestions. Please do not worry, this is a very typical reaction. You spent decades repeating the same phrase again and again, so of course, subconsciously it will be challenging in the beginning to replace the old story. My suggestion is to start with the strongest word in the sentence and find the opposite word to that. You might even use the help of the internet; just type "the opposite word to_____ " or "antonym of _____" in Google or any other search engines. Read through suggested words and pick the one that "speaks to you most." The reason I mention this is because I have seen my clients struggling with replacing their old programming because the subconscious was blocking them from changes. And sometimes I would throw some suggestions in the air just to get my clients started, but it is extremely important for you to find your own words.

3. Make a few sticky-notes and place them where you will see often: on the mirror in the bathroom, at your desk, on the fridge, and anywhere else you wish. In addition to the written statements, be

creative at helping yourself to memorize the new Auto Suggestions. Use the reminders in your calendar, create a screensaver or a poster on canvas.com, record yourself saying them, and listen when you exercise or sleep, etc.

4. Use the most sensitive time of the day for placing these new Auto Suggestions into your subconscious; that is in the morning, once you wake up, and in the evening, just before you go to sleep. While you will repeat those, make sure you also include feelings and emotions.

5. This is optional but very powerful: include positive and uplifting feelings and emotions into your new Auto Suggestions. Why? Because the more you feel, the more your subconscious believes that it is real and it will start helping you to get there. I am sure you have heard the phrase "fake it until you make it," so here I would like to suggest this: "cheat your mind until it believes that".

While the world was going through COVID-19 lockdowns and panic, I was travelling and exploring the Canary Islands in Spain. This is where I met Manel back in December 2020. Since both of us were free to travel anywhere and we got along really well, we spent a lot of time together. The day before Manel left to return to Brussels as his holiday was coming to the end, we were dancing in the room to some bachata music on YouTube. I clearly remember how tightly he was holding me and how much joy I had, as I hadn't danced for ages because of the situation we all were going through in the world. At one point, I started telling myself, "This is how I am going to feel when I dance with my husband." While we were dancing, I was visualizing dancing with my husband. It was so magical, it was so joyous, it felt so good that words can't describe that. As I kept repeating that through the dancing, I felt a much stronger connection with Manel, despite that we had only met two weeks ago and at the time, there were no feelings involved. But I truly felt like it was a dance with my husband. Of course, I didn't tell anything to Manel. I knew he was leaving the next day and I would continue to explore the Canary Islands so most likely, that will be it. We all know that travel romances can grow into something bigger, but let's face the reality— it's not an every-day story.

On the 27th of August 2021, we got married in a small church in Canillo, Andorra. It was a private ceremony with just us, witnesses, and a priest with a photographer. We wanted that day to be our day.

Did I see that coming at the time of repeating to myself, "This is how I am going to feel when I dance with my husband?"

NO!

But the feelings you have always attract the events you desire. Law of attraction works in exactly the same way as gravity: you can't see, smell or touch it, but it's there. You trust gravity, you respect it and don't abuse, you just have faith in it. Just trust the gravity of attraction.

What are YOU choosing to repeat to yourself, knowing that IT WILL HAPPEN?

# OLGA GEIDANE

**About Olga Geidane:** Olga is an International Speaker, an Event MC/Host, Facilitator, Mindset Coach, a Best-Selling Author, and a Regional President of the Professional Speaking Association in the UK. She is a host of Olga's Show and A World-Traveler.

Olga helps ambitious people to unlock their extraordinary performance and their true, authentic side. She is passionate about helping people to live their best lives. Olga knows how tough it is to be broke and unfulfilled in life: at the age of 24, just after her divorce, Olga came to the UK from Latvia with no spoken English, with just £100 in her pocket and a 2.5-year-old son. Olga is a very inspirational survivor: she went through abuse, betrayal, cheating, financial loss and emotional breakdown. Matt Black (Business Model Innovation & Disruption Consultant - Snr. Advisor to CEO CSO CCO COO - Author & International Public Speaker) said: "Olga really takes it up a notch beyond anything I have seen before. She is one of the bravest people I have ever seen on stage. If you are looking to book a speaker or attend a talk that will be inspiring, challenging and leave you wanting to take action... She is perfect."

Author's Website: *www.OlgaGeidane.com*
Book Series Website & Author's Bio: *www.The13StepstoRiches.com*

## *Paul Andrés*

# HACK YOUR HABITS

I found myself paralyzed, as my thoughts raced feverishly in my head, while nothing but stillness was seen outside. Sitting in my car, engulfed by the darkness of night, I stared blankly in front of me. No sound could be uttered. No muscle could be moved. Just a blank stare, racing thoughts, and darkness. As what seemed like an eternity passed me by, it was only when my thoughts began to overflow in my mind and cascaded against my now moistened cheeks, that I found myself coming up from the fog and making sense of the talk going on in my head. "You are such an idiot!" "No one will ever care about you as much as you care about them." "You should keep your mouth shut and stop asking questions." "It's your fault this happened." "You deserve this."

This dialogue went on and on. I berated myself for an hour in that car, after learning that my latest romantic interest had cheated on me again. But the truth was, I had been berating myself for something or another since before I could even remember. I had adopted the idea that love and sex were transactions, and somehow believed, "I was of less value than most." So I had to try harder, offer more, and be better than anyone else. Because if not, I would be lied to, completely mistreated, cheated on, and discarded. I was twenty-one years old. Abruptly single, and left with only a bag of clothes and my car to my name. How did I let this happen? Oh, that's right! I deserved it.

I wish I could say that everything changed that night. That I had learned from my past and moved forward in a triumphant transformation. But sadly, that was not my path. Instead, I spent the next few years truly diving into what it means to be human. How we are who we are. What we do to become that. And what power we have to shape who it is we truly want to become. What I learned was all our power begins and ends in our minds. The foundation of what we are and who we will become all starts with our self-talk. The way to be aware and control our self-talk is through the power of Auto Suggestion. I spent years reading stories of how people changed their lives simply by changing the way they spoke to themselves, using Auto Suggestion. Self-esteem was created from nothing, love that was lost was found, and rags-to-riches stories were no longer just fairytales. All of this was possible through being aware and choosing the way we talk to ourselves. It was one of the biggest aha's of my life.

Napoleon Hill said it best, "The law of auto-suggestion, through which any person may rise to altitudes of achievement which stagger the imagination, is well described in the following verse: "If you think you are beaten, you are, If you think you dare not, you don't. If you like to win, but you think you can't, it is almost certain you won't. If you think you'll lose, you're lost. For out of the world we find, success begins with a fellow's will—It's all in the state of mind. If you think you are outclassed, you are. You've got to think high to rise, You've got to be sure of yourself before you can ever win a prize. Life's battles don't always go to the stronger or faster man, but sooner or later, the man who wins is the man WHO THINKS HE CAN!"

For years, I had told myself that I was less than. That I deserved every bad thing that came my way. That it was always my fault. That I owed someone something for any affection given. That love was a transaction and my worth was too low to ever purchase the unconditional kind. All of this was a blow so big I nearly knocked myself out. But after the rubble settled, I realized that knowing this was actually powerful. This meant that if I could say these things to myself and create so much negativity within my life, then the opposite should also be true. It has to be possible for me to switch up the words from negative to positive and see positivity sprout up in my life as well.

And slowly but surely, just that happened. I began to believe in myself and my abilities. I secured my dream apartment, landed my dream job, and began dating someone who truly loved me. Using five easy steps, I truly changed my life and do the same with my clients today. There's nothing as satisfying as taking control of your life; watching all the negative, heartbreak and hurt melt away, as all the positive possibilities and purposeful future begins to bloom.

### My 5 Steps

*Get Verbally Woke*

Spend thirty consecutive days, becoming fully aware of your own self-talk. Notice all of your negative self-talk, and don't be ashamed or embarrassed by how often the negative creeps in. I promise, we all seem to be drowning in the negative when we first become aware.

*CANCEL! CANCEL!*

The first step in any transformational process is to first acknowledge the negative behavior, but what happens after you shine a light on the ugly negatives in your mind? Get rid of it! Clear the internal screen.

Step two in the process is simple. Whenever negative self-talk is noticed, immediately follow it up internally or externally, whichever you feel comfortable with or situation allows, with the words "Cancel! Cancel!" By canceling the negative self-talk immediately, you are directly teaching your mind to become more aware of what you don't want and ingraining the ability to cancel out the negative internally.

*Words of Affirmations*

After noticing your negative self-talk and canceling it from your mind, it is key to replace those thoughts with positive dialogue. Using positive words of affirmation to replace the negative self-talk is a key step in the transformational practice of Auto Suggestion. If our mind listens to exactly the words that we choose to talk to ourselves, then being intentional and specific with positive words that affirm us, our intentions, and our desired outcomes is everything.

*What You See is What You Get*

When it comes to the brain, words are powerful. But to truly have complete buy-in, what we imagine must match the story we are telling ourselves. To completely cancel out the negative self-talk and create real change that affects our lives, we must say it and see it, to believe it. Creating images that match the words of affirmation we use to replace the negative self-talk is exactly the one-two punch we need to create true chance in our lives. When you tell yourself something is, and you can see yourself in that exact scenario where that is true, your mind will begin to do everything in its power to make that a reality. This is that little bit of fairy dust to help Auto Suggestion fly and create true change in your life.

*Rinse & Repeat*

Repeating and implementing the three previous steps into your daily practice of living is sure create a positive change in anyone's life. Just look at mine! But like with every new habit, the transformation practice of using Auto Suggestion to positively impact your life will take time. So be patient, be intentional, and be positive. Make Auto Suggestion a constant in your everyday life. Reclaim your power and stop letting life happen to you. Start designing the life you deserve and remember, practice always makes perfect.

Complete Process. Notice the negative self-talk and CANCEL it! When you hear your internal dialogue creep into fear, doubt, hurt, and self-loathing, immediately fire back, "CANCEL, CANCEL!" And instead reframe those thoughts using positive words of encouragement, support, and love.

Example: *"Of course I messed that up. I'm an idiot!"*

CANCEL! CANCEL!

*"I'm human, and I am growing and learning every day. Every day, I am better and better."*

# PAUL ANDRÉS

**About Paul Andrés:** Paul is an award-winning conscious entrepreneur, visual storyteller, and intuitive coach. From digital and interior design, to business clarity and personal growth coaching, to social justice advocacy and volunteering, Andrés is proof that aligning your passions with your purpose is the true magic to success. He currently devotes his time to helping awakened entrepreneurs and heart-centered creatives design the life they deserve through personal and professional coaching and consulting, as well as shedding light on uncomfortable topics that bring awareness to the social justice issues of today as the host of his video podcast, In Your Mind. Andrés is also a two-time #1 best-selling author. You can catch him as a featured guest speaker at events across the country.

"Home is so many things, but ultimately, it's where life happens. It's where we sleep and grow a family, it's where we play and grow professionally, and it's where we learn and grow within. Each home plays a key role in helping us design a whole life—the life we all deserve." — Paul Andrés

Author's Website: *www.PaulAndres.com*
Purchase Book Online: *www.The13StepstoRiches.com*

## Paul Capozio

# LEARNING TO DESIGN THE LIFE I DESERVED

I'm excited to share my thoughts with you in this exciting chapter, mostly because this topic can be somewhat enigmatic and downright metaphysical. We do not even remotely comprehend the power of the human mind and we can do so much with it already. Even you have limited belief in things like the law of attraction, manifestation, or thinking yourself well, it still works. We can get glimpses of proof that this is real if we look for them in our daily lives. Many of my esteemed co-authors in this book series have done a tremendous job in outlining this topic for you, before and after me, so I'm going to go a slightly different route.

Here is the curveball: you need to learn one thing first before you can get this right. Exaggeration is the gateway drug. How powerful is your use of exaggeration, even in its mildest form? Come on, we all do it! Have you ever told a joke or a story in which you feigned anger, happiness, or fear, just for more effect? Have you ever embellished the details of an event? I once caught a fish "THIS BIG!" Each time, the hands of the storyteller get wider and wider.

Are you aware that in exaggeration, many of your limiting beliefs were born? Exaggeration is the true double-edged sword; what have you told yourself to get you where you are. You drop an ice-cream cone and say, "This always happens to me!" But does it, really? Yet, you are telling your subconscious what to know about the frequency of your ice-cream-cone-dropping ratio compared to the rest of the population of the civilized ice-cream-cone-eating world! Guess what? You now have a much greater chance of dropping your very next ice-cream cone. And when you realize this, you are not the only witness to your clumsiness, but the impact of that emotion further increases that probability. You are now an ice-cream-cone-serial killer!

The flip side to this is that the more reinforcement, visualization, and emotion you put to a positive thought and desire, the greater the probability. Don't believe me? How many unemployed teenagers do you know that are walking around with the latest twelve-hundred dollar smart phone because they must have it!

Did you notice I said you are telling you subconscious what to "know" about your dropping ice-cream cones? It's not what to "think" knowing is concrete, effective, and deliberate. The issue is that our brains do it automatically with certain things and not with others. There is not enough space here, nor am I the right person to go into the science and art of this, but there is enough meat on this bone so you can get my meaning.

Your subconscious does not decide good or bad. It eats what you feed it and responds with what you told it you want. Even if that want is a really, really bad day. You will be sabotaging yourself constantly until you get a handle on this process. We have all manifested bad stuff. What do you want? What do you really, really want? Think of your subconscious like a young child; what you say in front of them will most definitely be repeated and usually in front of people you wish did not just hear what they just heard. Your success is being held back by what you told yourself years ago.

When you tell a story with embellishments, it will become ingrained each time you tell it and you will believe it. It becomes part of your personality and belief system. I was reading Jerry Seinfeld's book "Is this *Anything*" and he wrote about his joke writing process. How he crafts it and then refines it over time based on reaction, and then he incorporates it into his act.

We all do that same thing with our subconscious. How about the role of the Joker in the Batman film series? Do you know Jack Nicholson told Heath Ledger to be careful; this role is dangerous to your mind? Nicholson said it was a bad experience for him emotionally. Who truly knows if that role had that type of an impact on Ledger, but it may have added to his negative mental state. Brilliant performance, but would he still be alive if he didn't take it on at that time of his life and be so invested?

### No Honey you're wrong!

Do you know that the vast majority of our memories about events that happened to us are not accurate? Tell a story in front of your family, longtime friends, or your significant other and you're bound to hear things like, "It didn't happen that way" or, "That must have been before we were married, sweetheart, that wasn't me!" These misremembrances affect our whole subconscious processing in incremental movements. I call it indexing or layering. There is no killing a fly with a sledgehammer— here, you need to build this up in layers, peeling away the bad and building up the good.

But for those who can feed the subconscious a steady diet of positive messages and beliefs, fortunes are made. Many of you are experts on the negative side of this equation, you can recognize it when you are in "Woe is me" mode. Good news! That means you're halfway there. This is especially true if you are getting good negative results! Have you told yourself recently that this is going to be a really difficult day and had one? Eureka! You're a pro!

## The Voices in your head are yours!

We have all had a traumatic experience or two in our lives. Maybe a bad car wreck, a fall, or something worse. If that traumatic event resulted in a physical injury, it will stay with us forever, compounded by the injury and the healing process. Were you out of work, paralyzed, or did you lose a loved one? The physical injury heals relatively quickly, but it reinforces the mental injury and results in a part of our calculations in future choices and decision making. In the future, when we dream or think about the event, our brain releases the same chemical cocktail that it did at the time of the event. Our body relives the experience all over again. These are your clues to the power of this process. Did you ever physically cringe at a memory, that of an embarrassing moment? Can you now understand how much power we are talking about here? My job is almost done. I'm trying to make the invisible visible for you to make this concept more relatable, show that you already have it in you, and for many, you need to correct what you are feeding yourself.

## How to hack our bad habits to unlock effective Auto Suggestion.

So you have the power to do this, don't you agree? Good! You cannot half-believe in Auto Suggestion. If you do, you are already doing it incorrectly. Like a great golf swing, knitting, or if you have ever watched a worker on an assembly line, that mesmerizing repetition becomes a ballet of muscle memory. Your brain must develop this ability for positive Auto Suggestion and blocking negative commands. You need to exercise it to where it becomes habit. To do this, use what works for you. It can start as affirmations and visualizations. See the money in your bank account, smell the leather of that chair in the corner office. See yourself ringing the bell on the Nasdaq as you take that crochet-potholder business public. Whatever it is, see it, feel it, and smell it. I'm not a vision board guy (because my mom never let me play with scissors), but they work.

The Ferrari picture on the fridge works because it's positive, unless you're a Lambo person.

The bad thoughts are going to come flying into your mind at this point, so it's going to take a commitment with lots of starts and restarts. When the flying monkeys of bad thoughts come in, just say "Fly, my pretties" and let them find another Dorothy to pester. You need to break those tendencies. I used to keep a rubber band on my wrist. It was actually one of those Lance Armstrong rubber bracelets. I would snap it hard when those thoughts came into mind. I would even honk my car horn to break the negative thought pattern. Not a smart thing to do, I'll say in hindsight. Randomly beeping your horn in the New York City traffic gets people testy! But then again, I'm six foot two inches tall and two-hundred forty-seven pounds, so guide yourself accordingly. My suggestion is go with the rubber band. You will need it to wrap around the wad of cash that will be in your pocket with all your newfound success!

All kidding aside, I strongly urge you to take this chapter seriously. This is one, if not the most important, part of your success plan. Regardless if your success quest is business, relationship, or child-rearing, you need to feed your subconscious in a healthy manner. You can train, role play, and read all the best business books, but nothing will propel you forward like mastering this superpower. The best part is you can already do this somewhat instinctively. Why am I so confident in you? Because I know you are already manifesting what you don't want.

# PAUL CAPOZIO

**About Paul Capozio:** Paul Capozio was born in Hoboken, New Jersey and grew up on the streets of Hudson County. At 35, he was recruited to be the President of Sales and Marketing for a 350-million-dollar human resources firm. In 7 years, he drove the top line revenue of that firm to over 1.5 billion.

Capozio owns and operates Capco Capital, Inc., an investment and consulting firm. The majority of Capco's holdings are of manufacturers and distributors of health and wellness products and human resources firms. Capco provides sales consulting and training, helping companies increase sales through traditional and direct sales disciplines. Making the invisible visible and simplifying the complex is his stock and trade.

A dynamic public speaker, he provides motivation and "meat and potatoes" skills to those in the health and wellness field who do not consider themselves "salespeople," allowing their voices to be heard above the "noise."

He is a husband of 32 years to his wife, Linda. He is also a father and grandfather.

Author's Website: *PaulCapozio.com*
Purchase Book Online: www.*The13StepstoRiches.com*

## Robyn Scott

# WE ALWAYS GET TO CHOOSE!

Auto Suggestion is what I feel we all should strive to have. Auto Suggestion is the benefit and/or outcome of observing one's own thoughts and patterns. Disrupting the auto response we've always acted upon, we have a choice, in every single second, of how to use the information coming into our minds. Over the past week, I have been amongst the most brilliant minds I believe to be in the world right here, right now. In the now is the only reality there is. It may actually exist in milliseconds as I navigate forward trying so hard to break the shackles that seem to elude us as soon as we observe their existence. In this scenario you are changing the auto response to an auto suggestion to maneuver through our subconscious to create true, real, legitimate change from our conscious mind into our subconscious absolutely and positively INTENTIONALLY!!

CAN YOU IMAGINE? How much more power do we posses, then?

This is a perfect example. Horror movies. Yep, that is not a fun thing for me. It never has been. Some of my kids I believe enjoy horror movies so very much. "Wait, what? Mom is terrified of scary movies?? Oh man, those are my favorites now!" I know this has been a conversation more than one of them has had! They find it so hilarious when I literally jump out of my seat! They laugh when I scream, and they giggle when I cover my eyes and plug my ears. I get very scared, to say the least. Now ,I am completely aware that when we entered the movie theater, there was not a masked murderer with a huge knife, or a swarm of killer bees nesting above our heads. We are completely safe. I am aware. That does not matter during the movie. Once the house lights go down and the movie begins, within minutes it feels real to me. The more swept up in it I get, the fear truly starts to build. Nothing has changed in my physical state. Not one thing has been added to my experience except the pictures I am watching up on the screen. I've left the movie theater with sore knuckles from holding on to my arm rest so tightly. I've spilled gallons of drinks and acres of popcorn. I have bruised my shins on the chairs in front of me. I get swept up in the illusion, the "picture," the story, and the music is always an enormous part of the scare. I learned long ago that it is not enough to just cover my eyes. I put my thumbs in my ears, my fingers slightly open in front of my face and have total control of what I want to experience in this situation. I can listen and see the scary. I can choose to just listen to the movie. I can listen and peek through just one of my fingers, or not listen and choose to peek. In all the scenarios, I have every option open to do what I choose. I tell my husband it is such a waste of time and money. He loves seeing me get scared and I must enjoy it because I keep going. My mind reacts to what is happening regardless of what I do. I can observe the reaction and feelings and as soon as I am in my "observer's chair" (thank you so much Dave Blanchard!). I have control!

We all get to CHOOSE our next move. In every second, of every day, we get to choose what happens next. We can choose the easy way. Even though that has not served you for years, most likely, or we can STOP, OBSERVE, and CHOOSE. One of my favorite lines from Napoleon Hill's *Think and Grow Rich* is, "Skepticism, in connection with ALL new ideas, is characteristic of all human beings. But if you follow the instructions outlined, your skepticism will soon be replaced by belief, and this, in turn, will soon become crystallized into ABSOLUTE FAITH. Then you will have arrived at the point where you may truly say, I am the master of my fate, I am the captain of my soul!" Nothing is easy when you first start doing it. We have all learned though. I was talking with a friend and realized that learning how to walk is the perfect example. When you first learned to walk and you fell down, what did your parents say? "STOP! Stop right there. You fell down, you cannot try that again, it is way too dangerous!" Can you even imagine? Nope, no way. So why is it so different from this principle? Here are my suggestions for Auto Suggestion implementation.

1. Become curious about YOU! Who are you really? What do you want? Why do you desire it?

2. Activate your imagination through visualization. Get quiet and still, and let your mind wonder, not wander, focusing on the desire. Have fun and enjoy the possibilities.

3. Commit to practice morning and evening rituals. Humans crave routine, gosh darn it! I am still practicing this one. I know it is super-duper important though!

4. Intend for the best, and be flexible with the rest. Roll with the punches. They will always be there. You got this, though. Be adaptable, coachable, and humble.

5. Be where you aspire to be, with people who model success to YOU. Surround yourself with successful positive people. You will learn so much by watching those we aspire to be like.

6. Double-down on your reaffirmations during vulnerable times. It is way too easy to slip back into old patterns and programs. If you observe yourself doing it, give yourself grace (unless it's the umpteenth time you slip back (that's another principle).

7. Experience your Auto Suggestion statements. Adding epic music and even an essential oil or scent can deepen the emotion behind

your statements. While envisioning them in your mind, having pictures or even money to hold will strengthen and deepen the subconscious connection.

8. Release control and have unwavering faith that all you desire is working for you. Let it go and keep moving forward! I only have to suggest you are listening to a song by a girl with long white hair who can use her powers to make ice and snow. I won't tell anyone else you are singing it in your head.

"It's impossible for a man to learn what he thinks he already knows."
-Epictetus

As aware beings, we know we are the only ones who can make ourselves do anything. Knowing this is crucial to the Auto Suggestion principle. Instead of rolling your eyes at your husband for the sixth time you have heard that joke, look at him and give him a genuine smile. (Yes, I am talking to myself on this one). Instead of losing your cool in the car because someone cuts you off, send some love and prayers for safety for all on the road. The next time you start to believe you are not worth it, immediately shut that one down and know that you deserve EVERYTHING!

You can keep reading that one until it sticks, ok?

"Your ability to use the principle of Auto Suggestion will depend, very largely, upon your capacity to concentrate upon a given desire until that desire becomes a burning obsession." -Napoleon Hill

# ROBYN SCOTT

**About Robyn Scott:** Robyn is the Chief Relationship Officer for Champion Circle. She manages the prospecting program for Divinely Driven Results. Scott is a Habit Finder Coach and has worked closely with the president, Paul Blanchard, at the Og Mandino Group. She is also a certified Master Your Emotions Coach, through Inscape World. Scott is commonly known in professional communities as the Queen of Connection and Princess of Play. She has been working hard for the past 9 years to hone her skills as a mentor and coach.

Scott strives to teach people to annihilate judgements, embrace their own stories, and empower themselves to rediscover who they truly are. Scott is an international speaker and also teaches how to present yourself on stage.

Her first book, *Bringing People Together: Rediscovering the Lost Art of Face-to-Face Connecting, Collaborating, and Creating* was released in August of 2019 and was a bestseller in seven categories.

Author's website: *www.MyChampionCircle.com/Robyn-Scott*
Book Series Website & Author's Bio: *www.The13StepsToRiches.com*

## Shannon Whittington

# YOU HAVE TO BELIEVE IT

As professionals, many of us have been conditioned to see achieving personal success as something completely "serious." We view ambition as an arena that's "business-only," with no room for anything childlike, spontaneous, or whimsical. Maybe we were shamed by a parent or a teacher who told us we needed to "grow up," or life dealt us so many obstacles that we became jaded. Regardless, we're left with the idea that in order to be successful, you have to be in "super-serious grind mode" twenty-four seven, but what if I told you that the secret to your success actually lies within embracing your innermost child and playing a game inside your own mind?

Auto Suggestion, or the medium for influencing the subconscious mind, might be my favorite item in my success toolbox. Instead of relying on things like intense analysis, hard logic and crunching numbers (as important as those actions may be), Auto Suggestion gives you the chance to manifest your goals by using the power of your imagination. The mind is a fertile playground where you can achieve anything or become anyone. The more you visit that mental playground, the more your thoughts become actions, which lead to making your dreams come true.

How do you use Auto Suggestion to your benefit? Here are a few tips that work for me, and I'm confident that if you give yourself permission to have fun a little bit every day, they'll work wonders for you, too.

## "I AM"

When it comes to achieving your goals, the single most important phrase you can ever use is "I am." What is it you want to be? Tell yourself, silently or out loud (though I recommend doing both), "I am a published author / a CEO / a partner to an amazing person / whatever it is you want to be." If you repeat this simple phrase enough, even if the logical part of your mind knows you haven't achieved your goal yet, your subconscious won't recognize the difference. You'll start thinking, speaking, and acting as if you already are who and where you want to be, and eventually, with enough determination and hard work, it will come into fruition.

As a personal example, I want to be a full-time public speaker with an eight-figure income. So, every day when I wake up, when I take my dog on a walk, and right before I go to bed at night, I say phrases to myself such as, "I am a speaker...I speak full-time...I make eight figures a year speaking to people and inspiring them." Even though I'm currently a nurse and a student, whenever somebody asks me what I do for a living, the first thing I tell them is that I'm a speaker, because that's what I want to manifest as reality.

Do you want to be out of debt? Repeat to yourself, "I am financially free." Do you want to write a successful book? Say, "I am a published author" before you even get out of bed. Do you want to make it as an actor, a businessperson, or a medical professional? Say, "I am [insert dream job here]" when you're at the grocery store or getting your mail. By repeating this simple phrase, as silly or awkward as it might feel at first, you are already on your way to becoming who you're destined to be.

### Visualize It

In conjunction with using the "I am" repetition, it's important to also use the theater of your mind to actively visualize who and where you want to be. Before I drift off to sleep, for instance, I imagine myself on stage alongside all my favorite public speakers, the ones who have inspired and motivated me for decades. But not only am I sitting among them; I belong on that stage with them. I am without a shred of doubt, on their level.

But I take it a step further. I also visualize what the stage looks like, how big the audience is, what I'm wearing that night, and the feeling of being clipped with my mic before it's my turn to speak. I visualize delivering a pitch-perfect performance, using my words and my story to impact and inspire everyone in that room to transform their lives in the best way possible. I visualize being complimented by each one of my speaking colleagues, some of who even invite me to speak at high-profile events they're hosting. And as I play this visualization in my mind, I go to sleep happy, excited and full of optimism, with an influenced subconscious turning its gears to make this dream come true.

## Be patient

As powerful as Auto Suggestion may be, it isn't a "get rich quick" scheme. It's a practice that takes time to properly cultivate and use in conjunction with the many other tools needed to achieve success. To make your fantasy a reality, you must also be grounded enough to know that it will happen when it's meant to.

This, unfortunately, also means you will face rejection. In fact, I'd even go as far as saying you will never experience true success or happiness without a healthy amount of rejection and hardship, first. Are you looking for a fulfilling relationship on a dating site? Be prepared for a lot of potential suitors to "swipe left" (and for many you don't want to "swipe right"). Do you want to be a successful author? Know that your manuscripts will end up in plenty of publishers' recycling bins. Want to be financially free? Expect the unexpected to happen as you slowly chisel away at your debt.

I don't intend to say all of this as a pessimist. In fact, when I get rejected for speaking opportunities, I do not see it as the universe telling me "no," but as it steering me in the direction and at the pace I'm supposed to go. Think about it like this: When you're waiting in line at the post office, and the customer three spots ahead gets to be served before you do, do you consider that "rejection" by the postal worker? Of course not. It simply isn't your time yet. If you apply that same mindset to not getting the job you want or the chance to go out with the person you've been crushing on, you do yourself no favors by taking it personally. The universe is still in your favor, even while you're "waiting in line."

**You have to believe it**

You've now got your key "I am…" phrases, you're projecting your dreams front-and-center in your mind, and you're aware that you'll receive a healthy amount of rejection before you get what you want. What's left? Simply put—believing. I don't just mean believing that your dreams will come true, as important as that mindset is, but also that you are worthy of the journey of achieving anything and everything you want. You have to feel it in your bones, to know that deep down you are who you want to be, and that no matter how many times you've been told "no" or how long the process takes, that you are destined to achieve your desires.

So many of us have been conditioned to doubt ourselves. Throughout our lives, people have told us that we should keep our dreams narrow, that we should make pleasing others a priority, and that doing anything for ourselves to cultivate joy and fulfillment is selfish and reckless. When we're fed negative ideas like this for long enough, we're destined to believe them, and instead of manifesting our dreams, we manifest darkness and uncertainty. We spend our days pushing against a brick wall thinking it's going to tumble down, fueled by the voices of others who thought so little of us.

By harnessing the power of belief in yourself, in your worth, in your ability to chase your dreams and become who you want to be, you will turn the volume down on those voices until they're practically, if not completely, inaudible. Those negative voices stem from those who didn't believe in themselves and only know how to exist by making others doubt their own power, but the powerful, almost terrifying, truth is that you are an embodiment of endless potential, and you must believe it.

I have manifested so many things in my life by ignoring the negativity and cruel criticism of others who were so full of self-doubt, by remembering what it was like to be a child. When someone felt the need to tell me everything I'm not or never would be, I escaped to the playground of my mind and said, "I am…" When they said I needed to "be more logical," I visualized my wildest dreams all the more. When I kept getting slapped with rejection for opportunities, with cruel behavior from small-minded people, I remained faithful to my very core that the universe had my back. Against every odd, I believed. And I achieved. And by giving yourself permission to play once in a while, you will too.

# SHANNON WHITTINGTON

**About Shannon Whittington:** Shannon (she/her) is a speaker, author, consultant, and clinical nurse educator. Her area of expertise is LGBTQ+ inclusion in the workplace. Whittington has a passion for transgender health where she educates clinicians in how to care for transgender individuals after undergoing gender-affirming surgeries.

Whittington was honored to receive the Quality and Innovation Award from the Home Care Association of New York for her work with the transgender population. She was recently awarded the Notable LGBTQ+ Leaders & Executives award by Crain's New York Business, as well as the International Association of Professionals Nurse of the Year award. Whittington is a city and state lobbyist for transgender equality.

To date, Whittington has presented virtually and in person at various organizations and conferences across the nation, delivering extremely well-received presentations. Her forthcoming books include *LGBTQ+: ABC's For Grownups* and *Kindergarten for Leaders: 9 Essential Tips For Grownup Success.*

Author's Website: *www.linkedin.com/in/shannonwhittington and on YouTube at ShannonWhittingtonConsulting-for 101 LGBTQ videos*
Book Series Website & Author's Bio: *www.The13StepsToRiches.com*

## *Soraiya Vasanji*

# ALIGNMENT

An Arabic word we use often in our home growing up is "Naseeb", which means fate or destiny. If it is in "your cards" dealt by the Universe or God, then it shall happen. In other words, "it shall be so." Repeating this in my mind or hearing it said by my family, especially my mom, always comforted me because at some point, my subconscious or inner core truly believed that when we work hard, play hard, and leave it in God's hands, what we are meant to receive shall be so. We don't know why something happens or why something doesn't happen, but instead of feeling stuck about "the why," it helps me to focus on seeing what is positive and what I have gained in the process, even if I wasn't expecting it. This was certainly the case when we lost our twin daughters, but if I never had that experience, I would not be able to be the empowerment coach that I am today: supporting women on their journey of creating the family portrait they have etched on their hearts. While we are going through something, it is challenging to see the gifts; but leaning in on this theme has allowed me to see that everything that happens in our lives is for us or is happening through us for others. It was the first time that I realized everything had set up around me systematically and was flowing through me—true alignment. In this context, life's equation of abundance is not only about fate. We get to support and encourage or manifest what comes up in our lives by our daily actions. The way to influence how we show up in life and to move us in the direction of our dreams is to influence our thoughts and actions by self-suggestion on a subconscious level.

Language is powerful. The words we say out loud and the words we have on repeat in our minds influence our conscious, subconscious and unconscious choices, and ways of being or personality patterns. There was a period in my life when I was my own worst critic. The voice in my head was mean and negative, and slowly started chipping away at my confidence. Often, in my workshops, I would share with others how my inner voice was so mean that she earned the infamous title of President of the Mean Girls Club. Our words are like water flowing over rocks and, over time, they create deep grooves in the rocks. These rocks are our thoughts and beliefs, and these words get so ingrained in us that the beliefs are chiseled into us. It takes creating new pathways of understanding, with new words, to shift out of the old ingrained patterns of thinking. Leaning into my faith, biopsychology/neuroscience background, and leadership development programs, I began to unhook and rewire my words and thoughts, and largely began utilizing the power of language in my favor. Here again, my subconscious has supported this new alignment and reinforced how I speak to myself. By using affirmations and truly repeating and believing that each one of us deserves to be on our side and our own best friend, I have changed the voice to positive (or at least silent)! It is a process and one that I now feel truly aligned with as myself. We have the power to build ourselves up, knock ourselves down, and rebuild or reinvent at any time. The power of our words and utilizing both the conscious behaviors and subconscious powers of the mind allows us to achieve anything and become anyone we desire. It is within you!

How does it all come together? Auto Suggestion or self-influence works with our conscience to manifest what we truly desire in our hearts. Many times, fears and scarcity thinking hold us back and get in the way of how we show up in life, and that creates limits around us. Truly tapping in and believing with every fiber in your body that something is going to happen for you works when we are actively working on it, as well as when we are idle or on sleep mode, if you will. Pulling this as a metaphor of a mobile phone, in the background, data is being sent and received, messages are being uploaded and downloaded, sent, filed, and archived. Similarly, our brain is moving information, storing, downloading, filing, and filtering, and when our subconscious works on our behalf we are creating alignment with our dreams and pinging the universe to support it happening. For instance, repeating "just show up" allows me to move from inaction to action. Taking the pressure off and just choosing in. It has allowed me to have confidence when I am not feeling my personal best. This was the case when I attended a grief-counseling workshop and wasn't sure what would happen. I took the pressure off by influencing myself to just go and see how it would be. The importance of using these types of words is that I already on some level knew that everything would be okay, and it quieted the internal self-preserving monologue to stay home and be safe. The gifts I received and also shared allowed others and myself to heal. Without using the repetitive reframe of Auto Suggestion, it may have been more challenging to break the guarded environment of home and attend the workshop.

The power of affirmations, mindfully practicing gratefulness, breath work, and embodiment work can all support planting new seeds in our mind that work on the conscious and subconscious level. Have you ever wanted something really badly? Have you ever had a huge goal that you thought was unattainable? In these moments, it is imperative to find alignment and trust in ourselves that it is happening, it has happened, and it is so. Think about how you act when you think you don't have or can't access what you want? Now, think about how you act when you think you do have what you desire? When we come from this latter place, that one-hundred percent is possible and that is it coming in some shape or form, we start to signal all levels of our consciousness that reinforce how we behave, how we think, and how we show up in life. This is manifesting and Auto Suggestion aligned to bring out what we desire most.

One of my desires was to be successful and contribute in a positive, powerful way to uplift and impact happiness, education, and ultimate joy in society. Another desire was finding my soulmate. Growing up, I knew all the traits I was looking for in a partner. I kept telling myself that when I find the person I will know. I will just know! I don't know exactly how I will know, but I will know and leap with all my heart. My husband, Nadim, laughs at this because I tell him I knew from the moment I met him, that he was my better half. I tease him and say, "I saw your forehead, and I knew you were my partner for life; my prince to the charmed life we will create together." It may seem cheesy, but I can tell you that there was considerable clarity, confidence, and alignment of knowing that happened leading up to this point. I manifested this opportunity to meet my soulmate, in what I believe was early on in life during my freshman year of college. Embracing the princess storyline, I had declared that I would find my prince early in life and he would be wicked smart, kind, loving, generous, and handsome. However, I didn't just say this flippantly or think about it occasionally. Just as I called forward my success and worked hard at gaining knowledge and using my skills to rank up in life, I was daring the universe and crafting my thoughts as though I had already met him. It was playing in the unconscious, subconscious, and conscious even before I knew that this is what was happening at the time. Thinking about the declaration and calling it forward so that the choices I made with studying hard, writing my college applications, choosing my school, going to school, putting myself out there, all were parts of my journey that laid my path across Nadim's path one fine day. When I saw him, alarm bells rang out, my heart skipped a few beats, and I knew—I just knew. Looking back, I believed it was possible.

I believed it was part of my Naseeb and therefore, I was just doing my part to draw it forward and draw it out. This is the power of influencing our thoughts and decisions. Some may think it is "woo woo," and in my experience, a little woo never hurts when really all it is, is alignment.

# SORAIYA VASANJI

**About Soraiya Vasanji:** Soraiya Vasanji is a Certified Professional Coach (CPC), Energy Leadership Index Master Practitioner (ELI-MP) and has a Master's in Business Administration (MBA) from Kellogg University. She inspires women to be present, not perfect, ditch what doesn't serve them and create their best messy life now. She loves sharing her wisdom on mindset, the power of language, self-love, self-worth, and leadership principles. She is the founder of the Mommy Mindset Summit series where she interviews experts on topics that interest moms so they can create a life of authenticity, abundance and joy and show their kids how to have it all too. Soraiya currently offers professional coaching services to women on their journey of creating the family they envision.

Soraiya is married to her soulmate, has a four-year-old daughter, and lives in Toronto, Canada. She is a foodie, a jet-setter, and loves collecting unique crafting and stationery products!

Author's Website: *www.SoraiyaVasanji.com*
Book Series Website & Author's Bio: *www.The13StepstoRiches.com*

### Stacey Ross Cohen

# AFFIRMING YOUR REALITY

*"Use your mind to create the circumstances you want created."*
—Napoleon Hill, *"Think and Grow Rich"*

Napoleon *Hill* emphasizes that mindset is a formula for success. But how do you cultivate the right mindset? The answer is Auto Suggestion—your secret ingredient to a happier, more productive life.

## What is Auto Suggestion?

In its simplest form, Auto Suggestion is a form of self-hypnosis where we use a cue or prompt to shift our thoughts and behavior. It's based on the premise that our thoughts influence our subconscious mind. After all, our thoughts shape our reality, and can be our biggest ally or obstacle. If you feed your mind positive thoughts, it will yield positive results. But the same is true for negative thoughts.

If you thought Auto Suggestion would be as simple as flipping a switch though, think again. It's more like swimming against a current. *Indeed,* we have tens of thousands of thoughts per day, and The National Science Foundation estimates that approximately 80% are negative. But while we can't control our thoughts, we *can* train our minds for success.

I have an aversion to the words "I can't." If you regularly engage with a negative thought like "I can't," chances are you won't succeed. Even *your* body language will show these negative feelings, from your facial expression to your posture. This is why I empower my staff to think like problem solvers, not problem spotters.

Positive thoughts also yield many benefits outside the professional realm, like good health. My mom was given three months to live after suffering a massive heart attack, but blew the doctors away by living another 17 years. Why? Her *positive* attitude. *She* was determined not to be defeated by her illness. One of my closest friends, Susan, is similar. Susan was diagnosed with Stage 3 breast cancer at age 37, and her doctor told her the situation was grave. Her response, *"What are you talking about?"* Now in her late 50s, Susan is healthy and cancer-free.

Even for us positive people, however, negative thoughts still do rear their ugly heads. My own struggles have taught me tried and true *techniques* on how to break the pattern of negative thoughts, which I will share with you in this chapter.

### Make a Conscious Choice

"Where focus goes, energy flows," Tony Robbins famously says. This adage is especially relevant here. It means, "You are the creator of your thoughts. It's your call what you want to direct your attention to. So choose wisely, because what you focus on expands and intensifies."

Those who choose to focus on the bad tend to experience more of it. We all know a "Debbie Downer" who always has new health issues or can't hold down a job. These people often blame external circumstances when the real problem lies within. But when we consciously shift our focus to positive goals and actions, the sky becomes the limit.

When you make the choice to think positively, also make the choice to be kind to yourself. Practicing self-compassion makes the Auto Suggestion process a lot easier. It allows you to enter a "flow state," where one positive thought leads to another.

Once you make the conscious choice to think positively, make a routine of it. A promise is one thing; a regimen is another. Let this be your inspiration: About five years ago, I visited a K-8 independent private school nestled in the Sonoma, CA, wine region for a story I was writing for *Huff Post*. The school abounds with inquisitive students, supportive families, and progressive faculty and staff. Their secret? A commitment to positive thinking at an early age. Each day begins with mindfulness practice. Two minutes for Kindergarten students, building up to 20 minutes by the time students are in the fifth grade. Research indicates that mindfulness, (defined as "a moment-by-moment awareness of our thoughts, feelings, bodily sensations, and surrounding environment" by UC Berkeley's Greater Good Science Center) yields better concentration, reduced anxiety, and heightened social skills. If you're seeking a helping hand with mindfulness, try using meditation apps like Calm and Headspace.

### Embrace Positive Affirmations

As you pursue your commitment to Auto Suggestion, it's important to add affirmations to your toolkit. Affirmations are simple *phrases* that you repeat regularly to internalize and emphasize thoughts, like "I am strong." I personally use affirmations to ace new business opportunities, grow my agency, and empower my team.

But this wasn't always so. Five years after launching my agency, Co-Communications, I was ready to throw in the towel. My daughters were both in elementary school and I had no work-life balance. I was working 75 hours a week. Enter Valerie, a brilliant management consultant I met through a women's business organization, who helped me adopt a different mindset.

On a hot summer day in Stamford, CT, I confided in Valerie that I could no longer handle the stresses of running a business. With her charming British accent, she started to ask me questions about my business, like *"What is your profit margin? What is your overhead?"* I looked at her blankly and told her that I'd need to compile these numbers. She replied, "You are *not* going back to corporate. You excel in marketing. But it is time to shift from an entrepreneur to a business woman."

Valerie offered to coach me on how to scale the business and work smarter. My first homework assignment was to prepare a *spreadsheet* of agency accounts parsed by monthly retainer amount and monthly time investment. This revealed a startling truth. One of the largest agency clients, a national real-estate brokerage, was actually not profitable due to time overages.

Valerie urged me to speak to the client and raise the retainer. But I was apprehensive. Valerie persisted, "Ask for more money or drop the client." So I developed a six-month analysis of my work and followed Valerie's advice. The result? The client totally understood and asked by how much the retainer should be increased.

This moment was the turning point—I became a true business owner. More importantly, I got my life back, boosted my confidence, and developed my first affirmation. That same year, I had a deep yearning to hit the million-dollar mark. So Valerie encouraged me to use the positive affirmation, "I will have a million dollar business by the end of the year." And guess what? It worked! It wasn't magic, of course. The affirmation was accompanied by hard, smart work. But the affirmation helped make that work possible.

If you're seeking an *affirmation* but need inspiration, consider one of these:

- My potential to succeed is limitless
- I am a success in all that I do
- My life is a gift and I'm grateful for everything that I have
- I'm open to new adventures in my life
- My business is growing and thriving
- I am grateful for my family and friends
- My needs and wants are important
- I'm worthy of love
- I am conquering/defeating my illness
- I act with courage and confidence

### Use Visualization

Images tend to be more *powerful* than words, and this holds true in the realm of Auto Suggestion. Napoleon Hill said it best. "If you do not see great riches in your imagination, you will never see them in your bank balance."

Learn how to use visualization, the practice of creating vivid and desirable images in your mind. Indeed, "Seeing is believing" and "visualize to materialize" are more than just motivational phrases; they are proven and effective *psychological* methods backed by science. Just ask the Olympians and professional athletes who use visualization to focus on, and then achieve, victory.

To get started, create a detailed vision board with pictures, words, and quotes. You can also blend visualization with affirmation by writing your affirmations on Post-It notes where you spend a lot of time, like the car or your desk. Another idea are *printed* "affirmation cards" that you can keep in your wallet. My close business colleague uses this. Once, when I was feeling defeated about a new business pitch, he handed me a card that read, "I am successful at whatever I put my mind to."

These are just a few of the tactics you can use to master Auto Suggestion and unlock the power of positive thinking. There are countless others, from regular exercise, to journaling, to listening to more uplifting music. I listen to ambient music and often find that it increases my performance and creativity. No matter what tools you pick, make sure to stay the course. Because with a positive mindset, anything is possible.

# STACEY ROSS COHEN

**About Stacey Ross Cohen:** In the world of branding, few experts possess the savvy and instinct of Stacey. An award-winning brand professional who earned her stripes on Madison Avenue and major television networks before launching her own agency, Stacey specializes in cultivating and amplifying brands.

Stacey is CEO of Co-Communications, a marketing agency headquartered in New York. She coaches businesses and individuals across a range of industries, from real estate to healthcare and education, and expertly positions their narratives in fiercely competitive markets.

A TEDx speaker, Stacey is a sought-after keynote at industry conferences and author in the realm of branding, PR, and marketing. She is a contributor at *Huffington Post* and *Thrive Global*, and has been featured in *Forbes, Entrepreneur, Crain's* and a suite of other media outlets. She holds a B.S. from Syracuse University, MBA from Fordham University and a certificate in Media, Technology and Entertainment from NYU Stern School of Business.

Author's website: *www.StaceyRossCohen.com*
Book Series Website & author's Bio: *www.The13StepsToRiches.com*

*Teresa Cundiff*

# UNWITTINGLY USING AUTO SUGGESTION

As I read Napoleon Hill's chapter on Auto Suggestion, I found myself stumped on where to begin to share with you my thoughts on the subject. I realize that we are only in book three of this incredible series, but you may have already discovered that I am not an author who is going to blow smoke up your skirt. I really began to apply myself to thinking about when I have used the practice of Auto Suggestion in my own life.

There are those occasions when we "speak things into existence" right? When we will say something out loud and then maybe someone in the room will say, "Don't say that out loud, you'll make it happen!" And that's usually meant about something bad. But things like that happen frequently, and we will never know if our speaking about them made them happen or not, but the feeling is still there that our giving voice to a thought in our head made an action occur. Am I right?

The one thing that I know I placed in my subconscious mind that has been true for thirty-two years as of this writing is that I was going to be married one time. Or maybe it was just sheer stubbornness! I talked about this in my chapter in the first volume of this series, Desire, because it was also a deep, burning desire I had to marry once, which of course meant that marrying the right man was the key. I, of course, had several opportunities to marry the wrong man. I can honestly say though, that I had said over and over again that, "I only wanted to be married once, I only wanted to be married once, I only wanted to be married once." That very thought played in my head for years. I was using the principle of Auto Suggestion and had no idea there even was such a thing.

Where are you applying the principle of Auto Suggestion? You might not even know that you are and are just like I was thirty-something years ago. So think about it for a minute. I have devoted more time to thinking about it as well. I have always said I would be a stay-at-home mom, as well. This is more of an action than Auto Suggestion, yet my husband and I made that happen without resorting to eating spaghetti and peanut butter every night.

I faced sexual abuse in the home as a latchkey kid, and there was no way as an adult I wasn't going to be in the home to be the primary caregiver and protector of my children. The result has been two amazing men who are stellar individuals. What a great by-product of a decision made based on such trauma and hurt suffered by me. Auto Suggestion? Maybe. Determination and will? Most definitely!

Napoleon Hill presents these words at the beginning of his chapter on Auto Suggestion, "There are no limitations to the mind except those we acknowledge. Both poverty and riches are the offspring of the mind." It is amazing to me that in 1937, he was talking about such things. These two sentences still are concepts that I struggle to wrap my mind around in 2021. If I'm being totally transparent with you, I have yet to discover and release the total power of my mind on my own business, but I have seen Auto Suggestion work for me, and I want riches to be the offspring of my mind. What about you?

Bring your attention to a heightened awareness of using Auto Suggestion into your everyday life. I feel like it's an incredible power that we all have available to us that we don't tap into! We each have a subconscious that stands at the ready to serve us, but without knowing how to exercise it properly, we have no idea what we are carrying around right inside our heads. I certainly didn't until I read *Think and Grow Rich*.

However, action must accompany the principle of Auto Suggestion. This much, I know is true. Was I going to find my Mr. Right without actively dating men? Of course not! That would be ridiculous, you say! So, while on my quest to only be married once, I was dating, and the time would arrive in the relationship when that voice inside my head would say, "He's not the One!" Most of the breakups were messy because most of the relationships were long. One breakup involved the police.

When I was a senior in high school, I was in a relationship that became abusive. I'll call him Bobby because that will be his name when I write my book about my life. I was in swing choir and honor choir because I have always been a singer. We were returning from a singing engagement at another high school in an adjacent county, and I was getting off the bus with an arm full of costumes and walking toward my car. I saw that Bobby had parked down the row from my car, and I thought he could plainly see that I had my arms full of heavy clothes and that I needed to put them down.

When I got to my car, I opened the driver's door and put the clothes in the back seat, and when I lifted my head out of the car, Bobby grabbed me by the neck and threw me up against the car. Next, he threw me into the driver's seat and shoved me over into the passenger seat. He got into the driver's seat, but my legs were still trapped on the driver's side because of the stick shift (yes, I drove a stick shift like a boss!). By this time, everyone was off the bus and watching the show. My choir director had made it out to my car by then and had caught Bobby's leg in the car door and said, "Bobby, I'll break the g*%damn thing off!"

We ended up sitting in my car talking after all that drama, and he talked me into leaving with him. He left his car there, and we drove off. Unbeknownst to me, some of my dear friends went to my house and told my mom what had happened. She didn't wake up my dad to tell him what happened, she just picked up the phone and called the cops. By the time the police found us, we were back at Bobby's house, and he was down on his knees begging me to forgive him for his behavior.

The situation outside Bobby's house looked really bad because two cops showed up in two separate cars. His parents had answered the door, and they said the police were at the door looking for me. My mom was there, too. The police said, "Miss Landers, we realize you're eighteen and can make decisions for yourself, but your mother was concerned for you, so we are here to see if you want to go or if you want to stay." My answer was, "I'll go." As I walked past him and out the door, Bobby grabbed my hand and said, "Marry me. Please, marry me!" And I said, "Bobby, I can't marry you." And I got in my car and left.

I had been trying to break up with Bobby, but hadn't been able to get away from him. This was my chance to finally end it once and for all. However, he did stalk me for some time after that as my senior year came to a close. He was three years older than me. He committed suicide in 1995. When I spoke to his mother upon learning about his suicide shortly thereafter, (we were living in England at the time), she said, "You know, he always loved you best." I just didn't know what to do with that.

So, there's a story about one of the men I could have married since I keep alluding to it. I was eighteen when all that happened. I would have had no business getting married at that age. I didn't get married until I was twenty-six, which is another reason I attribute to still being married to the same man. Having been in bad relationships, you know a catch when you find one!

There is so much stuff that our minds are constantly bombarded with every second of every day. Safeguard what you let get absorbed by your conscious into your subconscious! Let me encourage you to reinforce in your mind, using Auto Suggestion, the things that are most important to you. There have probably been times in your life when you used Auto Suggestion but didn't even know it. See what a powerful thing it has been in your life? Wonder what else there is? Stay with this series as we explore the rest of the *13 Steps to Riches*!

# TERESA CUNDIFF

**About Teresa Cundiff:** Teresa hosts an interview digital TV show called Teresa Talks on Legrity TV. On the show, she interviews authors who are published and unpublished— and that just means those authors haven't put their books on paper yet. The show provides a platform for authors to have a global reach with their message. Teresa Talks is produced by Wordy Nerds Media Inc., of which Cundiff is the CEO.

Cundiff is also a freelance proofreader with the tagline, "I know where the commas go!," Teresa makes her clients' work shine with her knowledge of grammar, punctuation, and sentence structure.

Teresa is a two-time International Best-Selling Contributing Author of 1 Habit for Entrepreneurial Success and 1 Habit to Thrive in a Post-COVID World. She is also a best-selling contributing author of The Art of Connection; 365 Days of Networking Quotes, which has been placed in the Library of Congress.

Author's Website: *www.TeresaTalksTV.com*
Book Series Website & Author's Bio: *www.The13StepsToRiches.com*

## Vera Thomas

# OUR WORDS AND VISION MATTER

"Thoughts are things,
and we are what we think about everyday"
Words matter
Be careful what words we hear and the words we say.
We can think ourselves into happiness, misery, or pain
With the words we say and the words we claim
The power of choice is in our hands
It does not matter whether others understand
Who we choose to be
All that matters Are the words we say
and what in our mind we see.

The power of Auto Suggestion is REAL! Growing up I heard "You are stupid, dumb, fat, and ugly." "You are nothing, you'll never be anything!" Growing up hearing those words from adults as well as other children, how could I not believe them? As a child, we can only relate to what adults tell us, UNTIL we realize differently. As a result of what I believed as a child and what I was told, during my elementary and high school years I was a mediocre student (high-C low-B average) because I did not believe I could do any better. I excelled in English because my English teacher in the tenth grade believed in me. The belief my teacher had in me was the beginning of my believing I could achieve.

My self-development required I change my thoughts about ME. I learned from what Eleanor Roosevelt said, "No one can make you feel inferior without your consent!"

To change what I believed about me required Auto Suggestions and visualization. It began with me falling asleep at night saying, "I am confident" over and over until I fell asleep. I did this every night for a few months. I wanted to be different from the words I heard others say about me. My confidence began to evolve as I sat and meditated on affirmations, and Auto Suggestions like, "I am wise, confident, and secure." "I can do all things through Christ who strengthens me." "I am healthy, wealthy and wise." "I am loving, kind, and enthusiastic about my life." These were a few suggestions I would repeat over and over in a setting of fifteen to thirty minutes per day.

I was able to graduate Cum Laude from college because of Auto Suggestions and finally believing that I am intelligent and can excel.

I had mentioned earlier in a previous book how I allowed my marriage to derail all the work I had done on myself to be the person I choose to be. I lost all that I had gained within the three years of my mentally, physically, verbally, and emotionally abusive marriage.

I had to start from scratch—all over again. It took three years. This time, I knew I needed to ensure my son never felt the way I did as a child or as a wife. I learned to address his behaviors, and not attack him as a person. He may have done something not meeting my approval; rather than call him stupid or any derogatory statement about him, I would address the behavior, affirm him as a person and discuss the issue and how things could be different. Auto Suggestion became very much a part of his life. As a toddler, I would have him saying affirmations. Throughout his elementary and middle school years, there was an affirmation on my bathroom mirror that I would have him repeat daily. "I am talented, intelligent, and creative."

One thing that becomes obvious, as the Auto Suggestions become an integral part of our being, is that others will see it and often comment on exactly what you have been suggesting for yourself. In middle school, my son sang "I Believe I Can Fly" at a school assembly. During his performance, there were people in the audience crying!

After the assembly, parents and teachers came up to me and said, "Your son, Miles, is so talented, intelligent and creative!" Wow, the very things I was instilling in him was evident to others!

Now a thirty-eight-year-old father, my son is one of the most confident, positive, and uplifting people I know! He works on instilling the same in his children.

I found that vision boards were another form of Auto Suggestions that encouraged me. Shortly after I left my husband and before the Lord told me to leave Los Angeles. I was introduced to vision boards (also known as treasure maps). At the time, I was regaining my confidence and working on becoming a better version of myself. Just before I left Los Angeles with my then three-year-old son, I took two poster boards and put everything I thought I would want on them and connected them together. When I returned to Ohio, I hung it on my bedroom wall and looked at it every day. A point I need to make is that while I completed the board in Los Angeles, the things on the board began to manifest AFTER I returned home to Ohio. Sometimes, there are things we are to do perhaps somewhere else.

The Auto Suggestions and vision board began to manifest. One of the things I affirmed was "A job training program that works." Shortly after returning to Ohio, I was hired as a career training specialist for the Job Training Partnership Association, where I prepared people for work, school, or entrepreneurship. I had over two-hundred clients, and the highest success rate in my department. Thus, a job training program that worked! I believe one of the reasons my success rate was so high, is because my clients completed a three-week career and personal development training. I insisted they choose one affirmation or Auto Suggestion that they would stand in front of the class and say out loud three times every day, at the beginning of each three hours session, for three weeks. Studies show that for any habit we want to form or break, we must claim the desired behavior for at least twenty-one days. I saw people gain confidence and control over their lives!

Any extended training that I do includes Auto Suggestions or affirmations. One time in particular, I created a training program for fathers who had been incarcerated and wanted to be more engaged in their children's lives. There was a young man who literally shook as he stood in front of the class during the first couple of sessions. His Auto Suggestion and affirmation was, "I am confident and secure in social situations." He would say it three times out loud for three weeks. At the end of the training, his family attended the graduation and commented on how he had changed and asked me, "What did you do to make that happen?" My response, "He did it, not me!"

Another example of manifestation is that on my vision board, I put myself on a large round stage with people all around it. I spoke at a rally in Washington, D.C., where I stood on a round stage with thousands of people surrounding it. Speaking in front of groups is my passion and continues to manifest.

I also realized that sometimes what we think we are representing could be something totally different. I thought I wanted to be involved in real estate, so I put a lot of houses on my board. I became a board member for Habitat for Humanity and traveled throughout the country training with them. Thus, the houses. In another area on the vision board, I put a white house with two trees in the front yard. I was able to purchase a home and, without realizing, it happened to be a white house with two trees in front!

I indicated a college degree on my board. It took ten years for me to obtain my bachelor's degree and another five years for my master's degree. Between a full time job and being a single mother, it took time and it happened!

These are just a few manifestations from Auto Suggestion and vision boards. We can speak things into existence! Scripture confirms in Proverbs 18:21, "The tongue has the power of life and death." Are you speaking life or death into the lives of those around you? Are you lifting and encouraging yourself or beating yourself up with your words? Remember, it is all right to talk to yourself and to answer yourself. Questioning with "What did I say?" can be a concern!

Proverbs 23:7 says, "As a man thinketh in his heart, so is he." In fact, there are twenty-five scriptures that make reference to "As a man thinks in his heart..." You might want to google and read them.

What we say is most often what we get and then we say, "I knew that was going to happen!" Auto Suggestions can produce positive or negative results. Choose this day what will bring the most fulfillment in your life and to those near and dear to you.

I want to encourage you to speak life! Create Auto Suggestions or affirmations for things you want to change or acquire. If auto-suggesting seems challenging, YouTube provides them, and you can listen to them while you sleep! There are affirmations that will run for eight hours at a time.

The beauty of Auto Suggestion is you have a choice!

# VERA THOMAS

**About Vera Thomas:** Author, Certified Life Coach and Mediator, Speaker, Trainer and Poet. Producer of a weekly podcast/radio show "The Vera Thomas Show". She has worked with individuals, companies, non-profit organizations, schools, and churches engaging youth and adults.

Her experiences of enduring physical, emotional, and mental abuse as a child, rape, homelessness and surviving as a battered wife leaving her husband when her son was only 6 months old has fueled her passion.

Vera is available for companies who want to transform their teams or families who want to transform their lives.

Learn more about Vera on Instagram: @vera.thomas.779

Author's Website: *http://www.youtube.com/user/VThomas1117*
Book Series Website & Author's Bio: *www.The13StepstoRiches.com*

## Yuri Choi

# WRITE IT INTO EXISTENCE

"I am a sought-after mindset and performance coach for six, seven, and eight-figure entrepreneurs and high achievers. I help them to show up as the best versions of themselves, by helping them gain clarity, leverage their emotions, and language. I impact millions with my talks, meditations, and my teachings. I am traveling all over the world with my remote coaching business, and changing peoples' lives."

I typed these out as a part of my vision a few years ago on my MacBook in my Newport Beach studio. I had just quit my corporate job to follow my heart and my calling to help people and change people's lives for the better. I had just hired my first coach to help me shift my own mindset, get over my imposter syndrome, and start my entrepreneurial journey.

One of the assignments given to me by my coach was to write down my vision, even if it didn't seem reasonable yet. And actually, I was encouraged to write it down, especially if it didn't seem reasonable yet.

So I continued to write on this piece of paper. "I am a best-selling author, speaker, entrepreneur, and an unstoppable feminine force that leads with compassion, magnetism, and unconditional love."

I cringed at these words staring back at me. "Who am I to say these amazing and big statements about myself? Who am I to become an author, speaker, and a coach? I just quit my corporate job and I don't even know how I'm going to make this all happen yet!"

The coach's suggestion was that I read these out loud to myself, as if it was all already happening, and after reading Napoleon Hill's *Think and Grow Rich Confidence Formula,* as well.

I started calling this the Morning Mindset Reframe Formula, and I printed these out.

To be honest, I am not sure if I believed a word that I wrote on that piece of paper at that time. It all felt like a lie and it all felt not true.

But at the time, I didn't have any better ideas either, so I thought, "What the heck, what do I have to lose?"

So the morning ritual of reading these "ridiculous" statements out loud started. At first, it felt very awkward. As I read these out loud, I was scared that my neighbors would hear me and think I was losing my mind. I wondered what they would think if they knew that I was saying these clearly-not-true-statements out loud every morning.

Yet I continued to read them out loud.

To my surprise, a few weeks into this, something magical started happening. I noticed three things started to happen as I read these in the morning.

One: I started to feel something deep in my core get activated and energized by reading these out loud, once I started to get over the initial awkward stage.

Two: I started to notice that I thought about these visions more often throughout the day, and this would also energize me to take more inspired actions consistently towards my smaller goals.

Three: I started to notice my relationship to these visions that once felt ridiculous, start to shift to thinking that it could potentially become a possibility.

The first two years, I repeated these vision statements and the Confidence Formula out loud every morning hoping that it would not only start to seep into my subconscious, but also start to become my reality.

Four years later, I am grateful, pleasantly surprised, and excited to share that those once "ridiculous" statements have come true.

I started to develop skills and somehow create opportunities that would lead me to working with six, seven, and eight-figure entrepreneurs and high achievers, helping them develop an abundant mindset to create fulfillment in their lives. One of my clients was the CEO of Psych2Go, the largest mental health online magazine and YouTube channel in the world with millions of subscribers. He started to invite me to speak and do livestreams on his platform, which led me to sharing my talks and my meditations with millions of subscribers around the world. I am now a best-selling author of the series that this book that you're reading is a part of. Things just started to happen, just like I had repeated over and over again.

Imagine that a farmer plants a seed into the soil. Right away, the farmer might not know if that seed is going to sprout into anything. They might not even see the seed because now it is under the soil. But if the farmer continues to water the seed, believing that it will one day sprout into a full plant, continues to take care of the soil, and continues to nurture it, one day it will blossom into its full manifestation of its potential.

When we write down our visions on a piece of paper, it is as if we are the farmer of our subconscious mind, and we are planting a seed there. We might not immediately see the full possibility of what it can become, but we must trust that it is there and continue to water it and nurture it.

Auto Suggestion in this process is the part where we are nurturing and watering this seed of potential. At first, just like the seed, we might look at the piece of paper of with our vision on it, and may not be sure if it will fully blossom into anything. However, with faith, and with consistency of watering the seed, or repeating these statements out loud, these visions blossom into their full potential.

On a physiological level, as we repeat these visions out loud, we start to hear ourselves say them over and over again. Then we start to visualize these visions repeatedly. Then by saying these out loud, we start to connect our voice to our visions. As we involve all of our senses to creating these new realities, our subconscious mind starts to believe in the possibility more and more.

Do you also have visions and dreams that seem ridiculous to you right now? Are you willing to plant a new seed of possibility into the realm of infinite possibilities and in your subconscious mind, and consistently water it? And can you do it consistently, as I did, knowing that there really isn't much to lose?

If so, I would like to invite you to play with this concept that can massively change your life. I believe that this process of writing down our dreams and visions, then consistently watering and nurturing them, is the key to creating our reality in the way that we design it.

Today as I sit here writing this chapter in the middle of a national park in Utah, I can assure you that this works, as long as you have faith and you are consistent with it.

So if you're willing to dream, play, and test this out for your own visions, I invite you into these journaling questions below.

## Journaling & Exercise on Auto Suggestion

1. What are some big and unreasonable dreams that you've always had that you never had the courage to tell anyone before? Write them down, unapologetically. Write this in present tense as if they are already happening. Some questions that you can answer to journal might be, "What would be your ideal day? When I walk into the room, people are captivated by my energy. I am living my dream life and it looks like this."

   Now, decide for how many days you want to say this out loud for. (I highly recommend doing at least ninety days).

2. When would you like to repeat these out loud every day? You can either specify morning, after lunch, or before bed, or you can designate a specific time. You may also stack it with another habit you might already have, such as, "right after I brush my teeth."

3. Now, either take a picture of this page if you journaled directly on to this page, or type it out and print it, then place it where you have easy access to it every day. Then every day for the time that you committed to, say them out loud and start to see the magic happen! It may happen faster than you'd think!

# YURI CHOI

**About Yuri Choi:** Yuri is the Founder of Yuri Choi Coaching. Yuri is a performance coach for entrepreneurs and high achievers. She helps them create and stay in a powerful, abundant, unstoppable mindset to achieve their goals by helping them gain clarity and understanding, leverage their emotional states, and create empowering habits and language patterns.

She is a speaker, writer, creator, connector, YouTuber, and the author of Creating Your Own Happiness. Yuri is passionate about spreading the messages about meditation, power of intention, and creating a powerful mindset to live a fulfilling life. She is also a Habitude Warrior Conference Speaker and emcee, and she is also a designated guest coach for Psych2Go, the largest online mental health magazine and YouTube Channel. Her mission in the world is to inspire people to live leading with L.O.V.E. (which stands for: laughter, oneness, vulnerability, and ease) and to ignite people's souls to live in a world of infinite creative possibilities and abundance.

Author's Website: *www.YuriChoiCoaching.com*
Book Series Website & Author's Bio: *www.The13StepsToRiches.com*

GRAB YOUR COPY OF AN OFFICIAL PUBLICATION
WITH THE ORIGINAL UNEDITED TEXT FROM 1937
BY THE NAPOLEON HILL FOUNDATION!

THE NAPOLEON HILL FOUNDATION
WWW.NAPHILL.ORG

## Global Speakers Mastermind &
## Habitude Warrior Masterminds

Join us and become a member of our tribe! Our Global Speakers Mastermind is a virtual group of amazing thinkers and leaders who meet twice a month. Sessions are designed to be 'to the point' and focused, while sharing fantastic techniques to grown your mindset as well as your pocket books. We also include famous guest speaker spots for our private Masterclasses. We also designate certain sessions for our members to mastermind with each other & counsel on the topics discussed in our previous Masterclasses. It's time for you to join a tribe who truly cares about **YOU** and your future and start surrounding yourself with the famous leaders and mentors of our time. It is time for you to up-level your life, businesses, and relationships.

For more information to check out our Masterminds:
Team@HabitudeWarrior.com
www.DecideTobeAwesome.com

## BECOME AN INTERNATIONAL
## #1 BEST-SELLING AUTHOR & SPEAKER

Habitude Warrior International has been highlighting award-winning Speakers and #1 Best-Selling Authors for over 25 years. They know what it takes to become #1 in your field and how to get the best exposure around the world. If you have ever considered giving yourself the GIFT of becoming a well-known Speaker and a fantastically well known #1 Best-Selling Author, then you should email their team right away to find out more information in how you can become involved. They have the best of the best when it comes to resources in achieving the best-selling status in your particular field. Start surrounding yourself with the N.Y. Times Best-Sellers of our time and start seeing your dreams become reality!

For more information to become a #1 Best-Selling Author
& Speaker on our Habitude Warrior Conferences
Please send us your request to:
Team@HabitudeWarrior.com
www.DecideTobeAwesome.com

Hardback ISBN: 978-1-63792-208-8
Paperback ISBN: 978-1-63792-206-4